ASIAN AMERICAN HISTORIES OF THE UNITED STATES

CATHERINE CENIZA CHOY

BEACON PRESS
BOSTON

BEACON PRESS
Boston, Massachusetts
www.beacon.org

Beacon Press books
are published under the auspices of
the Unitarian Universalist Association of Congregations.

25 24 23 22   8 7 6 5 4 3 2 1

This book is printed on acid-free paper that meets the uncoated paper
ANSI/NISO specifications for permanence as revised in 1992.

Text design and composition by Kim Arney

Library of Congress Cataloging-in-Publication Data

Names: Choy, Catherine Ceniza, 1969– author.
Title: Asian American histories of the United States / Catherine Ceniza Choy.
Description: Boston : Beacon Press, [2022] | Includes bibliographical
references and index. | Summary: "Asian American Histories of the United
States illuminates how an over-century-long history of Asian migration,
labor, and community formation in the United States is fundamental to
understanding the American experience and its existential crises of the
early twenty-first century"—Provided by publisher.
Identifiers: LCCN 2022001429 | ISBN 9780807050798 (hardback) |
ISBN 9780807050804 (ebook)
Subjects: LCSH: Asian Americans—Social conditions. | Asian
Americans—History. | Asian Americans—Violence against. |
Asians—Government policy—United States—History. | United
States—Emigration and immigration—Government policy. |
Asia—Emigration and immigration—History.
Classification: LCC E184.A75 C516 2022 |
DDC 973/.0495—dc23/eng/20220118
LC record available at https://lccn.loc.gov/2022001429

my husband, Greg Choy,
and our children, Maya and Louis,
with love always

CONTENTS

PREFACE

Writing in the Years of Great Hatred

I write this book with a sense of personal urgency. Given the long-standing presence of Asian Americans in the United States, how is it that we find ourselves in the years, 2020 and 2021, in the midst of so much hate directed against us?

Throughout 2020, and most notably beginning in March when COVID-19 became a pandemic, anti-Asian, coronavirus-related racism was on the rise. It took shape in various forms of verbal and physical harassment, from bullying Asian American youth and spitting on Asian Americans to blaming us for the disease. This anti-Asian hostility also led to grave violence, such as the knife attack on a Burmese American family in Midland, Texas. The perpetrator blamed the family for spreading the coronavirus.[1]

As I write this in 2021, anti-Asian violence is all around us from New York City to Atlanta to Glendale, Arizona, to the San Francisco Bay Area. We bear witness to some of this violence in video clips shared on social media of Asian American elders just going about their day, taking a walk for some daily exercise or running an errand at a grocery, and suddenly being assaulted, knocked to the ground, punched in the face, dragged from a car in a purse-snatching gone awry. On March 29, Vilma Kari, a sixty-five-year-old Filipino woman who had emigrated from the Philippines decades ago, was brutally attacked in broad daylight in front of a luxury building in Manhattan.[2]

Some of these assaults have been fatal. After being pushed with a level of force that knocked him to the ground, eighty-four-year-old Thai immigrant Vicha Ratanapakdee never regained consciousness and passed away two days later.[3] Seventy-four-year-old Filipino immigrant, Juanito Falcon, died after he had been punched in the face and hit his head against the pavement.[4]

This anti-Asian violence is about misogyny as well as racism. Asian American women make up a disproportionate share of these attacks.[5] We grieved over the March 16, 2021, shooting and killing of eight people in Atlanta. Six of the eight dead were Asian American women. The shooter denied racial motivation, emphasizing his sex addiction. However, many Asian American women understood the tragedy differently, having experienced the ways that race and gender intersect to create the stereotypes that fetishize and objectify them.[6]

It's not solely the brute violence that plays out in my mind. In Juanito Falcon, I see my Lolo, my Filipino grandfather. In Vilma Kari, I see my Filipino mother walking on her way to church. I learn that this violence is also playing out in the minds of my own children. And that, in the victims of these attacks, they see me.

My son, who is away at college, calls my husband and me. "Are you okay?" he asks. He's seen the videos and news stories of this violence. He fears what I fear. For most of 2020 and in the first few months of 2021, it is as though it has been open season to harass and harm Asian Americans. As though we are less than human, our lives expendable.

This fear threatens in ways both internal as well as external. It creates tension in your head, it hurts your heart. Your thoughts race. *Will I or one of my family members be next? What will I do if it happens to me? Why is this happening?*

MISUNDERSTANDING AND DEHUMANIZATION

As an Asian American historian who has researched, written, and taught Asian American history for over two decades, I know that so much of what I am observing and we are experiencing in these times is not new. Anti-Asian violence in the United States has a history that spans over 150 years. So too does the objectification of Asian women, as does the association of Asian bodies with disease. That Asian American history may still seem like an unknown quantity—well, that has a history too.

Asian American historical scholarship and teaching have made incredible strides over the past three decades, most notably in US university and college departments and programs, book publishing, and academic professional organizations. Yet, despite this progress, a profound lack of understanding of Asian American history permeates our culture.

This lack of understanding has led to a *misunderstanding* of Asian Americans and our histories. Instead, generalizations about who we are pass for common knowledge. Asian Americans are whiz kids, innately good at math and memorization. As adults, Asian Americans are model minorities who do not complain. Asian American men are effeminate or asexual while Asian American women are exotic and alluring. All Asian Americans are successful.

Some might ask, what could be wrong with this? After all, aren't there stereotypes of every group of people and culture? And isn't much of this the most positive branding a group could hope for?

What's problematic about this misunderstanding is that it contributes to the dehumanization of Asian Americans. These one-dimensional depictions, even the seemingly positive ones, can turn sinister in an instant, comprising two sides of the same coin that can easily be flipped. Thus, Asian Americans may be considered model minorities at one moment, but then quickly transform into something menacing. An Asian American woman is a lotus blossom, but also a dragon lady. Both are attractive, but the dragon lady is a villainess.

I painfully observed this fine line between docility and danger during the research for my first book, *Empire of Care*, about Filipino nurses in the US. In the 1960s and 1970s, tens of thousands of Filipino nurses immigrated to the United States to alleviate critical nursing shortages.[7] Many Americans considered these women to be soft-spoken and friendly. Yet, in the 1977 case of *United States v. Narciso and Perez*, two Filipino immigrant nurses were wrongfully convicted of conspiracy and poisoning patients at the Veterans Administration Hospital in Ann Arbor, Michigan. Although they were eventually exonerated in 1978, Filipina Narciso and Leonora Perez characterized their experience as an American "nightmare."[8] In his book *The Mysterious Deaths at Ann Arbor*, author Robert Wilcox wrote about the case against them, highlighting the supposed inscrutability of Filipino immigrants: "Such was the enigma of the little Filipino: responsible, considerate, shy. But was it a veil hiding evil beneath?"[9]

Thus, this duality of being superhuman (e.g., the whiz kid, model minority) and of being subhuman (e.g., spreaders of the "China virus," "dirty Japs," and "slant-eyed bitches," as one witness referred to Narciso and Perez) has a history. Its endgame is to objectify Asian Americans as non-Americans and even non-human. Tragically, in times of crises, such as disease outbreaks and economic downturns, dehumanization lends itself to racial, classed, gendered, and sexualized scapegoating and the surge of anti-Asian violence that we bore witness to in 2020 and 2021.

This misunderstanding is in large part a legacy of the American past. Historically, Asian identity was set in opposition to the American one in an expanding cascade of so many national, state, and local laws. Nineteenth- and early twentieth-century immigration laws, such as the 1882 Chinese Exclusion Act and the 1917 Immigration Act, which created the Asiatic Barred Zone, literally attempted to keep Asians out of the United States. US Supreme Court cases, such as *Takao Ozawa v. United States* in 1922 and the *United States v. Bhagat Singh Thind* in 1923, rendered Japanese and Indian immigrants ineligible for US citizenship because they were non-white. Alien land laws in California then barred persons ineligible for US citizenship from owning land. Anti-miscegenation laws in Arizona, Nevada, Oregon, Utah, and other states prohibited interracial marriage between Asians and whites.

American popular culture played a formative role in portraying Asians as subhuman and superhuman threats. In the late nineteenth and early twentieth centuries, world's fairs and political cartoons disseminated ideas of Asians as uncivilized children in need of American tutelage, threatening hordes, and harbingers of disease and immorality. During the Golden Age of Hollywood, producers profited from featuring Asians as mystical evildoers intent on taking over the Western world.

This positioning of Asians in opposition to American identity and experience is perhaps most powerfully expressed through the erasure of their long-standing presence in the United States and their contributions to its various industries. When Asians in the United States contributed to the building of the nation through railroad construction, agricultural development, military service, and labor organizing, many of these contributions were erased or forgotten. One egregious, early historical example is the omission of Chinese railroad workers in the iconic photograph of the ceremony that marked the completion of the transcontinental railroad in 1869, even though they built half of it. Another is the historical record overlooking the leadership of Filipino American Larry Itliong in the United Farm Workers, and the sacrifices of many other Filipino American organizers in US labor history.

The legacies of legal exclusion, cultural stereotyping, and historical erasure haunt us in the twenty-first century. They help explain why no matter how hard Asian Americans work to assimilate and to demonstrate our patriotism, we find ourselves outside the American experience looking in. We are forever foreigners regardless of whether we are fourth-generation Chinese American and Korean American, like my children on their father's side, or whether we are third-generation Filipino American, like my children on my side.

Thus, despite over three decades of Asian American historical book writing, documentary filmmaking, and professional association conferencing, Asian American studies scholars including me encounter the following reactions to Asian American history: "Really? I didn't know that," and "I only learned a little about that in the one ethnic studies course I took in college."

Yet, at the same time, the tenacity of this outsider status coexists alongside significant Asian American breakthroughs in American politics. In 2020, Vice President Kamala Harris became the first Asian and Black American woman to be elected in this major leadership role. Rob Bonta became California's first Filipino American state legislator when he was elected to the California State Assembly's 18th District in 2012. In 2021, Governor Gavin Newsom chose Bonta to be California's attorney general, making Bonta the first Asian American man in this position.

Asian American breakthroughs are also taking place in American arts and culture. In 2021, Steve Yeun became the first Asian American to be nominated for an Academy Award in the Best Actor category for the movie *Minari*, about a Korean immigrant family seeking to settle in rural Arkansas. Writer and scholar Viet Thanh Nguyen won the Pulitzer Prize for Fiction for his novel *The Sympathizer* in 2016, and then, in 2020, became the first Asian American to join the Pulitzer Prize Board in the board's 103-year history. Actress, comedian, writer, producer, and director Mindy Kaling became well known for her role as Kelly Kapoor in the long-running NBC sitcom *The Office* (2005–13), a television show that Kaling also contributed to as a writer, an executive producer, and a director. In 2020, Kaling created the Netflix series *Never Have I Ever*, which features the life of an Indian American teen and has been hailed as a groundbreaking series that challenges Asian American stereotypes.

Thus, Asian Americans find ourselves at a crossroads. As we celebrate these breakthroughs, we remain targets of hate. How did we get here?

VIOLENCE, ERASURE, AND RESISTANCE

In this book, I reckon with this question by emphasizing three interconnected themes in Asian American histories of the United States: violence, erasure, and resistance. One of my major motivations for writing this book is to explain how we got here by documenting the 150-plus-year history of anti-Asian violence, and its intersection with misogyny and other forms of hatred. To document this history is to confront a time line of terror inflicted against Asian Americans in its various physical forms including lynching, arson, shooting, stabbing, vandalism, threats, scapegoating, spitting, shoving, and beating. This history is not solely about acts of wrongdoing, however. It is just as much about the impacts of this violence on Asian Americans' life chances, their strategies for survival, and their overall mental health and well-being.

It is painful for me to confront and write about these events. I wonder: Will emphasizing this topic only serve to further the trauma that violence produces? Perhaps. Yet, the alternative of denying its contemporary existence and its history is unacceptable. If we do not confront anti-Asian violence, it will continue. As James Baldwin instructs us: "Not everything that is faced can be changed; but nothing can be changed until it is faced."[10] Thus, what is at stake in foregrounding the history of anti-Asian violence in the United States is not solely the accuracy of US history, but also the well-being of an American future.

The second major theme of this book is the erasure of Asian American experiences. In the subsequent chapters, I highlight its various forms including photographic and other documentary forms of erasure, forgotten and secret wars, and commercial redevelopment that removes traces of peoples' and their communities' presence. Examples of forgotten wars include the little-known Philippine-American War that began in 1899, and America's secret war in Laos in the 1960s and 1970s. Histories can also be overshadowed by violence, as in the case of the 2012 mass shooting at a *gurdwara* (Sikh temple) in Oak Creek, Wisconsin. It coincided with and diverted attention away from what should have been a celebratory centennial commemoration of the oldest gurdwara in the US, founded in Stockton, California, in 1912.

Resistance, the third theme of this book, is the creative force that Asian Americans have wielded over time to survive violence, improve their livelihoods, and contest the erasure of their histories. It, too, takes shape in many forms such as creating mutual aid societies, building alliances to establish labor unions, demanding ethnic studies in schools, and shepherding new legislation. Resistance is also inextricably linked to the Asian American imagination and its creative, and not solely reactive, acts of will. Asian American creativity is expressed in both individual and communal ways, and history illuminates how they can intersect and overlap. Unknowingly, an individual's creative force of resistance sparks imaginative thinking and resilience beyond themselves and across generations. For example, Chinese detainees at the Angel Island Immigration Station sought to express their isolation and anger by carving poems on the barrack walls beginning in the 1910s. This creative spark lives on in the more recent performances of *Within These Walls* by the Lenora Lee Dance Company. In 2017, the performance took place inside and around the Angel Island Immigration Station, its choreography creating time and space for healing and compassion in the year commemorating the 135th anniversary of the 1882 Chinese Exclusion Act.[11]

HETEROGENEITY AND CHRONOLOGY

Finally, the book's title, *Asian American Histories of the United States*, makes a statement about two major issues in Asian American history: heterogeneity and chronology. Asian Americans are not a monolith. They are a heterogeneous group with multiple histories. While the concept of Asian American remains salient—as in the current surge in anti-Asian violence that impacts Asian Americans across ethnic and socioeconomic lines—many Asian Americans feel marginalized or even invisible within the category because of the sheer diversity that it belies. Hence, on social media, scholars have used #BrownAsiansExist to call for more substantive inclusion of Filipino and South Asian Americans, for example. They point out that the elision of the many different groups that comprise Asian Americans is deeply problematic.

The challenge of synthesizing the histories of the largest Asian American groups—Chinese, Japanese, Korean, Indian, and Filipino—before the passage of the Immigration and Nationality Act of 1965 was already daunting. Then the 1965 Act, with its more equitable immigration policies, exponentially increased the numbers of emigrants from even more Asian countries. For the past six decades, Asian migrations to the United States have ushered in distinctive demographic groups, such as highly educated immigrants and refugee populations. These more recent histories of migration and settlement have complicated Asian America's composition as well as its meaning.

In the early twenty-first century, diversity and growth continue to be the hallmarks of Asian America. A record 23 million Asian Americans trace their roots to more than twenty countries in East and Southeast Asia and the Indian subcontinent.[12] US-born descendants of Asian immigrants and multiracial Americans who identify as Asian American and at least one other racial category further contribute to this vast heterogeneity.

Another salient contributing factor to this incredible diversity has been the grouping of Asian Americans and Pacific Islanders together in umbrella categories such as AAPI (Asian American and Pacific Islander), APIA (Asian and Pacific Islander American), and APA (Asian Pacific American) in specific community organizations, educational programs, and US-government-sponsored celebrations. According to the national organization Empowering Pacific Islander Communities, "Native Hawai'ians and Pacific Islanders" refers to persons whose origins are the original peoples of Polynesia, Micronesia, and Melanesia. The grouping of Asian Americans and Pacific Islanders has a history that is over four decades long. It is used, for example, in the celebration of Asian Pacific American Heritage Month in May, which began as a US-government-sponsored celebration of Asian/Pacific American Heritage Week in 1979; the Asian and Pacific Islander American Health Forum, established in 1986, in order to improve the health of Asian Americans, Native Hawai'ians, and Pacific Islanders; New York University's Asian/Pacific/American Institute, which has featured public programs about issues facing Asian/Pacific/American communities since 1996; and the Stop AAPI Hate reporting center, founded in 2020 to document and combat recent surges of anti-Asian violence in the United States.

While I refer to these categories when referring to specific organizations and events that use them, this book focuses on Asian American histories. This focus is not meant to exclude Pacific Islander American histories. On the contrary, it acknowledges Pacific Islander American community leaders and scholars' call to identify and learn about Pacific Islander studies on their own terms, which foreground their experiences of indigeneity, sovereignty, and language revitalization in the contexts of US militarism and occupation, and connect them with Pacific Islander communities in other parts of the world. As Tavae Samuelu, the executive director of Empowering Pacific Islander Communities, observes, "AAPI is incredibly ambitious. It contends to cover and speak for some of the largest regions in the world. . . . In some ways, marginalization and erasure feel inevitable."[13]

Samuelu's observation is also relevant for the term "Asian American," which encompasses so many different communities. Asian Americans recorded the fastest population growth rate among all racial and ethnic groups in the United States between 2000 and 2019.[14] This growth compels us to reimagine and reconsider our assumptions about US geography. In 2019, the following states had the largest Asian American populations: California, New York, Texas, New Jersey, Illinois, Washington, Florida, Virginia, Hawai'i, Massachusetts.[15] However, some of the most dramatic growth of the Asian American population took place in North Dakota and South Dakota, states that one might think would least likely have an Asian American presence.

Asian American diversity in the United States is compounded by the growing socioeconomic divide within as well as across specific Asian American ethnic groups. In a report about the incomes of whites, Blacks, Hispanics, and Asians from 1970 to 2016, the Pew Research Center found that Asians had displaced Blacks as the group with the most income inequality.[16] Regional and linguistic identities from their homelands, generational differences between immigrant and US-born generations, local variations based on where one lives in the United States, and significant class divides—to identify only some of the major differences among Asian Americans—have resulted in a multitude of Asian American histories.

This book's title acknowledges the immensity of the challenge for one history to encompass this diversity and growth. I do not claim to incorporate every Asian American's experience nor do I think I would be able to do so in one book. Rather, one of my major motivations for writing this book is to narrate and to integrate less well-known stories about Asian Americans that spotlight specific ethnic group and thematic experiences, such as Indian, Korean, Filipino, and Cambodian Americans, as well as mixed race and adopted Asian Americans, among others. While these groups are sometimes mentioned in history books that aim to synthesize Asian American experiences, they are typically less featured despite their long histories, large and growing numbers, and increasing visibility in American culture and society.

The book's title, and its introduction, about the multiple origins of Asian American history, also suggest something else. There are many ways of making Asian American history. And, as with US history—which has featured the providential story of the arrival of the Puritans who established a city on the hill in New England, but now grapples with the tremendous diversity of historical actors and perspectives, and its contradictory and painful legacies of genocide, slavery, and imperialism—there is no singular origin story in Asian American history. My hope is that this book's emphasis on multiple Asian American histories will inspire and generate new ones.

After having taught Asian American history in universities and colleges for over twenty years, I've also listened to students express frustration with the way the subject has been conceptualized. A major concern relates to chronology, specifically the way that Asian American history moves forward linearly, beginning at one origin point in the past, such as the discovery of gold in California in 1848, and then ending approximately in the 1980s with the Asian American Movement for social justice or the resettlement of Southeast Asian refugees. The last week or perhaps even the final day of the Asian American history course concludes with scant attention to more contemporary issues. A similar pattern emerges in Asian American history books.

By contrast, this book features multiple temporal origins of Asian American history, beginning in 2020, with subsequent chapters moving back in time to other earlier points of origin. Each of this book's chapters moves backward and forward in time. In doing so, they illuminate connections among historical events hitherto unseen, such as the 1875 legislative act that catalyzed the objectification and fetishization of Asian American women in the Atlanta murders in March 2021; and the continuity of historic alliances between Black and Asian Americans, from Frederick Douglass's 1869 speech advocating for Chinese immigration to Yuri Kochiyama and Malcolm X's friendship in the 1960s.

Finally, I write differently in these years of great hatred, taking distinct writing approaches as a way to address the current moment. In this book, I write in the first and second person as well as the more traditional third person. I include an interlude, which is typically used in a play or other artistic work, and not in a history book. And I share personal experiences. This different writing style emanates from my previous writing across genres of creative nonfiction, essay, and scholarly monograph. But it primarily stems from my deep concern that the general public still has very little knowledge of Asian American history. I believe that this has to do with the way we write about history. Only through storytelling can the dates, names, events, and ideas make an impression that resonates with the reader.

I write because the stakes are high. The potential for further erasure of our Asian American histories by this pandemic is in our midst. We have experienced so many losses. Asian American loved ones are among the over nine hundred thousand COVID-19 deaths in the United States. With small business closures, the tastes, smells, sights, and sounds of some Asian restaurants are no longer with us. After a yearlong surge in anti-Asian violence, we have lost a sense of safety in the United States.

And so I write in the way I wish to live: without fear. I write with the desire to see our nation move forward with a sense of collective purpose that emphasizes compassion and care for all. From my research and teaching, I've learned that Asian American histories can illuminate the way forward.

THE MULTIPLE ORIGINS
OF ASIAN AMERICAN HISTORIES

When and where does an Asian American history of the United States begin? There is no singular origin story that begins in one time and one place and then progresses forward smooth like silk, linear like thread. Rather, the origins of Asian American history are multiple.

Asian American history begins in the here and now, as well as over 150 years ago in the mid-nineteenth century. It begins in Asian continental lands and waterways as well as in urban, suburban, and rural areas of the United States. The Asian American experience stretches back as well as forward in time and space. It crisscrosses over time periods and over lands, oceans, and waterways. Where and when we enter are complex questions.

Like a galaxy of stars, the multiple origins of Asian American history are distinctive, but most meaningful when collectively visible as in a constellation, revealing intricate connections that present new ways of seeing, understanding, and moving forward. Sadly, these origins have been erased, obscured, and forgotten in traditional histories of the United States. Yet, by calling attention to them, they shine brightly again.

Asian American history helps us remember.

ASIAN AMERICAN HISTORY BEGINS IN 2020 with the creation of the Stop AAPI Hate reporting center, and the research finding that Filipino nurses in the United States suffered a disproportionate and devastating toll from COVID-19. The Stop AAPI Hate reporting center launched on

March 19, 2020, in response to the alarming escalation of anti-Asian coronavirus-related harassment and violence.[1] On September 28, 2020, National Nurses United, the largest union of registered nurses, released a report with the finding that 31.5 percent of registered nurses who died from COVID-19 were Filipino American, although the group makes up only 4 percent of this labor force.[2]

These current events are better understood in historical context. The present-day association of Asian bodies with disease is not new. Asian American history illuminates that it is just the most recent example in a long-standing history of racializing Asians as disease carriers, beginning with blaming Chinese immigrants for smallpox outbreaks in the second half of the nineteenth century. The presence of Filipino nurses on the front lines of American hospitals is also not new, but rather part of a six-decades-long history of their mass migration to the United States to alleviate critical nursing shortages. Since the 1960s, Filipino American nurses have worked on the front lines of major disease outbreaks including the AIDS epidemic and SARS.

One new aspect of this contemporary history is the large number of Asian American healthcare workers in the United States, some of whom have experienced anti-Asian hostility because of coronavirus-related racism. In April 2020, *Time* magazine recognized Dr. Chen Fu, a hospitalist at NYU Langone Medical Center, in its series entitled "Heroes of the Front Lines." Dr. Fu pointed out this dilemma: "As an Asian-American doctor, it's tough to reconcile being both celebrated and villainized at the same time."[3]

ASIAN AMERICAN HISTORY BEGINS IN 1975 with the journeys of Southeast Asian refugees from Vietnam, Laos, and Cambodia across land-based regions and rivers of Southeast Asian nations, and subsequently across all fifty states of the United States in their resettlement. US involvement in the Vietnam War and the "Secret War" in Laos placed the lives of their Southeast Asian allies at risk. Thus, many Southeast Asian Americans are here in the United States because Americans were there.

Although US government secrets obscured Southeast Asian American histories, refugees and their descendants indelibly shaped the late-twentieth-century American landscape through the building of Little Saigons, the creation of small businesses from Vietnamese nail salons to Cambodian donut shops, and the preservation of their stories through literature and the performing arts in organizations such as the Diasporic Vietnamese Artists Network in California and the Angkor Dance Troupe in Massachusetts.

The history of Southeast Asian American refugees is dynamic. In the twenty-first century, the numbers of refugees from Burma and Bhutan, fleeing political and social persecution and discrimination in their home countries, dramatically increased. They composed the two largest refugee groups arriving in the United States in 2011. Many have resettled in the American South.[4]

ASIAN AMERICAN HISTORY BEGINS IN 1968 with the emergence of the Asian American Movement and its solidarity with the Third World Liberation Front. On November 6, 1968, a coalition of student groups, including Black, Asian American, Chicano, and American Indian students, went on strike at San Francisco State College to demand institutional change. Another strike erupted on the University of California, Berkeley campus on January 21, 1969.

Their demands, their political consciousness, and even the language that they used to identify themselves were new. In 1968, UC Berkeley graduate students Emma Gee and Yuji Ichioka used the term "Asian American" for the first time when they founded the Asian American Political Alliance in Berkeley.[5] To identify as Asian American heralded a new political sensibility that brought together different groups of people of Asian descent under one larger umbrella, distinct from previous ties defined by Asian country of origin, region, or hometown.

From the late 1960s to the 1980s, the Asian American Movement was a social movement for racial justice that led to the establishment of Asian American social services, arts organizations, and historical societies as well as curricular innovation. One of its major legacies was the creation of San Francisco State University's Department of Asian American Studies and UC Berkeley's Asian American and Asian Diaspora Studies Program. The demand for Asian American studies, the academic discipline that examines Asian American history, culture, and contemporary issues, reverberated across the United States. It resulted in the creation of departments, programs, and course offerings at the Claremont Colleges; the University of Texas, Austin; the University of Minnesota, Twin Cities; Oberlin College; the University of Illinois, Urbana-Champaign; the University of Maryland, College Park; Williams College; Binghamton University; New York University; and more. It lives on in the continuing struggles for Asian American studies in higher education as well as the K–12 curriculum.

ASIAN AMERICAN HISTORY BEGINS IN 1965 with the passage of the Hart-Celler Act, also known as the Immigration and Nationality Act of 1965. The 1965 Act created a more equitable ceilings system of immigration by giving countries throughout the world the same number of immigrant visas. In doing so, it was a major break from the United States' previous national origins system of immigration that had been in place since 1924. That system was overtly discriminatory, favoring immigration from northern and western Europe and virtually abolishing immigration from Asia. In the 1960s, American legislators did not foresee how the Hart-Celler Act would greatly increase Asian immigration. Yet, that is what it did.

Exponential growth would become one of the defining features of post-1965 Asian America, with immigration its driving force. For example, the Korean immigrant population grew from just 11,000 in 1960 to 290,000 in 1980, marking a 2,500 percent increase.[6] The Pakistani immigrant population also grew exponentially, from 30,000 in 1980 to 273,000 in 2015.[7] Increasing ethnic diversity would be another distinctive feature of post-1965 Asian America. The record 23 million people who trace their roots to more than twenty countries in East and Southeast Asia, and the Indian subcontinent, contribute to Asian Americans' incredible heterogeneity.[8]

The Immigration Act of 1965 established a preference system that determined visa allocation. While most of the preferences facilitated family reunification, others favored the immigration of professionals and workers with needed skills. Hence, the socioeconomic diversity of Asian immigrants also increased, with many of the immigrants being highly skilled and educated. While this diversity fueled stereotypes of Asian Americans as whiz kids and model minorities, it is more accurate to characterize post-1965 Asian immigration as having a dual nature. While many Asian immigrants were highly educated, many others were not. This socioeconomic diversity is illustrated by the prevalence of Asian American labor in the technology and healthcare industries as engineers and physicians, as well as in the beauty and food industries as nail salon and restaurant workers.

ASIAN AMERICAN HISTORY BEGINS IN 1965 with Filipino American agricultural workers and labor leaders initiating the Delano Grape Strike on September 8, 1965. The impact of the five-year strike was profound. It catalyzed the modern farmworkers' movement for fair wages, the right to organize, and the recognition of the dignity of their labor.

The United Farm Workers (UFW) emerged from the joined forces of the Agricultural Workers Organizing Committee, which was predominantly Filipino American, and the National Farm Workers Association, which was mostly Mexican American. Yet, while Mexican American labor leaders, most notably Cesar Chavez, and the participation of Mexican American farmworkers became more well known, the formative role played by Filipino American labor leaders, such as Larry Itliong, in the Delano Grape Strike has been for the most part overlooked.

In the 1960s, Filipino American agricultural labor organizing was not new, but rather a continuation of their decades-long struggle to be recognized and treated as fellow human beings throughout the first half of the twentieth century. Thus, while the 1965 grape strike provides a useful starting point regarding how various Asian American groups have organized throughout the twentieth century and into the twenty-first, it raises critical questions about how and why Asian American activists have become forgotten. This origin story also presents an opportunity to showcase how more recent work by historians like Dawn Bohulano Mabalon and legislators like Rob Bonta have created new ways to remember Asian American activists.

ASIAN AMERICAN HISTORY BEGINS IN 1953 with the international and trans-racial adoption of Asian children by American families. The plight of mixed race children born of Japanese and Korean women and American soldiers was the catalyst for this phenomenon. It transformed the United States into an international adoption nation.

In the 1950s and 1960s, many Asian international adoptees were isolated, oftentimes the only people of Asian descent in midwestern and rural areas. Yet, they are part of a longer US history of Asian American interracial unions and the regulation of interracial intimacies. This history includes Chinese-Irish marriages in the Northeast in the 1800s as well as nineteenth- and twentieth-century anti-miscegenation laws barring marriages between Asians and whites in many states. However, even during times of discrimination, interracial marriages were formed with couples getting married at sea or traveling to other states to evade anti-miscegenation laws.

International and transracial adoption, and interracial romances of the nineteenth to the mid-twentieth century were precursors to the incredible heterogeneity of the Asian American population today. This diversity includes mixed race individuals who identify with multiple racial and ethnic categories. Often dismissed as incomplete, multiracial peoples' wholeness deserves recognition, as noted in the 1993 Bill of Rights for People of Mixed Heritage, authored by clinical psychologist Maria P. P. Root.

ASIAN AMERICAN HISTORY BEGINS IN 1942 with the incarceration of 120,000 Japanese Americans in internment camps. Their incarceration took place without due process. Approximately two-thirds of the Japanese American internees were US-born. Most Americans know the date of December 7, 1941, "a date which will live in infamy," because of Japan's bombing of Pearl Harbor and President Franklin D. Roosevelt's speech the day after the attack. However, we should also remember February 19, 1942, the date that President Roosevelt issued Executive Order 9066. It led to the forced removal of Japanese Americans from the West Coast to assembly centers and subsequently their incarceration in internment camps in remote areas of California, Arizona, Colorado, Utah,

Arkansas, Wyoming, and Idaho. Racism and wartime hysteria fueled this denial of justice.

World War II was also a period of revolutionary changes for specific groups of Asian Americans as a result of wartime needs and US alliances with China, the Philippines, and India. These Asian Americans availed themselves of new employment opportunities, enlisted in the US military, and became Rosie the Riveters. These groups also gained US naturalization rights. Despite these progressive changes and geopolitical distinctions, the racial lumping together of Asian Americans resulted in their unequal treatment in the form of anti-Asian harassment and violence.

The impounding of over one hundred of Dorothea Lange's photographs of the evacuation and internment of Japanese Americans concealed a visual critique of this history. In the 1980s, Japanese American internees would bear witness, share their stories, and demand an apology and redress. They would work against the amnesia regarding this grave injustice and toward remembrance.

ASIAN AMERICAN HISTORY BEGINS IN 1919 with Korean delegates gathering in Philadelphia, the "cradle of liberty." They wanted the American people to know that on March 1, Koreans in Seoul had declared their independence from Japan. This history illuminates the imperial origins of Asian America, forged at the intersection of multiple empires—in this case, that of Japan and the United States. By the late nineteenth and early twentieth centuries, both nations had emerged as world powers through imperial expansion. In the second half of the nineteenth century, Japan colonized Hokkaido and Okinawa. Its imperial ambitions expanded and included colonizing Korea from 1910 to 1945. Although the Korean delegates appealed to American values of liberty and freedom, the United States was building an empire of its own. The nineteenth-century ideology of Manifest Destiny justified white American westward expansion across the North American continent and the Pacific Ocean. Hence, early Korean American history intersects with the histories of Filipino immigrants who migrated to the United States as a consequence of US annexation of the Philippines as well as the histories of Indian immigrants who fled British domination.

While Korean immigrant pioneers were relatively few in number, their impact on Korean independence was substantive. In Hawai'i and the US mainland, Korean immigrants coordinated an independence movement composed of no fewer than twenty-four organizations seeking to free Korea. A prominent immigrant pioneer was Korean independence activist Ahn Chang Ho, who is considered one of Korea's most important philosophical leaders of the twentieth century. After immigrating to the United States with his wife in 1902, he established mutual aid societies and political organizations to fight for Korean independence. In the 1910s, he left his family in California in order to campaign for independence and help establish the Korean Provisional Government in Shanghai. He passed away in Korea on March 10, 1938, after having been arrested and tortured multiple times by the Japanese for his activism.

Other Korean immigrant pioneers and independence activists were unable to return to their Korean homeland. However, the Korean government officially recognized some of them as patriots and re-interred their remains in Korean national cemeteries. One of these patriots, Choi Neung-ik, who is my husband's paternal grandfather, is now buried in Daejeon National Cemetery. In the United States, this history lives on today through the work of the patriots' descendants. They include Ralph Ahn, the youngest son of Ahn Chang Ho, who sustains this history through newsletters and gatherings of the Korean American Pioneer Descendants Society.

ASIAN AMERICAN HISTORY BEGINS IN 1875 with the Page Act, the US immigration law that prohibited the recruitment of unfree laborers and women for "immoral purposes." Although the law focused on the importation of prostitutes, it was enforced primarily against Chinese women. The Page Act illuminates a history of the United States, not as a nation of immigrants but rather increasingly more like a fortress. It was only the first of many federal immigration laws that were used to keep Asians out of the United States.

Another troubling legacy of the Page Act is the objectification of Asian and Asian American women that persists to this day. It is most visible through the history of stereotypes of Asian women on-screen as dragon ladies, lotus blossoms, and prostitutes. However, these popular representations have affected the real-life experiences of Asian American women in dangerous ways, making them targets of harassment and violence. Current congressmembers such as Representatives Judy Chu, Grace Meng, and Marilyn Strickland challenge these one-dimensional portrayals by breaking barriers in politics and by working to address inequities in Asian American and women's histories, among other areas.

ASIAN AMERICAN HISTORY BEGINS IN 1869 with the completion of the first transcontinental railroad in the United States. Connecting the Eastern Seaboard with the Pacific Coast, this event heralded US national progress and ingenuity. Chinese railroad workers constituted the bulk of the labor of the Central Pacific Railroad. They worked through harsh winters and mountainous passages, using dangerous tools and placing their lives at risk.

In one of the starkest examples of the erasure of Asian American contributions to US history, Chinese railroad workers were excluded from the photograph celebrating the joining of the Central Pacific and Union Pacific railroads in 1869 at Promontory Summit in Utah. Their exclusion was accompanied by increasing anti-Chinese hostility in the American West, expressed in the violent expulsion of Chinese from cities and rural areas and in discrimination in courts of law. This hostility had emerged soon after the onset of Chinese mass migration to seek gold in Northern California after its discovery in Sutter's Mill in 1848.

In 2014, photographer Corky Lee resisted this erasure of Chinese labor by taking a photograph of Asian Americans, including descendants of the Chinese railroad workers, at Promontory Summit on the 145th anniversary of the transcontinental railroad's completion.

The impact of this erasure runs deep. Over time, erasure would form an Asian American historical pattern. Tragically, it informs the present-day surge in anti-Asian violence across the United States beginning in 2020 and continuing in the first few months of 2021. The rise of verbal and physical harassment and violence against Asian American elders and women illustrates that this violence is tinged with the vulnerability of age and gender, factors that intersect with racist scapegoating in the age of COVID-19.

Beginning in March 2020 and throughout the remainder of the year, President Donald Trump and other high-ranking US politicians referred to COVID-19 as the "China virus" and, jokingly, as the "kung flu." For Asian Americans, however, it is no laughing matter. For us, it can be and has been a matter of life and death.

Thus, Asian American histories of the United States matter. Anti-Asian violence is a violence with a history. It is an outcome of a longer pattern of Asian Americans being treated as expendable objects. This is poignantly expressed in the ways many Americans do not see us as a central part of US history.

And so Asian American activists, artists, and scholars do the work that we do in order to fight against dehumanization. We document and preserve, imagine and create, research and write our histories and humanity into being.

ONE

2020: THE HEALTH OF THE NATION

I n late 2019, Americans had come to know of a new coronavirus from an outbreak in Wuhan, China. COVID-19, the official name for the respiratory disease caused by the novel coronavirus SARS-CoV-2 (severe acute respiratory syndrome coronavirus 2), then spread to other parts of the world with significant outbreaks in South Korea and Italy. Although US health officials, politicians, and industry leaders had been talking about the threat of novel coronaviruses for the past quarter century, beliefs in US exceptionalism, chauvinistic assumptions of the country's greatness, and the cultural emphasis on individual grit contributed to making many Americans feel invincible.[1] The US had dealt with multiple disease outbreaks in recent previous years, including SARS in 2003, Ebola in 2014–16, and Zika in 2015–16. Cases were relatively few in number compared with other parts of the world, and the majority of Americans were left unscathed.

However, on March 11, 2020, the World Health Organization declared that COVID-19 had become a pandemic. Americans could no longer take the health of the nation for granted. By mid-March, the death toll had surpassed one hundred, with coronavirus cases confirmed in every state.[2] On April 6, the number of deaths increased to ten thousand.[3] On May 27, it multiplied to one hundred thousand.[4] The United States became the epicenter of the pandemic, leading the world in the numbers of coronavirus cases and related deaths.

For Asian Americans in the United States, what unfolded was an American horror story of racism and xenophobia in addition to the existential threat of a deadly disease. On March 16, President Donald Trump first referred to the novel coronavirus as the "Chinese virus" on Twitter. Such inflammatory rhetoric stigmatized China and, by extension, anyone who looked Chinese. The Stop AAPI Hate reporting center launched on March 19, 2020. Between March 19 and April 15, 2020, the center had collected almost 1,500 reports of anti-Asian hate incidents.[5]

As hate incidents spiked, Asian American healthcare workers were on the front lines battling this deadly disease. Beginning in April 2020, stories about Filipino nurses who had died from COVID-19 started appearing in national news coverage. In September 2020, National Nurses United reported that COVID-19 was taking a disproportionate toll on Filipino American nurses.[6]

An Asian American historical lens is useful to understand why this is happening. While the creation of the Stop AAPI Hate research center is relatively new, the phenomenon of associating Asian bodies with disease outbreaks and anti-Asian violence is not. The devastating number of Filipino nurse deaths in this pandemic has garnered the public's attention, but Filipino nurses have been caring for American patients for six decades.

The intersection of these two histories exposes one of the unique tragedies of anti-Asian, coronavirus-related racism. Targets of anti-Asian hostility include Asian American healthcare workers who labor to save the lives of Americans in the age of COVID-19.

THE LONG HISTORY OF MEDICAL SCAPEGOATING AND ANTI-ASIAN VIOLENCE

The history of associating Asian bodies with disease outbreaks in the United States is in fact as old as the first mass wave of Asian migration. After the discovery of gold in Northern California in 1848, the numbers of Chinese arrivals in San Francisco increased. Their growing presence fueled anti-Chinese sentiment in the region and the state. Many white workers and politicians viewed them as economic competition and an alien race. Anti-Chinese sentiment also had biological and medical components that presented Chinese bodies as a weak and inferior race.

Tragically, the concurrent development of San Francisco's public health institutions in the second half of the nineteenth century furthered anti-Chinese sentiment. Their municipal reports blamed Chinese immigrants for smallpox outbreaks. As Dr. J. L. Meares, who served as a San Francisco health officer from 1876 to 1888, emphatically stated, "I unhesitatingly declare my belief that the cause is the presence in our midst of 30,000 (as a class) of unscrupulous, lying and treacherous Chinamen, who have disregarded our sanitary laws, concealed and are concealing their cases of smallpox."[7] San Francisco public health officials instituted measures that racially profiled Chinese arrivals at the city's port for smallpox outbreaks. These included quarantine, physical examination, the fumigation of clothing and baggage, and mass vaccinations.[8]

Even with these measures in place, the medical scapegoating of the Chinese extended to ethnic enclaves such as San Francisco's Chinatown. Dr. Meares repeatedly referred to Chinatown as a "cesspool" and "nuisance."[9] The San Francisco Board of Health's annual reports from 1876 to 1877 did not mince words when they depicted Chinatown as a health threat, referring to it as a "moral and social plague spot," a "sanitary curse," and a region "contaminating the atmosphere."[10]

While public health reports presented a scientific and authoritative voice to a social discriminatory narrative about Chinese bodies as disease carriers, popular culture spread these medicalized horror stories to the general public. The San Francisco magazine *The WASP* commissioned artist George Keller to draw anti-Chinese political cartoons that expressed the downfall of the United States as a result of Chinese immigration. One of these illustrations was titled "A Statue for Our Harbor."

Published in 1881, "A Statue for Our Harbor" depicts the Statue of Liberty as a Chinese laborer wearing tattered clothing, a human skull at his foot, and an opium pipe in his hand. His queue, or traditional ponytail, is prominently displayed emanating from the back of his head as a slithering snake-like object, while a rat tail peeks out from behind the human skull. Blackened skies warn readers of what is to come to the United States if the Chinese continue to arrive in "our harbor." Asian sail boats, known as "junks," outnumber the steamboats in the water. This classic representation of "yellow peril," Western fears of Asian invasions and the resultant downfall of Western civilization, is clarified through the following capitalized words that emanate from the Chinese laborer's head in lieu of Lady Liberty's crown: "FILTH, IMMORALITY, DISEASES, RUIN TO WHITE LABOR." In 1882, one year after the publication of "A Statue for Our Harbor," Congress passed the Chinese Exclusion Act, which barred the immigration of Chinese laborers to the United States and made the Chinese ineligible for US citizenship.

While medical scapegoating of Chinese immigrants justified their exclusion from the United States, the belief in Western medical superiority contributed to the nineteenth-century American doctrine of Manifest Destiny—the divine right of the United States to expand westward across the continent and the Pacific Ocean, and into the Philippines. Although Filipino nationalists had been fighting for their independence from over three centuries of Spanish rule, the United States annexed the Philippines in 1898. In his proclamation of "benevolent assimilation," President William McKinley posited that, unlike Spanish conquerors, Americans came as friends. Evidence of American goodness included bringing Americanized public health to the Philippines.

Benevolent assimilation relied on a racial and medical hierarchy, however. Dr. Victor Heiser, who became chief quarantine officer in the Philippines in 1903 and later served as director of health in the Philippine Islands until 1915, described Filipino bodies as "incubators of leprosy." In a 1910 article, he presented Filipinos as a primitive people with little hope of progress if not for American tutelage: "We are practically cleaning up these Islands, left foul and insanitary and diseased by hygienically ignorant peoples. . . . We are draining the land, as it were, before beginning the constructive health projects which are going to make these people the strong and healthy race we intend them to be."[11]

Although Japan, like the United States, was emerging as a global power through imperialism, the pattern of associating Asian bodies with the threat of disease also applied to the growing numbers of Japanese immigrants in California. In early twentieth-century Los Angeles, public health officials, such as Dr. John Pomeroy, stoked fears of Japanese immigrants, many of whom were farmers, by linking their presence to food-borne diseases such as typhoid. He proposed increasing public health staff to surveil Japanese farms.[12] In a 1920 issue of the California magazine *Grizzly Bear*, Dr. Pomeroy titled his article on Japanese immigrants "Japanese Evil in California."[13]

In 1910, when US Public Health Service physician M. W. Glover found that many Indian arrivals at Angel Island's Quarantine Station had hookworm, the threat of disease became grounds for the movement to exclude them from entering the United States. The 1914 congressional hearings about Indian immigration included an article by Dr. Charles T. Nesbitt, health director of Wilmington, North Carolina, who wrote, "The Chinese, Japanese, and East Indians are racially alien to us. . . . History proclaims Asia as the fountain from which has flowed the most destructive pestilences that are recorded. Asiatic cholera, bubonic plague, typhus, smallpox, and malaria are reported weekly as being present in the ports of China, India, and Japan."[14]

The stereotyping of Asians as disease carriers obscured a historical truth about Europeans and European Americans. They too had contracted a variety of deadly diseases such as cholera and smallpox, and as settlers had brought these diseases to various places across the globe, such as the Caribbean and Central and South America in the sixteenth century and North America in the seventeenth century. There had also been smallpox epidemics in US Eastern cities. As historian Nayan Shah points out, in nineteenth-century San Francisco, "it was just as probable that smallpox arrived with European and American migrants traveling westward by rail."[15] However, it was easier to track and quarantine smallpox over the longer journey across the Pacific. And, when European immigrant laborers in San Francisco contracted smallpox, public health officials such as Dr. Meares expressed sympathy instead of disgust, diverting blame away from their bodies and emphasizing their misfortune in not being able to afford better housing.[16]

Asians and Asian Americans resisted the idea of Western medical superiority and the practice of anti-Asian medical scapegoating in a myriad of ways. In the early twentieth century under US colonial rule, Filipinos continued to consult indigenous healers, such as *curanderos*. From 1910 to 1940, Chinese detainees at the Angel Island Immigration Station wrote poetry on the barrack walls. One poem harshly criticized the invasive medical examinations: "I thoroughly hate the barbarians because they do not respect justice. . . . They examine for hookworms and practice hundreds of despotic acts."[17]

In 1921, Chinese merchants Hing Pang and Hee Fuk Yuen filed US federal lawsuits, criticizing immigration medical inspections that led to the denial of their reentry into the United States. Their lawyer, Jackson Ralston, argued that the targeting of Chinese arrivals was an "unequal administration of the law." Ralston noted that Caucasian passengers, regardless of their nationality or class, were not subject to microscopic tests of their feces as Asian travelers were—those traveling first-class being the only exception.[18] However, the federal appeals court and the Supreme Court affirmed that such practices were nondiscriminatory.

Asian Americans protested medical scapegoating because at stake was not solely their livelihood, but also their lives. Once they were labeled as filthy, immoral, and disease-prone, they became regarded as less than human and subject to harassment and violence. Key historical examples go back to the second half of the nineteenth century. In 1871, a mob of over five hundred people lynched seventeen Chinese immigrant men in the Chinese Massacre of Los Angeles. Local newspaper editorials condemning Chinese immigrants as immoral and inferior contributed to the brutality of these attacks.[19] In the 1885 Rock Springs Massacre in Wyoming, at least twenty-eight Chinese workers were killed, their homes and bunkhouses set on fire. Economic and social tensions pitted white immigrants—mostly Irish, Scandinavian, English, and Welsh—against the Chinese. Writer Tom Rea notes, "Although they worked side by side every day, whites and Chinese spoke separate languages and lived separate lives. They knew very little about each other. This made it possible for each race to think of the other, somehow, as not entirely human."[20] These events were not exceptional. In 1885 and 1886, over 168 communities in the US West expelled their Chinese residents, united in their vehemence that "the Chinese must go."[21]

Although the anti-Chinese movement in the Pacific Northwest was not as intense as California's, five days after the Rock Springs Massacre, a group of armed white men and several Native American men entered a Chinese camp in Squak Valley (now Issaquah in Washington State) and riddled their tents with bullets. Laborer Gong Heng was asleep in his tent when the shooting began. He described the attack: "So many shot fired it sounded all same [as] China New Year."[22] Three Chinese men died and several more were seriously wounded.

In Oregon and Washington Territory, a surplus of jobs lessened economic competition between white and Chinese residents. Chinese had been working in the lumber and railroad industries in Tacoma since the early 1870s. However, their more established presence did not protect them from intimidation and expulsion. In November 1885, several hundred white men armed with pistols and clubs rounded up Chinese, ordering them to "pack up and leave town by 1 p.m. or face unspoken consequences."[23]

In the early twentieth century, the majority of Indians, Koreans, and Filipinos worked in the agricultural, railroad, and lumber industries in the US West, and much of the animosity that they faced was linked to working-class labor competition. In 1907, a mob of five hundred white working men expelled South Asian migrant workers from Bellingham, Washington. They broke windows, threw rocks, and indiscriminately beat people.[24] An angry mob of white workers threatened Korean laborers with physical violence in Hemet Valley, California, in 1913.[25] Anti-Filipino riots took place in Exeter and Watsonville, California, in the 1920s and 1930s. In Exeter, white mobs roamed through Filipino agricultural labor camps, beating the laborers, smashing cars, and burning down bunkhouses.[26] In Watsonville, sexual as well as economic competition erupted in violence over Filipino men dancing with white women in taxi dance halls, resulting in the death of Fermin Tobera. White mobs roamed Watsonville's streets, beating or shooting Filipinos on sight.[27]

During World War II, although Asian American men served in the US armed forces and although Asian American women worked as Rosie the Riveters, Japanese Americans were racialized as an enemy of their own country. Their homes and businesses were targeted for arson, shootings, and vandalism. In 1942, 120,000 Japanese Americans were forcibly relocated and incarcerated in remote internment camps across the United

States. Two-thirds were US-born Japanese Americans who were incarcerated without due process.

Non-Japanese Asian Americans also experienced violence and harassment because they too were racially lumped together with Japanese. In her autobiography *Quiet Odyssey: A Pioneer Korean Woman in America*, about Korean American life in the early twentieth century, Mary Paik Lee recalled the following:

> Even after all the Japanese were taken away to concentration camps, other Orientals were subject to all kinds of violence. They were afraid to go out at night; many were beaten even during the day. Their cars were wrecked. The tires were slashed, the radios and batteries removed. Some friends driving on the highways were stopped and their cars were overturned. It was a bad time for all of us.[28]

Thus, despite the many differences in national origin, language, faith, generational status, and socioeconomic status of Chinese, Japanese, Filipinos, Koreans, and Indians, anti-Asian hate in the United States wove their fates together. The linkage between Asian bodies and diseases was only one strand of this pattern of hatred. Economic and sexual competition, imperial and colonial hierarchies, and wartime politics were others. At moments of various crises beginning in the second half of the nineteenth century, they incited egregious forms of anti-Asian violence in the United States.

These histories seep into our present.

ANTI-ASIAN HATE IN THE AGE OF COVID-19

On February 14, 2020, a bully physically attacked his classmate, a sixteen-year-old Asian American boy, in California's San Fernando Valley, accusing him of having the coronavirus and telling him to go back to China.[29] The case prompted Manjusha Kulkarni, the executive director of the Asian Pacific Policy and Planning Council (A3PCON); Cynthia Choi, co-executive director of Chinese for Affirmative Action; and Russell Jeung, a professor at San Francisco State University's Department of

Asian American Studies to ask California's Office of the Attorney General to host an online, anti-Asian hate reporting center. When the Office of the Attorney General was unable to do so, Choi, Jeung, and Kulkarni created the Stop AAPI Hate reporting center themselves, launching it on March 19, 2020.[30] The reporting center tracked and analyzed incidents of hate against Asian Americans and Pacific Islanders in the wake of the COVID-19 pandemic. Its website included a content area that enabled users to report a hate incident from a selection of twelve languages.

Stop AAPI Hate's founding emerged from a legacy of six decades of Asian American activism as well as a response to contemporary anti-Asian violence. Choi, Jeung, and Kulkarni were able to establish the reporting center relatively quickly because of the political infrastructure that activists had been building since the late 1960s as part of the Asian American Movement, a social justice movement that advocated for relevant community services and curriculum, among other causes.[31] Chinese for Affirmative Action was founded in 1969 with the mission to protect the civil rights of Chinese Americans and to advance multiracial democracy in the United States. San Francisco State University's Department of Asian American Studies was also created in 1969 as a result of student strikes led by the Black Student Union and Third World Liberation Front. A3PCON, which serves the needs of the Asian and Pacific Islander American community in the greater Los Angeles area, emerged from coalition-building among social service programs in the mid-1970s.[32]

In early 2020, as the coronavirus spread in China, Choi expressed concern about the impact on Chinese Americans, noting that public references to the "Chinese virus" were worrisome to members of Chinese for Affirmative Action.[33] Between March 16 and March 30, 2020, President Donald Trump used the phrase "Chinese virus" more than twenty times.[34] He also referred to COVID-19 as the "kung flu" in several presidential campaign rallies. White House press secretary Kayleigh McEnany defended the use of the term: "It's not a discussion about Asian Americans, who the president values and prizes as citizens of this great country."[35]

Asian American community leaders disagreed. Andy Kang, executive director of Asian Americans Advancing Justice–Chicago, criticized these labels: "With such an emotionally charged political atmosphere, it's irresponsible and reckless for our political leaders and candidates for our nation's highest office to engage in rhetoric that incites xenophobic scapegoating and violence."[36]

In 2015, the World Health Organization advised that new diseases ought not to be named after nations, economies, and people because of the stigma that becomes attached to them. Dr. Keiji Fukuda, WHO's assistant director-general for health security, noted that "this may seem like a trivial issue to some, but disease names really do matter to the people who are directly affected. We've seen certain disease names provoke a backlash against members of particular religious or ethnic communities. . . . This can have serious consequences for peoples' lives and livelihoods."[37]

Choi, Kulkarni, and Jeung feared that the assault on the Asian American teenager in the San Fernando Valley was not a singular incident. They were right. The Stop AAPI Hate reporting center collected approximately one hundred anti-Asian incidents per day during its first week of operation.

A major contribution of the center was its collection and analysis of qualitative as well as quantitative data on anti-Asian hate in its reports, the first of which was released on March 25, 2020.[38] Stop AAPI Hate reports highlighted stories from those who had directly experienced or observed hate incidents. Many of the stories captured not solely how anti-Asian hate was expressed, but also how it *felt*. They foregrounded Asian Americans' perspectives about their encounters with racism that have been neglected and dismissed.[39] In a story from Stop AAPI Hate's "Week 1 Report," an Asian American shared:

> I was not seen by the employee at my local post office where I have been a regular customer for over 20 years. After patiently waiting as she pointed to others behind me for nearly 45 minutes, I approached the desk when she prompted me to take several steps backwards in a very hostile tone. She had not requested [that of] any of the prior customers that had gone ahead of me, and they were also all non-Asians. The sting of her racism and coldness towards me made me feel less than and, frankly, dehumanized.[40]

In the center's "Week 2 Report," a story about online harassment poignantly revealed the psychological and emotional impacts of being the target of anti-Asian hate:

> Yesterday a teammate assumed I was Chinese even though I never said my race; all I said was "that is racist, I'm American FYI" when the teammate called me Chinese. He got everyone else on his team to join in and harass me. I feel ashamed almost to be Asian in America. It hurts. I was being called a "gook," being told "China has the highest suicide rates, you should think about that :)" or calling me "ling ling" and saying I eat dogs and spread corona virus.[41]

The Stop AAPI Hate reports also documented the wide spectrum of anti-Asian hate that was being expressed in the most mundane of situations—for example, while people were riding public transit or shopping in a store—and where there was sometimes no physical altercation but still a harmful expression of hate nonetheless. While the most egregious examples of anti-Asian violence made the national and local news, less sensational incidents did not. In its first two weekly reports, Jeung grouped stories of AAPI hate under the following categories: barred from specific establishments and transportation, coughed and spat on, verbally harassed, harassed online, physically assaulted, shunned, discriminated against at the workplace, and vandalism. In doing so, Stop AAPI Hate was able to present a more nuanced understanding of the hate that Asian Americans and Pacific Islanders were experiencing during the pandemic. Its data collection was also a form of advocacy, conveying to AAPI communities that they were not alone, and that their experiences mattered.

Finally, a major achievement of Stop AAPI Hate was raising awareness about the multiple trends in discrimination that Asian Americans and Pacific Islanders experienced in 2020. In the center's first national report, covering the period from March 19 to August 5, 2020, these trends included a gendered dimension. Women reported discrimination 2.4 times more than men. AAPI hate was also a nationwide phenomenon. Hate incidents came from forty-seven states, with California reporting 46 percent of the incidents, followed by New York (14 percent), Washington (4 percent), Illinois (3 percent), and Texas (3 percent).[42]

The center's national report further highlighted that, although Chinese were the ethnic group most targeted, 60 percent of the respondents were composed of non-Chinese, including Korean, Vietnamese, Filipino, Japanese, Taiwanese, Hmong, Thai, Lao, Cambodian, and mixed ethnicities. This trend reflects the significance of "Asian American" as a panethnic category in two distinct ways. First, it illuminates that an incredibly diverse group of Asian Americans was impacted by the stigma attached to the "China virus" because other Americans could not tell Asians and Asian Americans apart. Second, the Stop AAPI Hate reporting center's method of collecting data and presenting it in both aggregated *and* disaggregated ways shows that the shared experience of the AAPI community and the experiences of specific Asian ethnic groups are not mutually exclusive. Rather, it is important to pay attention to both.

FILIPINO NURSES ON THE FRONT LINES

The World Health Organization designation of 2020 as the International Year of the Nurse and the Midwife was meant to be celebratory. Tragically, it was a year of tremendous loss and grief. According to an investigative report by *The Guardian* and *Kaiser Health News*, nurses made up the largest percentage of US health worker deaths in 2020.[43] A September 2020 report by National Nurses United further revealed that among those deaths, a disproportionate number were Filipino nurses.[44]

Beginning in April 2020, multiple news stories reported that Filipino nurses had died from COVID-19. These nurses included Divina (also known as "Debbie") Accad, a clinical nursing coordinator for the Detroit VA Medical Center who had cared for American veterans for over twenty-five years; Celia Yap-Banago, who had worked for forty years at a hospital in Kansas City; and Araceli Buendia Ilagan, who died at the Miami hospital where she had worked for thirty-three years. Some of the nurses were only a few weeks away from retirement.[45]

In 2019, Filipino Americans were the third largest group of Asian Americans in the United States, with a population of over 4.2 million.[46]

One of their distinctive contributions has been decades of caregiving. Since the 1960s, over 150,000 Filipino nurses have migrated to work in the United States, constituting the largest group of foreign-trained nurses.[47] In 2018, nearly one in three foreign-born nurses in the US were Filipino.[48]

In states with a long history of recruiting foreign-trained nurses, such as California, Florida, Illinois, Massachusetts, New York, New Jersey, and Texas, Filipino nurses have been a highly visible labor force. In the mid-1990s, they made up 18 percent of New York City's registered nurses.[49] In 2016, Filipinos made up almost 18 percent of California's registered nurse workforce. Among younger nurses in California, they have been more predominant, with Filipino nurses representing nearly a quarter of nurses between thirty-five and forty-four years old, and more than one-fifth of RNs between forty-five and fifty-four.[50] These demographics suggest that the future of American nursing will continue to rely on Filipino nurses.

Despite their significant presence in US hospitals, Filipino nurses have been invisible in American culture even in television medical dramas. Some of the most popular TV dramas, such as *ER*, were based on public inner-city hospitals that were precisely the institutions recruiting nurses from the Philippines beginning in the 1960s. In 2018, the irony was not lost on Emmy Awards co-host Michael Che, who observed: "TV has always had a diversity problem. I mean, can you believe that they did 15 seasons of *ER* without one Filipino nurse? Have you been to a hospital?"[51]

Learning about the history of Filipino nurse migration to the United States is a way to resist their invisibility by acknowledging their long-standing presence. After the US annexation of the Philippines in 1898, benevolent assimilation policies led to the establishment of an Americanized training hospital system in the Philippines. American nurses trained Filipino nursing students in courses, such as practical nursing, the use of pharmaceuticals, and bacteriology, that followed a US professional nursing curriculum. Furthermore, Filipino nurse graduates had to demonstrate fluency in the English language in order to obtain *Philippine* nursing licensure. Americanized nursing training and English-language fluency prepared tens of thousands of Filipino nurse graduates to work overseas.[52]

Although American colonial officials had not intended to create a Filipino nursing workforce for export, US hospitals began to recruit Filipino nurses to alleviate nursing shortages in the second half of the twentieth century. The first mass wave of Filipino nurse migration took place under the US Exchange Visitor Program, a Cold War program established in 1948, that sponsored visitors from various professional backgrounds and from all over the world. However, Filipino exchange nurses and their US hospital sponsors began to dominate the program. Between 1956 and 1969, over eleven thousand Filipino nurses participated in the exchange program.[53]

The exchange program presented Filipino nurses with an opportunity to fulfill social and cultural longings. They had dreams of seeing a place with snow and where apples grow, another legacy of their Americanized education. The exchange experience also exposed them to working and living in the United States. During her exchange visit in New York City in the early 1960s, Epifania Mercado realized that she preferred living in the United States for economic as well as social and cultural reasons. Her salary as an exchange nurse was higher than her earnings in the Philippines, enabling her to help her family financially. "In the Philippines," she explained, "your salary is just enough for you."[54] She also enjoyed American outings: "You can go to Broadway, Lincoln Center. You have enough money to travel. There's always something going on."[55]

The predominance of Filipino nurses in US hospitals was catalyzed by three big changes in the United States during the 1960s. First, the establishment of Medicare and Medicaid in 1965 resulted in an increased need for nurses; second, the women's and civil rights movements resulted in new job opportunities for American women; and third, a more equitable immigration policy, called the Hart-Celler Act, was passed in 1965. Also known as the Immigration and Nationality Act of 1965, it established a preference system that favored the immigration of workers with needed skills. It enabled American healthcare institutions to recruit Filipino nurses to alleviate nursing shortages on a more permanent basis. In a 1969 advertisement in the *Philippine Journal of Nursing*, a Chicago hospital beckoned, "There's a job waiting for you."[56]

Meanwhile, in the Philippines, high rates of domestic unemployment and political instability pushed Filipino nurses overseas. The devaluation of the Philippine peso against the US dollar made the United States an especially attractive destination. By the early 1970s, a Filipino nurse in the Philippines needed to work twelve years to earn what she could make in the United States in one year.[57] This economic disparity would only worsen in the late twentieth and early twenty-first centuries.

Some Philippine government officials initially criticized Filipino immigrant nurses for abandoning their home country.[58] But, in the early 1970s, after observing the demand for Filipino nurses in the United States, Philippine president Ferdinand Marcos pivoted the country's development strategy toward a labor export economy.[59] The Philippine government began promoting the outmigration of Filipino nurses and other workers, most notably domestic workers and seafarers, to Europe, the Middle East, Canada, and other parts of Asia. Government officials later touted these overseas workers as the Philippines' new national heroes for the billions of dollars they remitted annually in foreign currency. This Philippine labor diaspora has also included the migration of Filipino nurses who have worked in the UK's National Health Service for decades. In December 2020, Filipino British nurse May Parsons made history when she administered the first COVID-19 vaccine outside of a clinical trial.[60]

Despite their long-standing contributions to healthcare delivery around the world, Filipino nurse migrants have historically faced numerous challenges including exploitive work conditions, fraudulent recruitment practices, racial and gendered scapegoating, restrictive licensing requirements, and language issues. Contrary to stereotypes of Filipino nurses' timidity and submissiveness, they have fought back.

In the mid-1990s, Woodbine Healthcare Center in Gladstone, Missouri, petitioned the US Immigration and Naturalization Service to hire Filipino nurses in its nursing home with the promise that it would employ them as registered nurses and pay them the same wages as American nurses. However, the Filipino nurses ended up working as nursing aides, and Woodbine paid them about six dollars an hour less than their US counterparts. Two Filipino nurses filed discrimination charges with the US Equal Employment Opportunity Commission and, in 1999, Woodbine agreed to pay $2.1 million to the nurses and their attorneys.[61]

Problems regarding language have occurred when the use of English in the workplace conflicts with the desire of Filipino nurse migrants to speak Filipino languages during work breaks and other noncritical work situations. In 2010, a group of sixty-nine Filipino nurses and medical staff members at the Delano Regional Medical Center shared a $975,000 settlement in a lawsuit filed by the US Equal Employment Opportunity Commission and the Asian Pacific American Legal Center. The Filipino nurses claimed that they were targeted to speak "English only" unlike other bilingual employees and described the workplace language policy as a source of embarrassment, shame, and harassment. Although the medical center insisted that it did nothing wrong, it had to conduct anti-discrimination training under the terms of the settlement.[62]

The predominant way Filipino nurses have responded to their challenges has been by organizing. Gina Macalino, an RN and California Nurses Association board member, observed, "There is a misconception that Filipino nurses are hard to organize. But if you go to any strike or any action where Filipinos work, the majority of the people you'll see on the line are Filipinos."[63] A recent study led by scholar Jennifer Nazareno supported Macalino's point. It found that a higher proportion of Philippines-trained RNs reported being part of a labor union or collective bargaining unit than their white US-trained counterparts.[64]

National Nurses United co-president Zenei Cortez was born and raised in the Philippines and migrated to the United States with her parents and siblings in 1974. As a leader of the largest union of registered nurses in the United States, she has been a staunch advocate for lower nurse-patient ratios and Medicare for all. Cortez's four-decades-long work history in bedside, direct-care nursing has given her a historical lens to view the shortcomings of the United States' early response to COVID-19. After photos of nurses in a New York City hospital wearing garbage bags as PPE (personal protective equipment) went viral in March 2020, Cortez decried the shortage of PPE for nurses: "We are in America, one of the richest countries in the world and, yet, nurses who have given themselves to the front lines are being denied something very important to protect ourselves and our patients. I have been a nurse for 40 years, and this is the first time this is happening."[65]

Beginning in the 1960s, Filipino nurses also organized local Philippine Nurses Associations from New York to Illinois to California that led to the establishment of the Philippine Nurses Association of America (PNAA) in 1979. Over the past forty years, the PNAA has welcomed and mentored new generations of Filipino nurses in the United States and provided them with professional development and leadership opportunities. Past PNAA presidents have become leaders in the broader US nursing profession, such as Lolita Compas, who has served as president of the New York State Nurses Association.

In 2020, the PNAA initiated a Heal Our Nurses Project to assess the well-being of their members and to amplify the voices of Filipino frontline nurses. Riza V. Mauricio, an advanced practice nurse intensivist, related: "Taking care of infants and children during this pandemic brought a lot of internal chaos. . . . Uncertainty and fear abound, especially as we are still learning about pediatric COVID symptoms."[66]

A major concern for Filipino frontline nurses has been about the risk of exposing their family members to this deadly disease. Evangeline Ver Vicente, an RN and member of the Philippine Nurses Association in Nashville, Tennessee, shared: "I pray every day that I will be safe and won't be able to transmit this bug to others and my family. For more than a month now, I wear a mask when I interact and see my family, especially my grandchildren. I am so eager to hug and squeeze them, but I am quickly reminded of the possible effect on them for me being a potential carrier. So, I stop and virtually hug them with a heavy heart."[67]

Filipino frontline nurses have responded to these challenges in creative and spiritual ways. Nurse Mauricio eased the anxiety of one Burmese mother, who did not speak English and whose baby had just been admitted to the hospital, by demonstrating and encouraging the mother to gently touch her baby's feet. Like Nurse Vicente, other Filipino frontline nurses have relied on prayer and spiritual beliefs to give them the strength to care for others. Arlin Fidellaga, an RN and Northern Regional vice president of the Philippine Nurses Association in New Jersey, recited the "Nurses Prayer" in a nine-day novena for those affected by the coronavirus, including healthcare providers. She and fellow members prayed:

> When we enter the room, allow us to project an image of confidence and warmth,
> So that our patients will feel at ease with us and trust our judgment.
> No matter how many times we see fear in their eyes, or recognize that they are in pain,
> Remind us that we should never become callous to their needs.[68]

During the pandemic, the needs of Asian American healthcare workers ranged from adequate PPE to the availability of mental health resources to combat a new deadly disease. They also included the need for safety from anti-Asian hate and violence.

CARING FOR OUR HEALTHCARE WORKERS

One of the tragic consequences of anti-Asian violence in the United States during this pandemic is that it has hurt American health workers of Asian descent. Incendiary rhetoric regarding COVID-19 as a "China virus" and the "kung flu" has belied the fact that US hospitals and other healthcare institutions have historically recruited many Asian healthcare workers during health crises. In 2018, US healthcare delivery relied on an immigrant workforce that made up a significant percentage—almost 18 percent—of healthcare workers. The majority of the 512,000 immigrant RNs in the US hailed from the Philippines, followed by India. Among the 269,000 immigrant physicians and surgeons, Indians were the top group, followed by those from China/Hong Kong, Pakistan, Canada, and the Philippines. Immigrants from China/Hong Kong and the Philippines were also represented among home health aides and personal care aides.[69]

Yet, Asian American health workers have not been immune to anti-Asian hate and violence. In an April 2020 video, Dr. Chen Fu, a hospitalist at NYU Langone Medical Center, reflects on how strange it is as an Asian American doctor during the pandemic and "being celebrated and villainized at the same time."[70] The video then cuts to a daily celebratory routine of car horns honking and people cheering at 7:00 p.m. to thank New York City's healthcare workers, while Fu notes solemnly, "At the same time I read on the news how people of my ilk are just experiencing tensions that they haven't experienced in modern history." Fu has experienced these tensions firsthand. He was stopped in the subway by a passenger who started to scream racial slurs at him, even though Fu was dressed in medical scrubs.

Filipino nurses have also been targets of anti-Asian hate. In late March 2020, San Francisco Unified School District nurse Kyle Navarro was unlocking his bike on his way to the post office to exchange a pair of glasses for a student. A man spat in the direction of Navarro, and then yelled a racial slur. Navarro reflected on the incident, "I was scared and I'm still scared. Navigating life as a queer person, I always have some level baseline of fear going out at any time. But even more so now."[71]

What should be done to end this fear, to stop Asian hate, and to heal from this pandemic? Navarro emphasized one path forward: access to comprehensive healthcare, including mental health services, for all Americans.

Despite the presence of so many Asian healthcare workers on the front lines fighting COVID-19, the history of associating Asians with disease is repeating itself. In an April 2020 interview for a *Berkeley News* story, journalist Ivan Natividad asked me the following questions: "How does this Asian xenophobia and racism impact other ethnic groups? How does it affect our attempts to combat the spread of COVID-19?" I responded:

> It's harmful to everyone. When Asians and Asian Americans don't go out in public to the hospital when feeling ill because they fear being the victims of anti-Asian hate crimes—that's a public health problem. While it is important that we modify individual behaviors, like washing our hands and keeping our distance from each other, we need everyone involved to make it effective. So, when you start blaming Asians or Asian Americans, it disrupts that collective response.[72]

The title of Natividad's article is "Racist Harassment of Asian Health Care Workers Won't Cure Coronavirus." It is an ironic message that demands our attention. Underlying it is a history lesson about the inefficacy of medical scapegoating that we've yet to learn in the twenty-first century. As I write, this pandemic is not over. Variants emerge. Anti-Asian hate and violence surge. At stake is the health of the nation.

TWO

1975: TRAUMA AND TRANSFORMATION

"I t is a beautiful country depending on where you look," writes Ocean Vuong in his semi-autobiographical novel *On Earth We're Briefly Gorgeous*. "Depending on where you look you might see the woman waiting on the shoulder of the dirt road, an infant girl wrapped in a sky-blue shawl in her arms."[1]

Vuong's writing compels us to look again. "A woman, not yet thirty, clutches her daughter on the shoulder of a dirt road in a beautiful country where two men, M-16s in their hands, step up to her. She is at a checkpoint, a gate made of concertina and weaponized permission."[2]

Before he became a critically acclaimed novelist, and before that an award-winning poet for his 2016 collection *Night Sky with Exit Wounds*, Ocean Vuong was born on a Vietnamese rice farm. The violence of the Vietnam War compelled his family to flee their home and their country as refugees.[3]

The family arrived in the United States when Vuong was two. His mother, grandmother, and an aunt raised him in a working-class neighborhood of Hartford. He attended public schools in the nearby town of Glastonbury, which were known to be among the best, if not the best, schools in Hartford County. In a March 2016 issue of the *Hartford Courant*, Connecticut's largest daily newspaper, an introduction to a photo gallery about life in the 1970s waxes nostalgic: "The good ol' days in Glastonbury. . . . Do you remember some of these places?"[4]

This is what Ocean Vuong remembers: "We literally erased ourselves to go to school [there]. . . . And there was shame with that, too, because I didn't know how to make use of it." Everyone had said it was a great school, but Vuong was less sure. "I don't know if it's that great. I feel like I'm judged before I step into any room."[5]

This is what Vuong's poetry and prose remind us: What is good—as in those "good ol' days"—depends on who is telling the story.

1975 marks a tumultuous year in Asian American history. It was the beginning of many journeys of Vietnamese, Hmong, Laotian, and Cambodian refugees to the United States. At the heart of the refugee's journey is the flight from persecution and violence in order to survive. The 1951 Refugee Convention, a United Nations multilateral treaty, defines a refugee as "someone who is unable or unwilling to return to their country of origin owing to a well-founded fear of being persecuted for reasons of race, religion, nationality, membership of a particular social group, or political opinion."[6]

Southeast Asian refugees fled from the aftermath of the Vietnam War, the Cambodian civil war and genocide, and the "Secret War" in Laos. They feared or experienced persecution because they had opposed communism and had allied with US-backed forces and governments. In short, they were *here* because Americans were *there*.

The Southeast Asian refugees who arrived in the United States had survived unspeakable terror. And they continued to encounter violence as they struggled to resettle and to breathe new life into their families and communities. Yet, just as American wars and policies have indelibly impacted Vietnamese, Laotian, Hmong, and Cambodian peoples and their homelands, so too have Southeast Asian refugees, their descendants, and immigrant generations transformed the US landscape with their labor and ingenuity, and their community organizing and creativity.

The massive influx of Southeast Asian refugees in the United States beginning in 1975 also dramatically changed US refugee policy from an ad hoc approach to a more intentional one through the passage of the 1980 Refugee Act. In recent times, refugees from Myanmar and Bhutan have been the largest groups of refugees in the United States.[7] Many of them have been employed as essential workers during the COVID-19 pandemic.

SECRETS AND WARS

Of the estimated two million people who fled Vietnam, Laos, and Cambodia, more than one million had been admitted to the US by 1992, constituting the largest refugee resettlement in American history.[8] Yet, while some of the experiences of their exodus and resettlement are well documented, ignorance of Southeast Asian American histories persists. In the 2020 documentary film *The Donut King*, about the predominance of Cambodian refugees in California's donut store industry, Susan Wahid of Rose Donuts & Café in San Clemente observes, "You would think by now most people would know about Cambodia, would know about the genocide, and would know about all the killing."[9] Yet, many of her customers don't even know where Cambodia is located.

This invisibility is partly the result of the ways that Vietnam and 1975 are popularly understood and remembered in the United States. 1975 marks the fall of Saigon, the year of America's loss of the Vietnam War to the country's communists. The defeat rattled American confidence. US involvement in the Vietnam War began with youthful optimism and an inspirational vision of service, embodied in President John F. Kennedy's iconic statement in his 1961 inaugural address, "Ask not what your country can do for you—ask what you can do for your country."[10] But as the war continued, it became an increasingly demoralizing war for the American soldiers who were being drafted into military service. In US history, another prominent theme is the bitter divisiveness on the home front, which included a robust antiwar movement. American critics noted the enormity of the social and economic cost. So many American lives were lost. Billions of dollars of funding for the Vietnam War could have been invested in the United States.

This plethora of controversial issues contributes to a US-centric history that has reduced Vietnam to a story about war and a consequence of the failed US strategy to contain the spread of communism after the Chinese Communist Revolution in 1949. This narrative erases the meanings and memories of Vietnam, Cambodia, and Laos as homelands, the beauty of their landscapes, and the diversity and humanity of their peoples. Another troubling outcome is the marginalization of Cambodian, Laotian, and Hmong refugees in US history. Their histories have been rendered invisible in large part because even though US military actions in Cambodia and Laos were part of the Vietnam War, they were covert.

Although Cambodia's head of state, Prince Sihanouk, tried to maintain the country's neutrality by severing ties with the United States in 1965, his policies allowed Vietnamese communists to use border areas and the port of Sihanoukville as supply routes. The United States bombed eighty-three sites in Cambodia between 1965 and 1969. In 1969, the bombing escalated. A covert US Strategic Air Command tactical bombing campaign of suspected communist base camps and supply zones involved carpet-bombing by US B-52s. The purpose of carpet-bombing, also known as "saturation bombing," is to inflict damage in every part of a targeted area just as a carpet covers every part of a floor. Although a 1970 coup put in place a Cambodian government that supported the United States, the bombing campaign continued until 1973, pushing Vietnamese communists deeper into Cambodia, and radicalizing more Cambodians against their government. An estimated 250,000 Cambodians lost their lives.[11] This destruction and devastation, combined with the withdrawal of US soldiers from South Vietnam, contributed to the fall of Phnom Penh on April 17, 1975, to communist forces, and the rise of the extremist government of the Khmer Rouge.[12]

The Khmer Rouge attempted to create a classless society made up of rural agricultural workers by destroying culture and traditions. The regime's leaders called this idea "Year Zero" and put it into practice by shutting down schools and universities, evacuating people from cities and moving them to rural areas, separating children from their parents and placing them in labor camps, abolishing money, and banning music. Professionals and educated persons were considered enemies of the state. Religious and ethnic minorities were singled out for persecution. Under Pol Pot's Khmer Rouge regime from 1975 to 1979, Cambodians endured forced labor, starvation, disease, and mass executions, after which the sites of these atrocities became popularly known as the "killing fields."

The Cambodian genocide led to the deaths of an estimated 1.5 million to 3 million people in a country that had a population of approximately 7 million in early 1975.[13]

The concealment of US military involvement in Laos is crystallized in the historical labels of the US "Secret War" in Laos and the US Central Intelligence Agency's sponsorship of a "Secret Army" of forty thousand of the country's Hmong hill tribesmen, a diasporic people and ethnic group. The "Secret War" and "Secret Army" were part of a broader US military effort to support the Royal Lao Government against the communist Pathet Lao army. The effort was an attempt to interdict traffic along the Ho Chi Minh Trail, a military supply route that ran from North Vietnam through Laos and Cambodia to South Vietnam, sending weapons, ammunition, and other supplies from communist-led North Vietnam to supporters in South Vietnam.

Southeast Asian refugees in the United States grapple with knowing these histories all too well from direct experience. Their descendants learn from what has been shared through familial and community-based stories. Some resist the secrecy that has rendered this history unknown by conducting their own research and crafting distinctive histories through poetry and other art forms as well as scholarship. Poet Monica Sok's 2020 debut collection of poetry, *A Nail the Evening Hangs On*, was inspired by her personal experience as a daughter of former Cambodian refugees, but also by the need to understand her collective history as part of a Cambodian diaspora. This is her hope:

> The U.S. secretly bombed Cambodia during the war in Vietnam, and this escalated the Khmer Rouge into power. This is not a mystery to me. If my readers learn anything by reading my book, I hope they learn that the U.S. is also responsible for what happened in Cambodia.[14]

These efforts to defy covert US military involvement relate to a different, albeit related, kind of war. As writer and scholar Viet Thanh Nguyen posits in his nonfiction book about Vietnam, *Nothing Ever Dies*: "All wars are fought twice, the first time on the battlefield, the second time in memory."[15]

FLEEING TO SURVIVE

It ought to be essential for all Americans to learn about the journeys that Southeast Asian refugees undertook to get to the United States. Many of their narratives have been published, such as the story of a Cambodian refugee known by the pseudonym of Bun Thab.[16] The Khmer Rouge had assigned him the task of writing down people's life stories each month. If their stories differed from what they had said the previous month, Bun had to report the discrepancy and "that was enough to get them killed."[17] One night, fearing for his own life, Bun fled with two friends. He witnessed one of his friends get shot and butchered to death. Bun hid underwater in a river as a communist soldier jumped over his head.

After some time had passed, he and his friend emerged. Holding hands, they started to walk again. They walked for two days with nothing to eat. Their discovery of a large turtle could have satiated their intense hunger. Yet, Bun related, "neither my friend nor I could bring ourselves to kill the turtle. Instead we prayed and promised the turtle, 'If you bring us good luck and take us to Thailand, we will not kill you. We will let you go.'"[18] They continued walking, carrying the turtle with them, until they reached Thailand, where an old man brought them to his house and his family gave them rice to eat. Bun recalled that he and his friend's stomachs were full, but their hearts heavy from the memory of their friend who had been killed. And although Bun eventually resettled in the United States, his trauma persists: "I still have nightmares of that Khmer Rouge jumping over my head, and I wake up shivering with fear."[19]

Bun Thab's story is but one of many narratives about arduous and harrowing journeys. Other first-person accounts describe a myriad of traumatic experiences, including individuals leaving only with the clothes they were wearing and being unable to tell family and friends about their escapes, witnessing the deaths of family members en route, encountering pirates in the Gulf of Thailand who robbed and brutalized them. The refugees with American contacts and who had fled via airlifts were considered to be the lucky ones. But this mode of escape was also perilous. In 1975, the first flight of Operation Babylift—the mass evacuation of orphans from South Vietnam to the United States and other countries—crash-landed and many on board died. The refugees who fled via land

and sea sometimes encountered unwelcoming authorities in Thailand, Malaysia, and the Philippines, which were the main countries of first asylum before their resettlement in the United States and other countries. Those refugees who were able to join these refugee camps further endured long and difficult waiting periods.[20]

The wide range of these experiences is often conceptualized as three migration waves, each taking place within a specific political context and having a distinctive socioeconomic composition. Beginning in 1975, the first wave's 130,000 refugees consisted of primarily South Vietnamese military personnel and their relatives. Many of them were well educated and spoke English. They had experience living in urban areas and had worked directly with Americans.

The second wave of refugees began arriving in 1978. It was a much larger group and socioeconomically more diverse than the first wave. Many were uneducated, poorer, and spoke little English. They hailed from rural areas. The Vietnamese refugees of this wave who fled by sea became popularly known as "boat people," although critics decry this label because it simplifies them as pitiful and obscures their heroic will to live.[21] The second wave was also more ethnically diverse. It included ethnic Chinese-Vietnamese, but also a large number of lowland Lao and highland Hmong. Many were Buddhists and animists, in contrast to the significant Catholic population of the first wave.

By the early 1990s, Southeast Asian refugee flows to the United States declined as formal refugee admissions programs, such as the Orderly Departure Program, ended. A third wave of Southeast Asians entered the United States primarily as immigrants utilizing the family reunification provisions of the 1965 Immigration and Nationality Act. It also included thousands of Vietnamese Amerasians (children born of US servicemen and Vietnamese women) as well as political prisoners.

In the early twenty-first century, new immigration and new generations born in the United States have significantly contributed to Vietnamese American growth and diversity. According to the Pew Research Center, the Vietnamese American population grew by 78 percent between 2000 and 2019. In 2019, 2.2 million people in the United States claimed Vietnamese ancestry, making the Vietnamese one of the six national origin groups, alongside Indian, Chinese, Filipino, Korean, and Japanese, that account for 85 percent of all Asian Americans in 2019.[22] The Cambodian, Hmong, and Laotian American populations also increased during this time. In 2019, the Cambodian American population numbered 339,000; Hmong Americans, 327,000; and Laotian Americans, 254,000.[23]

The concept of migration waves enables us to organize and generalize a large number of Southeast Asian refugee and immigrant experiences in the United States. But waves continue to move and take on new shapes. Southeast Asian refugee flows continued into the twenty-first century with the resettlement of a new group of Hmong refugees in Minnesota in the early 2000s.[24] This is a living history.

One might think that this historical ebb and flow of Southeast Asian refugees would make an impression on the general American population and impart lessons about wars and understanding about suffering. Yet, this is not what has happened in the age of COVID-19. Rather, ignorance and hate persist in the form of racial scapegoating.

In 2020, a hate note was taped onto a Hmong American couple's apartment door in Woodbury, Minnesota. It read: "We're watching you fucking chinks take the Chinese virus back to china. We don't want you hear infecting us with your disease!!!!!!!!!!" It was signed: "your friendly neighborhood." Woodbury is a suburb of St. Paul, a short distance to the Twin Cities, which houses the largest Hmong American enclave in the United States.[25]

The irony of the invisibility of Hmong Americans *even in Minnesota* is not lost on scholar Kong Pheng Pha, who writes and teaches about refugee migration with a focus on Hmong Americans. For Pha, it is but a reflection of the "larger and longer history of Hmong American structural eradication within U.S. history."[26]

AMERICAN HARDSHIPS

Refugee resettlement in the United States offered immediate refuge, but it also presented multiple challenges and crises. Refugees with less education struggled to learn a new language and make a living wage. Xang

Mao Xiong arrived in the United States from Laos in 1978. In an oral history, he explained, "I did not even know the difference between 'yes' and 'no' when I first came, yet I was required to find a job to support my family."[27] The English language was so different compared to the Hmong language, and adults struggled to learn what seemed to come easily to their children. Xiong continued:

> One problem I have had in learning English is that after I learned what one word means, I got all confused when I found that another word had the same meaning. For example, good, nice, beautiful, perfect have similar meanings. In Hmong, different words have different meanings. American English is very hard for us adults to learn. It is easy for our children, but not for us.[28]

In many refugee families, parent-child hierarchies flipped as children grasped the English language with more proficiency than their elders. They became the translators for all activities, the most important as well as mundane. For example, Genevieve Siri and her family arrived in the United States from Laos in 1976. Siri was only a first grader when she was called to interpret for a Lao family enrolling their child in school.[29]

Furthermore, refuge in the United States could not erase the memories of wars and the suffering that accompanied them. Southeast Asian refugees experienced depression and anxiety.[30] In the mid-1980s, the Centers for Disease Control began receiving reports of sudden unexplained death syndrome, or SUDS, among Southeast Asian—mostly Laotian and Hmong—refugee men.[31]

And, while some Americans welcomed Southeast Asian refugees, others scorned them as non-whites and undeserving foreigners. Vietnamese refugee fishermen clashed with white fishermen in Seadrift, Texas, culminating in the arrival of the Ku Klux Klan in the fishing village in 1979.[32] Racial tensions and violence also arose between Cambodian and Laotian refugees and Black, Latino, and white residents in poor urban areas, such as West Philadelphia. These racial hostilities partly stemmed from the way that Americans lumped Southeast Asian refugees with other Asian American groups who, in the 1960s and 1970s, were increasingly portrayed as successful immigrants and model minorities. In this context, the fact that Southeast Asian refugees in the United States received government and other public assistance was a source of resentment and misunderstanding.[33]

Southeast Asian refugees encountered intense anti-Asian harassment and violence in cities and urban neighborhoods that were grossly unprepared for the sudden influx of refugees needing assistance. Robert P. Thayer's 1990 report, titled *Who Killed Heng Lim?*, about the Southeast Asian population in Philadelphia, identified anti-Asian verbal and physical harassment as major problems. School-aged youth stated that racial epithets, such as "Chink," "ching chong," and "f**king Chinese," were regular occurrences.[34] Forms of physical harassment included assault, the throwing of rocks and bottles, vandalism to cars and houses, and arson. One Hmong American woman described the anti-Asian violence as ubiquitous and deadly:

> Everyone who can walk, between the ages of 6 and 85, has experienced it in some way. . . . I know old people who have been attacked and little children who have been attacked. . . . The situation is extremely bad. The level of hostility is very high. A lot of Hmong would agree. . . . That's why a lot of Hmong left the city. They started to feel that, if they didn't leave, then one day they could be killed.[35]

Such fears were not unfounded. In South Philadelphia in 1990, Timothy Meitzler struck Heng Lim on the head with a long piece of wood after calling him a "f**king Chinese."[36] Lim later died from the head injury. He had planned to become a doctor in Cambodia, but fled when the Khmer Rouge took power, making his way to a refugee camp in Thailand, where he stayed for two years before coming to the United States. The title of Thayer's report was inspired by Christine Choy and Renee Tajima-Peña's 1987 documentary film, *Who Killed Vincent Chin?*, about the 1982 murder of Chin, a Chinese American man, in Detroit. Ronald Ebens and his stepson Michael Nitz brutally beat Chin to death with a baseball bat, blaming him for the increasing competition from Japan's automobile industry in the United States, despite the fact that Chin was

Chinese American. According to witnesses, Ebens allegedly said to Chin, "It's because of you little m—f—s that we're out of work."[37]

In the 1980s and early 1990s, anti-Southeast Asian violence took place across the United States. A 1993 issue of the *CAAAV Voice*, the newsletter of the Committee Against Anti-Asian Violence, reported that Southeast Asians were bearing the brunt of anti-Asian violence. The story highlighted intense campaigns of violence against Southeast Asians in the Boston area that included efforts to drive them out of Dorchester in 1983 and 1987; multiple cases of arson targeting Cambodians in Revere; the 1985 beating death of a Cambodian man, Bun Vong, on his way home to Lowell; and the 1987 drowning death of a teenage Cambodian boy, Vandy Phorng, after being pushed into a canal lock. The story also spotlighted two horrific cases of anti-Asian violence in 1989. Before they pistol-whipped and killed Chinese American student Jim Loo in Raleigh, North Carolina, Robert and Lloyd Piche told Loo and his Vietnamese friends, "We had enough of you gooks in Vietnam." In Stockton, California, Patrick Edward Purdy, who had been obsessed with the Vietnam War, killed five children—four from Cambodia and one from Vietnam—in a shooting rampage at Cleveland Elementary School. According to the *CAAAV Voice*, "the non-acceptance of the American defeat in Vietnam plays a large part in the hostility towards Southeast Asians," despite the fact that the Southeast Asian refugees in the United States had been American allies.[38]

The poverty and violence of tough American neighborhoods and the helplessness of their parents and other elders pushed a number of Southeast Asian youths in the United States toward gangs for protection and a different kind of kinship. Some of these youths who are now adults have been deported or face deportation to their Southeast Asian nations of birth, even though they have completed their US prison sentences. According to the Southeast Asia Resource Action Center, two thousand Southeast Asian Americans have been deported from the United States since 1998. Roughly fifteen thousand currently live with a final order of removal, and about 80 percent of those removal orders are based on past convictions.[39] Most of these cases involve Southeast Asian Americans who came to the US as infants and toddlers, fleeing Southeast Asia as refugees with their families. Their deportations surged after 1996, when Congress passed the Antiterrorism and Effective Death Penalty Act and the Illegal Immigration Reform and Immigrant Responsibility Act, which enable the deportation of non-citizens for certain crimes, even if they were committed before the passage of the law.

Many of the Southeast Asian Americans who have been deported or are facing deportation are legal permanent residents. They face deportation for minor, nonviolent crimes, as in the case of Saroun Khan. He was about four years old when he and his parents arrived in Philadelphia in 1984. His parents did not speak any English. Khan felt as though he and his brother had to fend for themselves while in poverty. Khan's crime was to take an unlocked car for a joyride, an offense for which he had served time in prison. Yet, under immigration law, it is considered an "aggravated felony" and subject to deportation. In 2020, federal immigration agents arrested and detained him, putting him on track for deportation to a country that he hardly remembers.[40] Thus, violence persists for Southeast Asian Americans in the United States: as a young Southeast Asian person coming of age in Philadelphia in the 1980s, Khan had been bullied and robbed; now violence comes in the form of more recent government policies that engender fear.

Finally, the 1996 laws severely restrict the ability of immigration laws to consider Khan's individual circumstances before ordering deportation, further concealing the reasons why Khan and other Southeast Asian refugees are here in the United States and erasing what they have endured. What then of his and his family's history of fleeing war and genocide to survive, the histories of so many Southeast Asian refugees in the United States?

TRANSFORMATIONS

Just as US wars and policies indelibly impacted Vietnamese, Laotian, Hmong, and Cambodian peoples and their homelands, so too have Southeast Asian refugees, their descendants, and immigrant generations transformed the United States with their memories, their labor and their ingenuity, and the revitalization of their cultures. They have changed the contemporary American experience of the United States through their contributions to industry, government, and the arts.

One of the most recognizable ways that Southeast Asian Americans have shaped the landscape is through the building of ethnic enclaves. In 1988, California governor George Deukmejian officially designated the area in Orange County bordered by Westminster Boulevard, Bolsa Avenue, Magnolia Street, and Euclid Street as "Little Saigon." The sight and sound of the Vietnamese language and the smell of Vietnamese cuisine have contributed to making it a tourist destination. Yet, for Vietnamese refugees, who had left their homeland involuntarily and for whom there is often no return, these places have a deeper social and spiritual meaning. One of the ways that Little Saigon communicates a distinctive identity and presence reminiscent of Vietnam is through its architecture. Temples and other structures are built according to the principles of *phong thuy*, a Vietnamese form of feng shui. Familiar architectural forms such as arches and curved roofs, artifacts like Buddhist statues, and landscaping with plants and trees from Vietnam remind refugees and immigrants of the places they left behind.[41]

By creating a new place-based identity that forges connections between Vietnamese Americans and their ancestors, Little Saigon can be equally powerful for those who were born in the United States and those who were born in Vietnam but have little memory of their native country. Sometimes these connections are conceptualized in spiritual terms, for example, when this multigenerational community encourages those Vietnamese Americans living outside of Little Saigon to make a pilgrimage to the place, perhaps to attend the Tet festival and celebrate the Vietnamese Lunar New Year.

Some ethnic enclaves are not as architecturally visible, but still thrive. Silicon Valley offered Vietnamese refugees and immigrants a booming tech industry for manufacturing jobs and socioeconomic opportunity in engineering, while the businesses in San Jose's Little Saigon fulfilled cravings of home. Writer Beth Nguyen emphasizes that "if there's one thing that refugees and immigrants will never give up, it's their food culture."[42] Restaurants and groceries offering banh mi, pho, *banh xeo, com tam, cafe sua da*, produce, and snacks reminded them of the taste of home.

Music and video stores, fabric and clothing stores, and import shops served a similar purpose.

What began as a way to address communal longings would sometimes grow into stand-alone shops and even franchises. Lee's Sandwiches established a permanent location in San Jose in the early 1980s. It served the Vietnamese sandwich, banh mi, known for its textural contrasts of the baguette (crisp on the outside and airy inside), aromas of cilantro and meat, and flavor bursts from cool pickled vegetables against the heat of jalapeño peppers. In 2001, founder Chieu Le and his eldest son, Minh, expanded Lee's Sandwiches to offer Euro-style sandwiches alongside its banh mi options. It currently boasts over sixty locations across the United States.[43] And then there is the heartwarming comfort of pho with its foundation of long-simmered beef broth, rice noodles, meat, onions, herbs, and spices. Phở Hòa, which opened in San Jose in the 1980s, has expanded across and outside of the United States, with multiple locations in Washington, Indiana, Texas, Florida, and British Columbia, as well as California.[44]

It is not solely large concentrations of people and businesses that constitute a community. After Hurricane Katrina, one of the deadliest hurricanes in US history, devastated New Orleans in 2005, a relatively small Vietnamese American community in New Orleans's Village de L'Est returned to the city and rebuilt their community in the aftermath. Some observers attributed their resilience to innate Vietnamese family values and hard work ethic. Yet Asian American studies scholars cautioned against such ahistorical analysis, warning that it perpetuated a "model minority" stereotype.[45] Village de L'Est was a place that Vietnamese Americans had forged out of relatively recent refugee displacement and resettlement. It was a place that they could re-inhabit and build anew.

Sometimes the impact of Southeast Asian Americans in the United States is not through a geographically bound community, but rather through entrepreneurship. Ted Ngoy fled with his wife by military plane as Cambodia fell to communist forces. In California, he worked multiple jobs as a church custodian and gas station attendant until, one day, he tasted a donut, which he savored. It had reminded him of a Cambodian treat, *nom kong*. This discovery led to work at a Winchell's donut shop and eventually to Ngoy owning his own store. It sparked what would become Cambodian predominance in California's donut industry, what might be called a "pink box" revolution.

Ngoy went on to buy dozens of donut stores that he then leased to other Cambodian refugee families. Even with limited English proficiency, Cambodian refugees could make a living from operating a donut shop. Communication with customers could be limited to basic elements, like prices and the names of different donut types and flavors such as chocolate frosted and cinnamon twist. Ngoy used pink boxes to package donuts because it cost less than the traditional white boxes used by Winchell's and other donut shops. The pink box has since become the standard visual cue for a box of donuts in the United States.

Ngoy has received significant media attention regarding his donut empire, most recently in the documentary *The Donut King*. While the film features his refugee story and his family's economic rise in the United States, it resists romanticizing the American Dream through entrepreneurship. The documentary reveals that at the heart of each successful Cambodian-owned donut shop is an incredible amount of labor—the long working hours, seven days a week—which is often performed by refugee parents and their children.[46]

The resilience and innovation of Southeast Asian Americans can also be gleaned from their efforts in cultural preservation in music, language, and dance. In St. Paul, Minnesota, Hmong American adults gather to learn traditional funeral songs on the *qeej*, a reed pipe instrument, that dates back to 1100 BC. Music ensures the safe passage of those who die, so that their souls may return to their birthplace. According to student Be Vang, "The more you hear about it, the more it sounds like poetry. It's very heartwarming when you understand it."[47]

Since Southeast Asian American history and culture are often not taught in school, enrichment programs provide cultural continuity and help instill ethnic pride in children. Maysee Yang Herr is one of the creators of Camp Phoojywg, a youth program in Wisconsin that promotes appreciation and understanding of the Hmong language and culture. While the program is offered to all children, Herr observes increased pride among the Hmong children participants: "They were not quite as afraid to speak Hmong as they were before. And that says a lot."[48]

An example of Cambodian American cultural preservation is the artistic and educational work of the Angkor Dance Troupe. Angkor was the capital city of the Khmer Empire, which flourished from the ninth to fifteenth centuries. Tim Thou and a group of Cambodian refugees in Lowell, Massachusetts, established the Angkor Dance Troupe in 1986. Its goals include teaching students how to explain the history and tell the stories of the Cambodian people through the power of facial and body language, musical composition, and lyrical speech. In 2021, the Angkor Dance Troupe offered three courses remotely because of the COVID-19 pandemic. One course geared toward young Cambodian Americans features Cambodian cultural history and its relation to present-day issues.[49]

Southeast Asian American youth are leaders and organizers as well as students. Founded in 1988, the Lao Student Association at California State University, Fresno, aims to create a foundation where students can strengthen their knowledge through participation in various Lao cultural functions, such as an annual Lao Heritage Night. Students promote Lao culture through wearing traditional Lao clothing, dancing, and singing. But they also promote participation in American democracy by encouraging their social media followers to register to vote and by protesting against hate. In a May 15, 2021, Instagram post, they wrote: "We're glad that we could do our part and take a step towards change. Together we can fight and prevail to end hate crimes and discrimination in the United States. #unityagainsthate."[50]

Southeast Asian American women have organized as well, integrating cultural enrichment programs with community advocacy. The Hmong American Women's Association (HAWA) was founded in 1993 by a group of thirteen women in Milwaukee, Wisconsin.[51] Its initial programs included health education and literacy development. Since the early 2000s, its services have included providing individuals proficient in speaking Hmong, Burmese, Karen, and Chin as advocates for domestic violence and sexual assault survivors, with the broader goal of ending gender-based violence within the Hmong community. The organization also touts a Southeast Asian–specific LGBTQ program. And, in 2020, Leana Yang became HAWA's first openly Hmong queer-fem outreach and education director.

Education and leadership development are at the forefront of multiple Laotian American organizations. About 27 percent of Laotian Americans live with educational and financial disadvantages: 14 percent have attained a bachelor's degree and 41 percent live in poverty.[52] Thus, the Laotian American Society's most important annual event is its Education Award Ceremony. Established in 2005 and based in Suwanee, Georgia, the organization recognizes the achievements of Laotian grade school children and provides scholarships to rising seniors at its award ceremony. It reappropriates military code names in its outreach initiatives, such as Operation Lunchbox, for K–12 students of the Laotian community in Georgia. As the organization's website explains, "With school being out for the summer, many kids lose access to their school lunches. . . . We are making sure the kids are not left without a good meal."[53]

Leadership development has resulted in Southeast Asian Americans entering US government, including becoming elected officials. They include Mee Moua, who became the first Hmong American elected in a state legislature, serving in the Minnesota legislature from 2002 to 2010. Rady Mom also made history on November 4, 2014, by becoming the first Cambodian American to be elected to the state legislature in Massachusetts. Mom was born in Cambodia in 1970 and arrived with his family in the United States in 1982. He spoke no English, and credits his family's example, decades of community involvement, education, and a positive mindset for his success. After his political victory, he emphasized how important it was for younger generations to think differently: "We've never been taught to think positively. I'm going to do that. Here's proof: A man who didn't speak a word of English and can do this."[54]

Rady Mom mentored Tina Maharath, who became the first Asian American woman elected to the Ohio Senate in November 2018. The daughter of Laotian refugees, Maharath gained a reputation for her advocacy for underserved, troubled youth, and for people who have experienced trauma. She volunteered for many organizations, including Legacies of War, an educational and advocacy organization working to raise awareness about the history of the Vietnam War–era bombing of Laos.[55] During Maharath's political race, she acknowledged Rady Mom's support: "Fortunately, I am not alone. One of my mentors is . . .

Rady Mom (Massachusetts House of Representatives), who is also a former refugee."[56]

Finally, Southeast Asian Americans have transformed literary landscapes. In the 2002 groundbreaking anthology, *Bamboo Among the Oaks*, edited by Mai Neng Moua, first- and second-generation Hmong Americans share their perspectives on being Hmong in the United States. Moua created the anthology after noting the absence of Hmong stories in Asian American anthologies. *Bamboo Among the Oaks* was groundbreaking for multiple reasons, including the fact that Hmong culture is rooted in an oral tradition, and the Hmong had no written language until about fifty years before the anthology's publication. In an interview for the *New York Times*, Moua further explained the anthology's significance: "People who don't have a written tradition don't seem to exist."[57]

The desire for existence through narration also inspired the creation of *Little Laos on the Prairie*, an online storytelling publication. It emerged from the first annual Lao American Writers Summit in Minneapolis, held in 2010, when Danny Khotsombath and Chanida Phaengdara Potter were inspired to write about their experiences as Lao Americans raised in the American Midwest. *Little Laos on the Prairie* foregrounds the journeys of the people of the Laotian diaspora, who have been "layered beneath larger Asian nation narratives that are more commonplace to the public."[58] It calls for "words and stories written by us, and for us. Included, as well, are those that want to listen and learn. But don't interrupt us. It's our turn. We're getting Laod."[59]

Championing Vietnamese stories and passing them on to current and future generations drives the mission of the Diasporic Vietnamese Artists Network (DVAN). Founded by artists and scholars Viet Thanh Nguyen and Isabelle Thuy Pelaud in 2007, DVAN resists racist stereotypes linked to colonialism and war, while also celebrating the joy and pride of creating art in today's modern world. This emphasis on joy adds a distinctive dimension to Southeast Asian American histories, which are typically presented as traumatic stories.

Poet Monica Sok recalls how a school librarian chased her down the hall to give her the book *First They Killed My Father*, a memoir by Loung

Ung about the horrors of the Khmer Rouge regime. Sok characterizes the book as "survival literature" that helped her piece together her family's history, as it did for many Cambodian Americans of the 1.5 (people who arrived in the US as children and adolescents) and second generation. Yet, worried that restricting Cambodians to a trauma narrative tokenizes them, she asks: "How do we reimagine Cambodian American literature to include themes such as urbanism or sex or humor?"

And Sok wonders, what would have happened if the librarian ran to her to give her a book about a Khmer girl who lived on the moon? Or about a queer Khmer boy living in Phnom Penh whose dream was to dance? In the article "The Cambodian American Writers Who Are Reimagining Cambodian Literature," she along with Danny Thanh Nguyen, Angela So, Anthony Veasna So, and Sokunthary Svay discuss these questions, reminding us that there is no one way to be Cambodian.[60]

Southeast Asian American joy is a source of creative inspiration for Alexandra Huynh, a second-generation Vietnamese American who was named National Youth Poet Laureate in May 2021. Although she was initially hesitant to write about her Vietnamese identity—thinking it would be a clichéd story of immigrant parents silencing their American-born children—she changed her mind: "I realized I was meeting so much internal dissonance because I told myself that I could only write that story, but there is a lot of joy that comes from being Vietnamese American."[61]

REFUGEES IN THE AGE OF COVID-19

The massive and unexpected influx of Southeast Asian refugees beginning in 1975 changed US refugee policy. It transformed what was a largely ad hoc policy that had favored persons fleeing communist countries into a more intentional one, and it led to the passage of the 1980 Refugee Act. The Refugee Act adopted United Nations conventions and protocols that defined "refugee" as a person with a well-founded fear of persecution. It funded a new Office of US Coordinator for Refugee Affairs and an Office of Refugee Resettlement. The Refugee Act also raised the annual ceiling for refugees from 17,400 to 50,000 and created a process for reviewing and adjusting this ceiling.[62]

After passage of the act in 1980, US refugee admissions exceeded 200,000, then declined to 159,000 the following year, and ranged between 40,000 and 130,000 over the next thirty-five years, with the exception of the two years after the 9/11 attacks. The ceiling declined significantly under President Donald Trump, who set it at 15,000—the lowest refugee ceiling in forty years—in 2020.[63] In May 2021, President Joe Biden revised the ceiling to 62,500.[64]

In the twenty-first century, the numbers of refugees from Myanmar and Bhutan, fleeing political and social persecution and discrimination in their home countries, dramatically increased. They made up the two largest refugee groups arriving in the United States in 2011.

Many reside in the American South but also in the Northeast, Midwest, and West. In a 2014 report titled *Invisible Newcomers*, scholars Chia Youyee Vang and Monica Mong Trieu note that for these groups, limited English-language proficiency is a key socioeconomic barrier, among several others.[65]

Iowa is home to some ten thousand Burmese refugees, and many do not speak English. As a result, the majority work in Iowa's meatpacking plants, which pays higher than minimum wage without requiring English-language proficiency. In 2020, the community bore a disproportionate risk of contracting COVID-19 because, even though meatpacking plants had become hazardous workplaces for the transmission of the disease, President Trump invoked the Defense Production Act to classify meat plants as essential infrastructure that must remain open.[66]

In southeast Iowa's Columbus Junction, a meatpacking town of 2,300, the ethnic Chin community has grown to become nearly 20 percent of the population. According to an Iowa Public Radio news story by Kate Payne, at least 221 workers at one meatpacking plant there had tested positive for COVID-19, and two had died. Payne interviewed Pastor Benjamin Sang Bawi of Carson Chin Baptist Church, who has essentially been the main resource for this refugee community. He related, "If they don't go to work, how [will they] survive—that is a big question. . . . Of course, every family [is] concerned about that."[67]

· · ·

1975 is a touchstone for memories of war and displacement in Southeast Asian American histories. But it can and should also serve as a touchstone for transformation, a reminder that Southeast Asian Americans and new waves of refugees have contributed to the US economy, government, culture, and public policy. And they continue to do so. We would do well to pay heed to their stories and their challenges, because the COVID-19 pandemic makes clear that their lives and livelihoods are inextricably linked to our own.

THREE

1968: WHAT'S IN THE NAME "ASIAN AMERICAN"?

What's in a name? In Shakespeare's play *Romeo and Juliet*, the name does not matter as much as the quality of someone or something. But, for Asian Americans in 1968, the ability to call oneself Asian American was meaningful. To name oneself Asian American was to confront the racism and violence that had relegated Asian Americans as second-class citizens. To name oneself Asian American was an act of historical agency—the ability to make choices and, in doing so, to make history.

Many Americans take for granted the existence of Asian American identity. Yet, before Asian American became a category that one could check off in a box, or a heritage that Americans could celebrate in the US government-designated month of May, it was a radical consciousness that emerged in the late 1960s as part of the Asian American Movement. It signified a political sensibility that valued solidarity with Black, Chicano, and American Indian social justice movements in the United States and with revolutionary movements throughout the world.

While much of the Asian American Movement was new, Black and Asian American solidarity was not. The 1968 Black Student Union and Third World Liberation Front strike at San Francisco State College is part of a longer history of mutual support. This history challenges contemporary narratives that continue to pit Black and Asian Americans against one another.

The Asian American Movement's wide-ranging agenda led to many civic, cultural, and educational innovations. One of these innovations was the establishment of ethnic studies and Asian American studies in universities and colleges across the United States. Yet the struggle for Asian American studies in higher education and the K–12 curriculum continues.

NEW NAME, NEW STRATEGY

The contemporary general definition of "Asian Americans" signifies Americans of Asian ancestry. However, the name "Asian American" hasn't always been with us. It was born of defiance and a radical imagination in the late 1960s. In 1968, UC Berkeley graduate students Emma Gee and Yuji Ichioka coined the term "Asian American" when they founded the Asian American Political Alliance in Berkeley.[1] An anti-imperialist, anti-capitalist, Third World political organization, the Asian American Political Alliance fought for self-determination and liberation for Asian Americans.[2]

The name "Asian American" was a rejection of externally imposed categories of identity, such as the popular usage of "Oriental." Although some organizations of this period continued to use "Oriental" in their names, the term became increasingly outdated and smacked of Asian Americans' perpetual foreignness and their objectification as vases and rugs. It also recalled scholar Edward Said's concept of Orientalism, and its binary depiction of the East as primitive, static, and despotic, in contrast to the West's superiority, dynamism, and democracy.[3] Other seemingly affectionate names, such as the reference to Filipinos as "little brown brothers," infantilized them and reflected the unequal colonial relationship between the United States and the Philippines. Racial slurs—"chink," "Jap," "gook"—dehumanized Asian Americans. To call oneself "Asian American" defied these pejorative labels and claimed an American presence literally on one's own terms.

To be "Asian American" was also to claim a new collective vision. It imagined anew the relationship among diverse individuals of Asian ancestry by bringing them together under a broader Asian American identity. The breadth of this identity was a break from the past. Previously,

Asians in the United States primarily identified with their national origin or ethnic group, or even more specifically a particular Asian region, province, or hometown, or with their extended family or clan. In the second half of the nineteenth century, the first mass migrations of Chinese came from various districts of the coastal province of Guangdong in the Pearl River Delta. Pioneering Japanese emigrated from various prefectures such as Hiroshima, while Asian Indians hailed primarily from the region of Punjab. Language also divided them. As the largest group of detainees on Angel Island Immigration Station in San Francisco Bay, Chinese migrants carved poems written in Cantonese on the walls to express their disdain and despair. In the late 1920s, pioneering Filipino migrants spoke several languages including Ilocano, Visayan, and Tagalog.

Furthermore, an earlier strategy by Asian groups to counter anti-Asian hostility and attempt to gain acceptance in the United States was to distinguish themselves from one another. As they arrived in larger numbers in the late nineteenth century, Japanese immigrants did not want to be treated with the hostility and violence that the Chinese had suffered before them. Many of them also felt racially distinct and superior to other Asian groups such as Chinese and Filipinos. During this period, Japan was ascending as a world power with an Asian empire of its own. Japanese immigrants made conscious efforts to differentiate themselves from the Chinese through visible cultural markers, such as their clothing, and through public discourse in newspaper editorials.[4]

Yet, in the 1922 Supreme Court case *Ozawa v. United States*, the Supreme Court ruled that Japanese immigrants, or Issei, were ineligible for US citizenship. Takao Ozawa was born in Kanagawa, Japan, on June 15, 1875, and immigrated to San Francisco in 1894. He became fluent in English and practiced Christianity. Ozawa insisted that he was an American based on his industriousness and personal beliefs.

What's in the name "American"? Ozawa wrote: "In name Benedict Arnold was an American, but at heart he was a traitor. In name I am not an American, but at heart I am a true American."[5] The Supreme Court ruled otherwise because Ozawa was not white. Its decision upheld the 1790 Nationality Act that limited citizenship by naturalization to "free white persons." Ultimately, Ozawa's honesty and hard work could not overcome his Asian-ness. Race mattered. The court's decision enabled the exclusion of Japanese immigrants from the United States after the passage of the 1924 Immigration Act, which barred persons who were ineligible for US citizenship.

During World War II, when Japanese Americans on the West Coast were forcibly assembled and incarcerated in internment camps, Chinese, Korean, and Filipino Americans wore buttons identifying themselves. "I am Chinese" (or Korean or Filipino) was a short phrase that signaled what they were not. They were *not* Japanese Americans who were deemed enemies in their own country after the bombing of Pearl Harbor. Nevertheless, these buttons could not completely prevent the anti-Japanese racial harassment and violence directed at them.

By the 1960s, it had become clear that this "but we're not that other Asian group" strategy could only go so far. The contrasting strategy of Asian groups coming together to fight back and demand justice is what scholar Yén Lê Espiritu calls Asian American "panethnicity." Changing demographics facilitated a panethnic approach. Before World War II, Asian Americans spoke different languages. But by 1940, the US-born population of Chinese and Japanese Americans outnumbered the immigrant generation for the first time.[6] In the postwar years, increasing intergroup communication and contact also came from the breaking down of some economic and residential barriers. College campuses became a primary site for Asian American interaction. Among this new generation, Asian national differences and the old-world tensions that often accompanied them became less important.

The civil rights movement had exposed them to racial injustice. During Pat Sumi's visit to the American South with friends involved in the Congress of Racial Equality (CORE), the courage of young Black Americans to face the Ku Klux Klan at demonstrations made a deep impression on her. It galvanized her own activism, which included working on voter registration efforts in the South, antiwar organizing with GIs, and participating in the Eldridge Cleaver Delegation of antiwar Americans to North Korea, North Vietnam, and China.[7]

The Black Power movement, its substance and style of community-centered and confrontational politics, became a major source of inspiration.

In a 1969 essay, Amy Uyematsu described the emerging Asian American movement as an expression of "yellow power" and a direct outgrowth of the Black Power movement.[8] The Bay Area revolutionary group known as the Red Guard Party, founded that same year, modeled itself on the Black Panthers. They wore berets and armbands, created their own "10-Point Program" and serve-the-people initiatives such as a Free Breakfast program, and denounced police brutality in Chinatown. As Chinatown youth, they experienced joblessness and were increasingly targeted by the police. Alex Hing, one of its founders, recalled:

> A handful of us were closely following the Black Panther Party. They were arming themselves, and they were talking politics. At the time, we felt an extreme urgency because police were killing people, putting us in jail. My cousin was handcuffed and beaten to death in prison. People think this doesn't happen to Chinese people, nah. This was why armed self-defense wasn't just rhetoric, some macho thing we thought was cool. This is what we were facing.[9]

A global dimension—the idea of being part of the Third World majority—informed an empowering paradigm shift. In 1968, the Philippine American Collegiate Endeavor (PACE), a new student organization at San Francisco State College, declared: "So we have decided to fuse ourselves with the masses of Third World people, which are the majority of the world's people, to create, through struggle, a new humanity, a new humanism, a New World Consciousness, and within that context collectively control our own destinies."[10] Liberation and self-determination at home and abroad were major objectives. A racist society, silence, and neutrality, the major obstacles.

Activists added a transnational, Asian American racial dimension to the antiwar movement because they recognized that other Americans would not be able to tell them apart from the Vietnamese communist enemy whom the US military dehumanized as "gooks." Some Asian American soldiers became antiwar activists after suffering firsthand this affront of being lumped together with North Vietnamese soldiers. Their superior officers used them as examples of what the enemy looked like, telling non–Asian American recruits, "We kill people who look like him!"[11] Such racist abuse fueled their fears of being killed by fellow soldiers or being left behind by medevac teams. The horror of witnessing and participating in violence against people who bore a resemblance to their own families also took a psychological toll.

Philippine president Ferdinand Marcos's backing of US military actions in Vietnam and American presidents' continuing support of the Marcos regime, despite his dictatorial ambitions, motivated some Filipino American activists to work toward Philippine democracy as well as freedom from American racism. After Marcos declared martial law in the Philippines in 1972, they participated in various anti-martial law organizations in the United States.[12] One of these organizations was the KDP (Katipunan ng mga Demokratikong Pilipino, or Union of Democratic Filipinos). Founded in 1973, it was a revolutionary organization that advocated a "dual-line" program, calling for a national democratic movement in the Philippines and the establishment of socialism in the United States.[13]

From the late 1960s to the 1980s, the Asian American Movement was a social justice movement whose major aims were wide-ranging and ambitious. They included community-centered service programs, the humane representation of Asian Americans in arts and culture, and justice for victims of anti-Asian violence and Japanese American internment. Some of the movement's most impactful events included the protests against the eviction of Filipino and Chinese elders in San Francisco's International Hotel that was part of an "urban renewal" strategy to satisfy big developer interests in the 1960s and 1970s; the creation of Asian American activist publications, posters, and albums; campaigns for justice for victims of anti-Asian violence; and the Redress movement for former Japanese American internees.

Although it would take time—decades even—numerous contributions emerged from the ideas, actions, and sacrifices of these activists. These include the publication of *Gidra* magazine (1969–74) and *Roots: An Asian American Reader* (1971); the 1973 album release of *A Grain of Sand: Music for the Struggle of Asians in America*; the creation of the Asian American nonprofit organization American Citizens for Justice in response to the 1982 killing of Vincent Chin; the passage of the

1988 Civil Liberties Act that granted redress for surviving internees and a formal presidential apology; and, in 2010, a new International Hotel Manilatown Center in San Francisco.[14]

Like other social movements of the period, a major challenge was internal dissent within and across various groups. Revolutionary groups competed against one another. Activists within specific organizations disagreed over tactics and goals. Coalitions were built, but they were also fragile. Although the movement attempted to unite Chinese, Japanese, and Filipino Americans, who made up the three dominant Asian ethnic groups of the period, Filipinos felt marginalized by terms like "yellow power" and participated in Brown Asian caucuses at various Asian American national and regional conferences, such as the National Conference on Asian-American Mental Health in 1972.[15]

Sexism and homophobia challenged the centrality of race and racism in the movement. In a 1971 skit written and performed by women activists, the character "Sister" poses the question "What do you think of women's liberation?" "Brother 1" seems to support it, but then says: "Right on! Let's put it on a stencil and run it off for the conference. Here, sister, can you type it up (hands it to her without waiting for her to answer)."[16] Daniel C. Tsang came out at the 1974 Third World People's Solidarity Conference in Ann Arbor. He was active in gay and Asian groups but felt a sense of isolation in both. The gay groups were primarily white, and some Asian Americans were homophobic.[17]

Still, the similar experiences of anti-Asian violence, labor exploitation, and social discrimination created common ground. The study of history would occupy a special place in Asian American studies because it illuminated that these similarities existed over time. Activists' belief in the value of Asian American history and their critique of its erasure helped to unite them. As Asian American Political Alliance (AAPA) veteran Jeffrey Thomas Leong explained:

> What happened was that we in AAPA and other folks identified the lack of historical accuracy in the courses we were taking, how the Japanese internment was not even in the history books, how discrimination against Asian Americans, Chinese Americans, Filipino Americans also

was not in the history books. So we made it a high priority on our agenda to make changes within university and high school curriculum to include courses that covered those subjects.[18]

At stake was their very humanity. Steve Wong, a fellow AAPA veteran, lamented:

So much of Asian American history is not available in any kind of format. . . . Young people growing up, or even as I was growing up, we knew very little about our own background, our contributions, not only within the context of the United States, but internationally. And the struggles that we had to go through in order to be recognized in any kind of way that we too are human beings, that we have potential to do things that other people can do.[19]

Confronting histories of anti-Asian racism was difficult, but it was a first step toward healing and empowerment. Before he joined the Union of Democratic Filipinos (KDP) in the 1970s, Abe Ignacio had experienced so much racial taunting that he became ashamed of his Filipino heritage and wished he were white. His mindset shifted after taking an Asian American history class during his senior year of high school and reading *America Is in the Heart* by Carlos Bulosan, about the hardships of Filipino migrant laborers in the 1920s and 1930s.[20] This knowledge enabled Ignacio to understand the long history of racial injustice and helped him rebuild his self-esteem.

Such revelations reflect the heart of a beloved quote among Filipino American history advocates: "No history, no self. Know history, know self." This aphorism is based on an interpretation and translation of a famous quote by Philippine national hero Jose Rizal: "He who does not know how to look back at where he came from will never get to his destination."[21]

The significance of a relevant curriculum that featured the histories as well as contemporary issues of people of color contributed to galvanizing a student coalition at San Francisco State College in 1968 to demand ethnic studies.

BLACK AND ASIAN AMERICAN SOLIDARITY

November 6, 1968, at San Francisco State College was a watershed moment in United States history. It marked the beginning of the Black Student Union and Third World Liberation Front (TWLF) student strike, an action that would last five months and become the longest college strike in US history.[22] The TWLF was a multiracial alliance of Black, Asian American, Latino, and American Indian students who demanded institutional change. Its constituent organizations included the Black Student Union, Latin American Student Organization, Mexican American Student Coalition, Philippine American Collegiate Endeavor, Asian American Political Alliance, and Intercollegiate Chinese for Social Action.[23] Their activism led to the establishment of the College of Ethnic Studies.

The 1968 TWLF strike was not the first time that Blacks and Asian Americans had expressed solidarity with one another. Rather, this historical event is part of a long history of mutual support between these two groups that spans over 150 years. This support took shape in many forms including advocacy for immigration, union organizing, friendship in times of national crisis, and activism for civil rights.

Tragically, this history is not well known because both groups have been pitted against one another, an egregious example of which is the way that news stories in the late 1960s and early 1970s presented Asian Americans as model minorities at the expense of Blacks. In 1966, a *U.S. News & World Report* story titled "Success Story of One Minority Group in U.S." depicted Chinese and "other Orientals" as successful immigrants who suffered prejudice, but who did not complain, achieving success through hard work alone.[24] This seemingly positive branding was set in contrast to Black Americans, who were used as the example of an unsuccessful minority who protested hardship and relied on the government for help.

Asian American studies scholars have long argued that the model minority is a harmful stereotype, emphasizing that one of its most pernicious impacts is its construction of a Black and Asian American divide. Yet the association of Asian Americans as docile, model minorities persists, as does the perception of Black and Asian American enmity.

We can learn lessons from histories of Black and Asian American solidarity. A working time line could begin in 1869. By the time that abolitionist leader, orator, and author Frederick Douglass delivered his lecture titled "Our Composite Nationality" in Boston in December of that year, the movement to disenfranchise the Chinese was underway. In 1854, the California Supreme Court case *People v. Hall* had ruled that Chinese testimony against whites was inadmissible in court because the Chinese were an inferior race incapable of participating in "our Government."[25] Frederick Douglass made his support for Chinese immigration clear:

> I have said that the Chinese will come, and have given some reasons why we may expect them in very large numbers in no very distant future. Do you ask if I would favor such immigrations? I answer, *I would.* "Would you admit them as witnesses in our courts of law?" *I would.* Would you have them naturalized, and have them invested with all the rights of American citizenship? *I would.* Would you allow them to vote? *I would.* Would you allow them to hold office? *I would.*[26]

Douglass urged Americans to settle such matters with higher principles and not selfishness. "There are such things in the world as human rights," he reminded listeners. One of them was the right of migration, which belonged to all races, including the Chinese.

In 1899, a twenty-one-year-old Buffalo Soldier named David Fagen defected from the US Army during the Philippine-American War in support of Philippine revolutionaries, who had declared their independence initially from Spain and, subsequently, the United States. He became a guerrilla leader of such renown that Filipino soldiers called him "General Fagen."[27] Fagen had been part of the six segregated regiments of Black soldiers who were sent to fight in the Philippines. While some Black soldiers believed that fighting alongside non-Black Americans and demonstrating their loyalty would improve their situation in the United States—where Blacks were being routinely lynched in front of white mobs—at least one dozen Black soldiers fought on the side of the Filipinos. Black newspapers published letters from soldiers in the Philippines, such as Sergeant

John Galloway, who foreshadowed their interwoven fates: "The future of the Filipino, I fear, is that of the Negro in the South."[28]

Filipino and Black solidarity reemerged in the United States in the form of labor organizing in the 1920s and 1930s. In 1925, trade unionist A. Philip Randolph and the Pullman porters organized and founded the Brotherhood of Sleeping Car Porters. In the classic divide-and-conquer strategy, the Pullman Company hired Filipino train car attendants to disparage Black workers. Although the Brotherhood initially vilified Filipino "scabs," historian Barbara M. Posadas has found that its policy shifted to recognize the common plight of minority workers.[29] The Brotherhood welcomed Filipinos as members, declaring: "The only security of the Filipinos as well as the Negro Pullman porter is organizing as one common union."[30] Yet, recruiting Filipino attendants to join the union was a challenge. Some Filipinos rejected union membership as damaging and preferred to work with white society, while others doubted the Brotherhood's ability and commitment to protect Filipino jobs. The integration and leadership of Filipinos in the union made a difference. Attendant Cipriano Samonte understood the need for organizing after having migrated from the Philippines to Hawai'i and enduring harsh labor conditions on sugar plantations. Samonte led the organizing drive of the Filipino workers in Chicago, meeting with Filipinos on payday to talk about the importance of the union. After years of struggle, the Brotherhood was recognized as the union representing workers at the Pullman Company, signing its first contract in 1937. Samonte spent more than twenty-five years with the union, serving on the executive board of the Brotherhood of Sleeping Car Porters' Chicago division and its grievance committee.[31]

In times of national crisis, the seemingly ordinary gesture of friendship becomes extraordinary. Soon after Japan's attack on Pearl Harbor on December 7, 1941, the United States declared war on Japan. In February 1942, President Roosevelt issued Executive Order 9066, which resulted in the internment of about 120,000 Japanese Americans on the West Coast. They included Takashi Hoshizaki, who was detained at Pomona Assembly Center located on the Los Angeles Fairgrounds, about thirty miles east of downtown Los Angeles. Hoshizaki recalled a moment of joy and respite at the assembly center when his Black neighbors, the

Marshalls, traveled all the way to see him and his family, albeit through a fence, and to bring them apple pie à la mode. The Marshalls had a catering business and, decades later, Hoshizaki recalled with delight how they had skillfully baked the apple pie so as to create space between the crust and apple filling for the ice cream. "It was a real pleasure," Hoshizaki said.[32]

Hoshizaki was subsequently incarcerated at Heart Mountain internment camp in Wyoming, where civil rights, antiwar, gay liberation, and AIDS activist Kiyoshi Kuromiya was born in 1943. In the 1960s, Kuromiya participated in restaurant sit-ins in Maryland to protest those establishments that refused to serve Blacks and was brutally beaten by Alabama state troopers in Selma as he was leading a group of high school students in a march to the state capitol building in Montgomery.[33] Kuromiya developed a close friendship with Rev. Dr. Martin Luther King Jr. and his family. After King was assassinated in 1968, he helped care for King's children at the family's home.[34]

In 1948, Cecilia Suyat needed a job to support herself in New York City after having moved away from her Filipino family and her childhood home in Hawai'i. Suyat recalled that when she went to the employment office, "the clerk, she saw my dark skin, and she sent me to the national office of the NAACP."[35] Suyat became the secretary for Gloster B. Current, deputy executive director of the NAACP. She traveled to various cities where she attended conferences and took minutes. Like her fellow NAACP workers, she experienced being turned away from hotels, and credited local people who took them in: "We stayed in their private homes, and they fed us and treated us like kings."[36] Suyat played a role in the 1954 *Brown v. Board of Education* decision, typing and re-typing the NAACP's legal briefs over a four-year period as it honed its arguments for the landmark case that ended legal segregation in public schools. In 1955, she married Thurgood Marshall, then a civil rights lawyer and widower, who in 1967 would become the first African American Supreme Court justice. They remained married until his death in 1993. In a 2013 oral history interview for the Smithsonian Institution's National Museum of African American History and Culture and the Library of Congress's Civil Rights History Project, Suyat Marshall repeatedly described her work at the NAACP as a "blessing." It taught her about racial injustice in the United States and the hard work it took to end it. She reflected, "And as I look back today, we've come a long way. But we still have a ways to go."[37]

The daughter of Chinese immigrants, Grace Lee Boggs was a long-standing activist, author, and philosopher, who worked as a tenant organizer in Chicago before marrying James Boggs—a Black autoworker, writer, and radical activist—and moving to Detroit in 1953.[38] Together, they participated in the major social justice movements of the twentieth century for Black freedom, and dedicated themselves to workers', women's, and Asian American rights, antiwar campaigns, and environmental issues. In 1992, they helped found Detroit Summer, a community transformation program for youth that focused on planting community gardens, painting public murals, and holding intergenerational and peer dialogues. Grace Lee Boggs attributed her optimism to her participation in collective action. A centenarian, she continued to contemplate and write about revolutionary politics later in life, emphasizing the historical significance of Black resistance: "And I think it's very, very important that folks understand how much this country was founded on the enslavement of blacks, and how the resistance of blacks to that enslavement has been the spark plug for so many important developments."[39]

After moving to Harlem in 1960, human rights activist Yuri Kochiyama met Malcolm X, and their friendship transformed both of them. She was moved by his calls for Black liberation and began working with Black nationalist organizations in Harlem. As the FBI and police surveilled and repressed Black activists, Kochiyama dedicated herself to supporting political prisoners, "providing non-stop letter writing—often at two or three in the morning," and linking the plight of imprisoned political activists to her own internment in Jerome, Arkansas, during World War II.[40] In 1964, Malcolm X visited the Kochiyamas to meet Japanese *hibakusha* (atomic bomb survivors) and journalists on a world peace tour. He also sent the Kochiyamas postcards from his travels to Africa and other parts of the world. One of them, mailed from Kuwait on September 27, 1964, read: "Still trying to travel and broaden my scope since I've learned what a mess can be made by narrow-minded people. Bro. Malcolm X."[41]

In February 1965, when Malcolm X was assassinated at the Audubon Ballroom in Manhattan, Yuri Kochiyama was there. She had been in the audience waiting to hear him address the Organization of Afro-American Unity, which he had recently founded. After the burst of gunfire, she rushed to the stage, cradled his head on her lap, pleading with him to stay alive. Although a photograph of Kochiyama comforting Malcolm X was published in *Life* magazine, there was no mention of her by name, and only in recent years has there been mention of an Asian American in attendance at Malcolm's final speech.[42]

Black and Asian American solidarity existed well before the TWLF strike at San Francisco State College in 1968. As this brief history shows, some of these examples of mutual support continued after the 1960s, weaving together personal and collective time lines, and overlapping in ways that may surprise us because we never knew about them. In May 2021, a survey commissioned by the nonprofit organization LAAUNCH (Leading Asian Americans to Unite for Change) found that 42 percent of people in the US could not name one well-known Asian American. Not one Asian American name.[43]

What's in the names: Frederick Douglass, David Fagen, Cipriano Samonte, Takashi Hoshizaki, the Marshalls, Kiyoshi Kuromiya, Rev. Dr. Martin Luther King, Cecilia Suyat Marshall, Thurgood Marshall, Grace Lee Boggs, James Boggs, Yuri Kochiyama, Malcolm X? Histories of Black and Asian American solidarity that many of us did not know. Histories that we could not know because we never learned about them.

As a result, we find ourselves grappling with one-dimensional, tired and tiring stories that emphasize the animosity between us. In the age of COVID-19, we bear witness to the intense circulation of videos and images of Blacks committing violence against Asian Americans on social media, creating the notion that the surges in anti-Asian hate crimes and incidents are primarily a problem of Black-on-Asian violence. But, like the model minority, this too is a myth.

The University of Michigan's Virulent Hate Project, led by historian Melissa May Borja, analyzes news media to research trends in anti-Asian racism and Asian American activism. In a report on anti-Asian racism in 2020, Borja and researcher Jacob Gibson found that the majority of the offenders were identified as male and white.[44] In political scientist Janelle Wong's analysis of official crime statistics and previously published studies of anti-Asian hate crimes and incidents, she concludes that "the racist kind of tropes that come along with [the media coverage]—especially that it's predominantly Black people attacking Asian Americans who are elderly—there's not really an empirical basis in that."[45]

This is not to say that no tensions exist between these groups. They do. Nor that we should not have difficult conversations about the hostilities between us. We should. But what if the history about our communities' solidarity had been circulated with the same frequency and intensity? What if the examples of solidarity that emerged after the 1992 Los Angeles Riots among Blacks, Asian Americans, and Latinos had become common knowledge?

On April 29, 1992, the acquittals of a group of mostly white police officers who had been charged with the excessive beating of Black motorist Rodney King sparked civil unrest in Los Angeles. The bulk of the rioting in South Central Los Angeles took place in Koreatown. It resulted in the looting and destroying of more than 2,200 Korean businesses and $400 million in damages.[46] What Koreans call *Sa-i-gu*, or April 29, increased the public's awareness of Korean immigrants in the United States. Yet, it was an awareness primarily filtered through news media that accentuated Korean-Black interracial conflict.

In 2017, twenty-five years after the LA Riots, Rev. Samuel Rodriguez, president of the National Hispanic Christian Leadership Conference, Rev. Mark Whitlock, pastor of Christ Our Redeemer A.M.E. (COR) Church in Orange County, California, and Rev. Hyepin Im, president of Korean Churches for Community Development, coauthored an editorial rejecting the myths and prejudices that had divided their communities. Instead, they highlighted their friendship and the potential of working together: "Twenty-five years later, we choose to look back by celebrating all that we've accomplished since. We can get along. We can end biased policing. We can create jobs. We can end violence. We can see."[47]

The spirit of solidarity lives on in the Black Lives Matter movement. While Asian Americans have participated in public protests that typically take center stage in news media, their activism has also taken place behind the scenes in the more intimate space of family conversations. Letters for Black Lives "began as a group of Asian Americans and Canadians writing an intergenerational letter to voice their support for the Black community." Their letters constitute a set of crowdsourced, multilingual, and culturally aware resources that create space for dialogue about racial justice, police violence, and anti-Blackness in Asian American families and communities.[48]

Beginning in 2016, the letters in English have since been translated into twenty-six languages. A new set of letters was created in 2020 in response to demands for justice for George Floyd, Dreasjon Reed, Tony McDade, Breonna Taylor, and Ahmaud Arbery. Both the 2016 and 2020 sets of letters include a South Asian American edition. "Dear family and friends," begins the letter in the 2016 edition. "We need to talk." It then makes direct connections between Black and South Asian American communities:

> In fact, stereotypes directly impact members of our community as well. The media shows us as foreigners with thick accents. We get called names in schools and on the streets. Airport security stops us, and some of us are profiled as terrorists because of our clothes or our religion.
>
> Sometimes, anti-Black racism also puts us in danger. In 2015, Sureshbhai Patel came to Alabama from India to care for his grandson. He was taking a walk outside when a White neighbor called 911 to report a suspicious "skinny Black guy" on the street. The police went on to assault Mr. Patel, who spoke little English. *He was left partially paralyzed, spending months in the hospital.* The police officer was never convicted of any wrongdoing, even though the entire incident was captured on video.[49]

The spirit of working toward unity lives on in the struggle to stop Asian hate. After an elderly Chinese American woman was set on fire in Brooklyn in August 2020, rapper China Mac organized They Can't Burn Us All protests. In February 2021, as attacks on Asian seniors continued to surge, he teamed up with Bay Area rapper Mistah F.A.B. to promote unity in their communities. In a joint television interview, China Mac emphasized the need for dialogue: "We're having our own conversations within the Asian community, but there's not enough conversations being had with people of other communities, specifically with the Black community."[50] And Mistah F.A.B. acknowledged that "there are many people that stand in solidarity with us, against our adversity, and our obstacles that we fight as Black people. And here it is, our turn to show that we're in solidarity with our Asian brothers and sisters."[51]

The history of Black and Asian American solidarity gives us not only a lens to view the past but also a way to reimagine our future.

ASIAN AMERICAN STUDIES NOW

The 1968 TWLF student strike led to the establishment of the College of Ethnic Studies at San Francisco State University. Today, the college houses five departments that offer degrees in Africana, American Indian, Asian American, Latina/Latino, and race and resistance studies. A TWLF strike on the University of California, Berkeley campus beginning in January 1969 resulted in the creation of UC Berkeley's Department of Ethnic Studies, which consists of four undergraduate programs—comparative ethnic studies, Asian American and Asian diaspora studies, Chicana/o and Latina/o studies, and Native American studies—and a PhD program in ethnic studies.

The demand for Asian American studies, the academic discipline that examines Asian American history, culture, and contemporary issues, reverberated across the United States. It resulted in departments and programs at the Claremont Colleges; the University of Texas, Austin; University of Minnesota, Twin Cities; the University of Illinois, Urbana-Champaign; the University of Maryland, College Park; State University of New York at Binghamton; New York University; Duke University; and other schools.

Yet, the struggle for Asian American studies in higher education continues. Although San Francisco State University and UC Berkeley recently commemorated fifty years of ethnic studies, including Asian American studies, journalist Agnes Constante reported in 2019 that Asian American studies programs can still be hard to find.[52] According to the College Board, only twenty-five US colleges and universities offer majors in Asian American studies.

The struggle for Asian American studies in the K–12 curriculum also continues. When history curricula include aspects of Asian American history, they typically devote only a few sentences to Chinese labor on the transcontinental railroad and Japanese American internment, if at all.[53] In 2021, Illinois senator Ram Villivalam and Representative Jennifer Gong-Gershowitz introduced the Teaching Equitable Asian American Community History, or TEAACH, Act (HB 376). The act aims to present a more holistic picture of US history by adding Asian American history to the Illinois School Code beginning in the 2022–23 school year.[54] Legislators in New York, Connecticut, and Wisconsin have introduced similar bills.[55]

These efforts stem from the urgent need to address the surge in anti-Asian hate and violence since 2020. The frequently raised question—What can we do to stop this and move forward?—typically elicits responses such as participating in bystander training and donating time and money to Asian American organizations. These actions are undoubtedly important. However, the conundrum of why this violence happens over and over again remains. A root cause is the phenomenon of not knowing Asian American history, the long-standing tragedy of anti-Asian scapegoating, and Asian American contributions to US culture, economy, and government. How can we begin to change what we don't know? How can we affirm Asian Americans as human beings if we don't even know their names?

FOUR

1965: THE MANY FACES
OF POST-1965 ASIAN AMERICA

Sometimes stories that we read in our youth about other countries, cultures, and peoples change the trajectory of our lives. We may not realize it at the time, but decades later, we can trace the emergence of an inspired path. During those impressionable years, we become aware of distinct places—new worlds—that transport us into a place that we now call home.

In Krishna Chandrasekhar's case, he started reading magazines and journals about the United States while he was a high school student in India. "I was fascinated by the United States," he recalled.[1] Soon after earning his medical degree, Chandrasekhar decided with two other doctors to immigrate to the United States. A complex interplay of individual and collective curiosity, professional limitations in India, and employment opportunities in the United States had propelled them to take a chance and work abroad.

On June 28, 1970, Chandrasekhar departed from Madras, India, for Buffalo, New York, where he completed his residency at Mercy Hospital. In the headshot that accompanies his interview for the First Days Project—a project, presented by the South Asian American Digital Archive (SAADA), which shares stories of immigrants' and refugees' first experiences in the United States—we see Chandrasekhar's face from those first days. Looking straight into the camera, he looks smart and determined. His long hair is pulled away from his face, and neatly styled into a bun on top that you might miss seeing if you looked at the photo quickly. His glasses with black rims on the top and clear frames (which in the twenty-first century have become retro chic), crisp, buttoned-up white shirt, and dark tie with a subtle diamond pattern complete the seriousness of his look.

Sometimes what brought us to the United States had less to do with our own youthful dreams, but rather was a path laid out for us by a family member. In Lakshmi Kalapatapu's story, the family member was her husband, Venu, who had begun working in Minneapolis, Minnesota. In 1974, she and their two young children departed from Hyderabad, India, and joined him in the heartland of America. Kalapatapu may not have been the first of her family to arrive in the United States, but her first days were no less adventurous. In her interview for the First Days Project, she recalled, "I came with one small suitcase and two small boys—a four-year-old and an 18-month-old—and that was a very big change for me."[2]

One of the biggest changes she experienced had to do with the weather. Although Kalapatapu had arrived in Minneapolis on a summer day, the subsequent snowstorms made an impression. She recalled, "That year, the snow didn't stop until May of the following year. That was really something."[3] While Minnesotans were used to this type of climate, perhaps taking it for granted, Kalapatapu was struck by its beauty: "All day long, I would sit at the window with my two boys and watch the snow fall. . . . I enjoyed that time very much."[4] The photo that accompanies her First Days Project interview complements these sentiments. You see her in a long winter coat, standing with her two young boys, who are sporting puffy down winter jackets. They appear to the left of the frame alongside freshly shoveled mounds of snow. The faces of Kalapatapu and the two boys are a bit blurry, but she appears to have a hint of a smile.

And sometimes what brought us to the United States was not solely an individual or family adventure, but rather the country's new law. The passage of the Immigration and Nationality Act of 1965 enabled both Krishna Chandrasekhar's and Lakshmi Kalapatapu's immigration. Before passage of the 1965 Act, anti-Asian hostility infused US immigration policies, and immigration restriction and exclusion had cast a shadow over the Asian American experience. As Chandrasekhar noted, "When I became a doctor, in 1965, for the first time since 1924, [the US] relaxed the immigration rules for foreigners; previously only people of European descent could come to America."

Krishna Chandrasekhar and Lakshmi Kalapatapu are two of the many faces of post-1965 Asian America.

THE IMMIGRATION AND NATIONALITY ACT OF 1965

The Immigration and Nationality Act of 1965 ushered a major transformation of the United States. It abolished the national origins system that had favored immigration from northern and western Europe since the 1920s. The new immigration system continued to restrict immigration, setting a ceiling of 290,000 annual visas, with 120,000 from the Western Hemisphere and 170,000 from the Eastern Hemisphere. However, it prioritized family reunification. Immigrants who were immediate relatives of US citizens, such as spouses and minor, unmarried children, were not subject to quotas or numerical limitations. The 1965 Act created a more equitable system to the extent that it limited annual emigration from any one country to 20,000.

The Immigration and Nationality Act of 1965, also known as the Hart-Celler Act for its congressional sponsors, established a preference system that emphasized the reunification of other family members—such as the adult, unmarried children of US citizens—and the immigration of workers with needed skills. The initial preference system consisted of seven preferences. A non-preference category was also created, under which a person who invested $40,000 in a business could qualify for immigration to the United States. Although the 1965 Act has been modified—the third and sixth occupational preferences became part of a larger employment-based immigration system in 1990, for example—it continues to be the basis of US immigration law in the twenty-first century.[5]

The Immigration and Nationality Act of 1965 is a legacy of the civil rights movement, linking the histories of Black freedom struggle and contemporary immigration. It prohibited discrimination on the basis of race, sex, nationality, place of birth, or place of residence in the issuance of immigrant visas.[6] Yet, despite its historical significance, it is not well known. On the fiftieth anniversary of its passage in 2015, multiple observers noted that the Immigration and Nationality Act is overshadowed by other major civil rights legislation such as the Civil Rights Act and the Voting Rights Act.[7]

In light of some Americans' insistence that the United States is a nation of immigrants alongside others' persistent hostility toward immigrants, it is time for post-1965 immigrants—their contributions and struggles—to step out of the shadows and take center stage. As a result of their immigration, the face of America has changed.[8] It is more Asian as well as Latino and African.

Although some legislators expected the 1965 Act to increase immigration to the United States, the increase they expected was from Europe and not from Asia, whose emigration numbers grew exponentially. In 1960, persons of Asian ancestry in the United States numbered less than one million. By 2019, that number had increased to over twenty million.[9] Post-1965 immigration catalyzed this dramatic numerical growth. As a result, a much larger percentage of Asian Americans—57 percent—were born in another country, compared with 14 percent of all Americans.[10]

The faces of post-1965 Asian America are also changing. South Asians and Southeast Asians account for the majority of Asian Americans, while Japanese Americans account for a much smaller share of the population than they did a century ago.[11] Many of these faces are of immigrant women, whose larger numbers helped balance a gender ratio in Asian American communities that once favored men.

The Pew Research Center's demographic profiles of national origin groups present one lens to view the dramatic growth and diversity of post-1965 Asian America. Whereas pre-1965 Asian American communities were predominantly Chinese, Japanese, Filipino, Indian, and Korean, nineteen origin groups make up the vast majority of Asian Americans since then. In addition to those initial groups, they now include Vietnamese, Pakistani, Thai, Cambodian, Hmong, Laotian, Bangladeshi, Nepalese, Burmese, Indonesian, Sri Lankan, Malaysian, Mongolian, and Bhutanese. According to Abby Budiman and Neil G. Ruiz's analysis of US Census Bureau data, six origin groups—Chinese, Indian, Filipino,

Vietnamese, Korean, and Japanese—accounted for 85 percent of all Asian Americans in 2019.[12]

Eleven of the nineteen origin groups more than doubled in size between 2000 and 2019. These include the Pakistani population, which grew from 204,000 to 554,000. However, some of the smaller origin groups, such as Bhutanese, Nepalese, and Burmese, stand out because they experienced the fastest growth rates, growing tenfold or more during this span. The Nepalese population increased from just 9,000 to 198,000.[13] By contrast, Japanese have had the slowest growth rates among Asian Americans since 2000. Thus, while the largest groups shape the demographic characteristics of the overall Asian American population, disaggregated data, unique histories, and distinct migration and settlement patterns demonstrate that each origin group deserves analysis on its own terms.

In the midst of these sheer numbers are two more faces of post-1965 Asian America. One belongs to Tariq Akmal, who departed from Lahore, Pakistan, in 1984 when he was eighteen years old and arrived in Pullman, Washington. The other belongs to a girl who departed Chitwan District, Nepal, in 2004 when she was nine years old and arrived in San Pablo, California.

Before arriving in Pullman, Akmal had landed in Chicago at O'Hare International Airport. In his interview for SAADA's First Days Project, his memories are infused with strong sensory experiences of sight, smell, and taste. Although he was familiar with large airports, having traveled to Europe, he was struck by the incredible expanse of O'Hare against the color of the sky, which appeared to be even bluer in this new place, and the smell of the concourses that he later realized had come from the industrial strength cleansers used in those days. In Washington State, his cousin picked him up from Spokane's airport and, on their way to Pullman, stopped at a county fair, where Akmal tried a corn dog for the first time. "I never knew what a corn dog was even," he recalled.[14]

The wondrous quality of the United States that Akmal had noted during those first few days had been forged by his previous positive interactions with "well-educated Americans who were so open to new ideas, who were so progressive."[15] He also experienced the welcoming and friendly nature of Americans as he went through the customs and immigration line during that first day. "A grandfatherly looking gentleman with a nice white mustache" had opened Akmal's passport and said, "Welcome home, son."[16] Akmal had hoped that this would be the American spirit that he would encounter everywhere he went in the United States, but soon realized that that was not the case, and his overblown hopes became tempered by disappointment.

The first days of the nine-year-old girl who immigrated to California from Nepal were also filled with wonder and disappointment. She was disappointed that the "big buildings and fun stuff" of New York City that she had seen on television were not to be found in San Pablo. Yet, she was in awe of her first BART (Bay Area Rapid Transit) train ride that brought her and her family from San Francisco to San Pablo in forty-five minutes. She had never been on a train before. Coming from a "developing country," such a fast transportation system "just felt new."[17]

The girl soon learned that her new community was a violent place. One day when her parents were away from home, she saw the ice cream man getting beat up and robbed for twenty dollars, and she wondered why anyone would "make someone bleed" for such a pittance. The contrasting grandeur and despair of the new country shocked her but did not dampen her curiosity. She learned the English language by watching *Tom and Jerry* cartoons and Bob Ross's *The Joy of Painting* show, and by studying the dictionary because she loved spelling bees. Within a few months of arrival, her father and mother started working in the fast-food industry, so the girl became the household cook for her parents, her younger sister, her uncle—with whom they were staying—*and* his three roommates. The need to cook nurtured her passion for food and inspired new ambitions. Watching Food Network stars like Rachael Ray and Emeril Lagasse made her want to become "really, really famous," and inspired her to role-play the host of her own cooking show in front of an audience consisting of her sister. Although she requested that her name be withheld from her First Days Project interview, and no photos of her or Akmal accompany their respective interviews, their vivid storytelling present themes of the post-1965 immigrant experience both unique and universal.

The 1965 Act initiated new waves of immigration that increased the number of female immigrants. Alongside new emigration policies in Asian-sending countries and changing social attitudes about female international migration, these waves contributed to balancing the predominantly male composition of Chinese, Filipino, and Indian communities that had settled in the US before 1965. Sometimes women immigrated to join their husbands and other family members. Other times, they were the ones to pioneer the immigrant trail by utilizing the occupational preferences of the new system.

One of these women was Viji Raman, who was born in Cochin, in the southern state of Kerala in India.[18] She arrived in New York City in 1969 and initially resided in Rochester, New York, where her husband completed his medical residency. Her family relocated to Houston, where Raman together with six other women founded the organization Daya—which in Sikhism signifies compassion—to provide culturally specific services for South Asian women impacted by domestic violence. Its first service activity was establishing a volunteer helpline. Since it began in 1996, the organization has grown, and its idea of who is a survivor and the many types of abuse it addresses have expanded. In 2021, as Daya commemorated its twenty-fifth anniversary, the organization paid tribute to Viji Raman in a blog post titled "Women We Admire." In it, Raman acknowledged her immigrant background and shared her hopes for future generations:

> As a first generation Indian American, I know firsthand the challenges that immigrants have faced. Struggling to balance life, living in two cultures, gave me a unique perspective about life. Moving forward, I'm focused on the legacy I want to leave for my daughter, son, grandsons, and granddaughters. I want them to feel comfortable in their own skin. I want my grandsons to respect boundaries and understand the meaning of consent. I want to teach them that sexism is neither cool nor funny. I want to have conversations about empathy and healthy relationships.[19]

The occupational preferences for workers with needed skills facilitated the immigration of Filipino female medical professionals, most notably nurses, to alleviate critical shortages in inner-city public hospitals as well as rural healthcare institutions.[20] The high demand for nurses contributed to a healthcare–industry ethnic niche for Filipino immigrants in general and the rise of immigrant women-owned healthcare businesses specifically. The research of medical sociologist Jennifer Nazareno spotlights the growing number of Filipino immigrant women in Southern California who have become private owners of government-subsidized small businesses in the long-term care industry. These women provide care to some of the most impoverished—as well as cognitively and physically disabled—elderly populations. While Filipino immigrant women entrepreneurs have created an important safety net for the most vulnerable in the American healthcare system, they are under tremendous stress to provide quality care within limited budgets. For example, Regina, the owner of a government-subsidized six-bed residential care facility, could not afford to hire any staff members initially. She recalled:

> When I first opened my board and care in 2006, I remember sleeping on the floor by the door for two weeks straight because one of my first residents would wake up in the middle of the night and keep saying "Help me, help me . . ." But she was confused, physically unstable, so I was afraid she might fall. . . . I told her daughter that it was so difficult for me to care for her, but her daughter did not have anywhere else to take care of her because of her SSI [Supplemental Security Income]. So I took care of her for almost a year. So I was the employer, caregiver, licensee, maid . . . you name it! Sometimes you know the kids are fighting too and you're in the middle. They only pay $1500 but want best care. Some of them, some of the kids tell you, do your job, that that's what we're paying you for . . . and they don't even know how hard it is to take care of mom.[21]

In the first few decades after the passage of the 1965 Act, the occupational preferences and non-preference category facilitated the immigration of highly educated Asian medical professionals and engineers as well as business investors. Their backgrounds created a simplistic perception that Asians were innately good at particular occupations and skills, especially in STEM fields. If the Asian American faces you encounter are predominantly those of STEM college students or employees, you might get that impression. Unfortunately, such notions reinforce the model minority stereotype and the cultural expectation of Asian American socioeconomic success. They also obscure the dual nature of post-1965 Asian immigration, which includes less educated persons who are not part of the highly specialized STEM workforce.

The dual nature of post-1965 Asian immigration is partly a product of the 1965 Act's prioritization of family immigrants who did not necessarily have highly educated backgrounds, investment capital, and specialized skills. In the twenty-first century, income inequality among Asian Americans has become more pronounced. Researchers Rakesh Kochhar and Anthony Cilluffo note that, from 1970 to 2016, the gap in the standard of living between Asians near the top and the bottom of the income ladder nearly doubled. Asians have displaced Blacks as the most economically divided racial or ethnic group.[22]

The growing number of undocumented Asian immigrants and their vulnerability to exploitation further contribute to the presence of Asian Americans in low-paid, precarious work. Undocumented Asian immigrants are often rendered invisible by the perception that undocumented migration is a Latino issue and a unique problem related to the US-Mexico border. However, according to scholars Karthick Ramakrishnan and Sono Shah, one out of every seven Asian immigrants is undocumented. In the United States, there are approximately 1.7 million undocumented Asian immigrants, accounting for about 16 percent of undocumented immigrants in the country.[23] The number of undocumented Asian immigrants has tripled since 2000.

The numerical caps of the post-1965 immigration system and increasing visa backlogs for both family-based and occupational preferences gave rise to this phenomenon. For example, by 1970, the waiting period for a "third preference" occupational visa—for skilled workers and professionals—was already thirteen months. In 1970, an immigration amendment allowed foreign workers to fill permanent positions in the United States through a temporary H-1 visa that migrants could receive in significantly less time. These two factors—the extraordinary wait times that can be decades long for immigrant visas, and the expiration of various temporary visas for work, study, or tourism—have contributed to the increase in undocumented Asian immigration.

Another face of post-1965 Asian America is Anthony Ng, who came to the United States from the Philippines as a twelve-year-old. Ng is a DACA recipient. The Deferred Action for Childhood Arrivals program, or DACA, protects undocumented immigrants who were minors upon arrival from deportation and allows them to work and study in the United States. After graduating from the University of California, Irvine, Ng worked at the nonprofit civil rights organization Asian Americans Advancing Justice–Los Angeles, advocating for the protection and expansion of immigrant rights. Ng spoke to the *Washington Post* in 2017, a few days after President Trump announced that the program would end. When asked whether he felt ignored because Latinos are the face of the immigration debate and if that even mattered, Ng responded:

> It really does matter. When you feel invisible, you don't feel connected, you feel isolated. Acknowledging that there are diverse immigrant communities—there are black immigrants, Asian immigrants, LGBT immigrants—means a lot of those folks hold those identities. The first time I met other undocumented Asians, I felt I was understood; I didn't have to explain myself.[24]

The Supreme Court blocked President Trump from ending DACA, but the program's status remains uncertain.

The struggles of Asian immigrants in low-wage and precarious work are often hidden behind the model minority stereotype and the emphasis on post-1965 professional immigration. Restaurants and other food services, and nail salons and other personal care services are two of the major industries that employ them. In the 1970s and 1980s, the labor and entrepreneurship of Vietnamese, Korean, Chinese, Nepali, Tibetan, and Latino immigrants and refugees transformed nail salons from an elite, luxury service to a more accessible, affordable one.[25] In 1996, state licensing exams were translated into Vietnamese in some metropolitan areas, reflecting the predominance of this group. Korean women were pioneers in New York's nail salon industry, with over two thousand Korean-owned nail salons in the metropolitan area.[26] By the late twentieth century, manicurists had become stereotyped as "quiet Asian women working in sweatshops," reflecting a racial, gendered, and classed hierarchy separating the cheap salons from the high-end ones.[27] The seemingly glamorous side of this multibillion-dollar industry belies its exploitive work conditions.

The story of Minh, the twenty-nine-year-old daughter of a Vietnamese nail salon worker, bears witness to the intergenerational toll of low-paid work. According to Minh, her mother had been an accountant, but started working in the nail salon industry after Minh's father's auto parts business had folded. Her mom thought that the industry would offer more job security, but she barely earned enough money from paychecks and tips to support herself, even though she was working over forty hours per week, five days a week. Despite the hazards of working amid chemicals and fumes from nail polishes and removers, her mom did not have healthcare. As a result, Minh worked multiple jobs to pay for her own college tuition so as not to burden her mother. Minh lamented, "I am angry seeing older Vietnamese women exploited in this industry on a larger level. As a society, we must ask why it is okay for Vietnamese and other immigrant women to fill the nail salon industry across the United States."[28]

Higher education, specialized skills, and financial capital are among the privileges of immigrant professionals and investors. They fuel images of successful Asian Americans who do not need any help. These perceptions often exclude Asian Americans from discussions about diversity, equity, inclusion, and belonging. However, according to Buck Gee and Denise Peck of the nonprofit Ascend Foundation, Asian success is an illusion. In their analysis of the leadership pipeline in the Bay Area technology sector from 2007 to 2015, they found that Asians were the largest cohort of professionals yet the least likely among all races to become managers and executives.[29]

Furthermore, Asian women were the least likely among all other racial groups to become executives. They face a "double glass ceiling." "It turns out that the racial gap accounts for more of the disparity than the gender gap alone," Peck says. "What that means is if you are an Asian woman, then not only do you suffer from the gender pay gap, but you are also heavily penalized for being Asian."[30] With increased awareness of these leadership ceilings and gaps, companies and organizations can collectively as well as individually address these disparities. Including Asian Americans in these discussions is a basic but integral step forward.

Finally, the post-1965 period is marked by many cases of anti-Asian hate and violence that predate the surge beginning in 2020. These include a spate of violence targeting South Asians in New Jersey in 1987. In September of that year, Navroze Mody was taunted and brutally beaten to death by a group of youths in Hoboken. Mody had just been promoted to a managerial role at Citicorp. A few days later, another Indian was beaten into a coma on a busy street corner in Jersey City Heights.

That same year, a note threatening to drive out the Indian community in Jersey City, penned by a hate group known as the Dotbusters, was published in a local paper. The group's name refers to the bindi, or dot, that Indian women wear on their foreheads. The bindi has familial, social, and spiritual meanings. It can signify marriage, self-realization, and piety. Yet, in the midst of this violence, its meaning had tragically changed for Lalitha Masson, a gynecologist who had emigrated from India in 1966. Masson stopped wearing her bindi and opted for Western-style dress instead of her Indian saris. She hoped this would make her less of a target.[31]

EVERYWHERE AND NOWHERE

Just as there is no singular face that represents the United States, post-1965 Asian America is composed of many faces. They labor in various sectors and in diverse jobs within industries. Their faces include those of physicians in hospitals and caregivers in nursing homes, of massage therapists at spas and nail technicians in salons, of chefs and dishwashers in high-end and mom-and-pop restaurants, of high-tech engineers and computer factory assembly workers in Silicon Valley.

Writer Janice Lobo Sapigao's debut book of poetry, *microchips for millions*, weaves binary code, English, and her family's Philippine language, Ilocano, to make visible the thousands of immigrant women who help produce our ubiquitous tech devices, yet who we rarely acknowledge.[32] It is dedicated to her mom who, in the poem "the assembly line," works in the shadow of Silicon Valley.[33] In the poem "the tech museum of innovation of 2012," Sapigao refers to an exhibit called "reface," which combines visitors' eyes, noses, and mouths to create various expressions. The poem ends with the question: "even though we are small do you see us?"[34]

As of 2019, Asian Americans reside in every region, with the majority living in the West (45 percent), yet they also have a sizable presence in the South (24 percent), Northeast (19 percent), and the Midwest (12 percent). Nearly a third (30 percent), or roughly 6.7 million, live in the state of California. The states with the next largest Asian American populations are New York, Texas, New Jersey, and Washington. A closer look at growth rates, however, would shift our attention to North Dakota and South Dakota, which between 2000 and 2019 saw the fastest increases in Asian American populations. Indiana, Nevada, and North Carolina also saw significant growth.[35]

From this data, we might conclude that Asian Americans are everywhere. And, yet, we are nowhere. Nowhere to be found in American history textbooks, minus a few sentences about Chinese laborers building the first transcontinental railroad in 1869 or Japanese American internment during World War II. Nowhere on Hollywood movie and American television screens—again, with few exceptions. Consider the number of Hollywood films with an Asian-majority cast. One of them, *Crazy Rich Asians*, was released in 2018, twenty-five years after the previous one, *The Joy Luck Club*, in 1993. Before *Joy Luck Club* was *Flower Drum Song* in 1961.

In a 2021 study, *The Prevalence and Portrayal of Asian and Pacific Islanders Across 1,300 Popular Films*, scholars Nancy Wang Yuen and Stacy L. Smith and the USC Annenberg Inclusion Initiative found that nearly 40 percent of the films reviewed had no Asian and Pacific Islander (API) representation at all. And of those API characters who did make it on screen, 25.3 percent died, often violently, by the end of the film. In the study, the juxtaposition of these findings with data on anti-Asian hate incidents during 2020 and 2021 is haunting.[36] And it begs the question: Can one acknowledge a people's humanity if one does not see them as multidimensional human beings in popular culture?

Many Asian Americans grapple with the complex messages that they should just work hard, be quiet, and not make waves in a nation that values speaking up and standing out. These messages partly stem from American societal expectations of the model minority. Sometimes, these messages come from our own family or community members, many of them immigrants, a result of their cultural values of modesty and respect of authority, but also their experiences of American nativism and racism.

Yet, there is also a history of Asian Americans' resisting immigrant invisibility. Sharing their stories for SAADA's First Days Project is but one example. SAADA launched the First Days Project in 2013 because it realized that stories of immigrants' and refugees' first experiences in the United States were not systematically being collected, preserved, and shared with others.

Immigrant health practitioners have documented their contributions to healthcare delivery on online media platforms, such as Zócalo Public Square. Before the emergence of COVID-19, post-1965 immigrant professionals worked on the front lines of the AIDS epidemic. After studying dentistry in India, Jayanth Kumar pursued a dental residency training program in the New York State Department of Public Health. He started his public health career during the onset of the AIDS epidemic. At that time, no one knew that AIDS was caused by the HIV virus. Dentists started observing people who had unusual ulcers and tumors called Kaposi's sarcoma in the mouth but did not know how to manage or treat this condition. Kumar was part of the New York state health department's team studying this problem and addressing the transmission of the disease. The department recommended that all dentists should wear gloves, masks, and eyewear for treating patients. Prior to the study, dentists were not wearing gloves while treating patients. Later, this guideline to wear gloves, masks, and eyewear—which we may take for granted in a dentist's office today—became a requirement through regulation.

In the essay he contributed to Zócalo Public Square's inquiry on how immigrants are making healthcare delivery more holistic and human, Kumar reflects:

I was able to see the impact of this policy, which within a short period of time made all dental offices improve their infection control practice—not only for HIV and AIDS, but also for other diseases like hepatitis B. The policy really transformed the way infection control is practiced in dentistry and dramatically reduced the transmission of infection in dental settings. That experience exposed me to the power of making big, system-wide changes in dental care.[37]

Kumar led one of these big changes, developing guidelines for oral health care during pregnancy that are now adopted in many states. Previously, pregnant women had difficulty obtaining dental care during their pregnancies.

Asian influences, from meditation to herbal medicine, have shaped the booming, trillion-dollar wellness industry. However, for Ka-Kit Hui, the integration of Eastern and Western medicine is not about profit, but rather the goal of making people all over the world healthier. In 1968, Hui departed Hong Kong and arrived in Los Angeles to study chemistry at UCLA. He initially aimed to introduce the Western world to a new drug derived from the Chinese herbal pharmacopoeia, following in the path of the 2015 Nobel laureate Tu Youyou, who discovered artemisinin, the anti-malarial drug derived from a Chinese herb used for fever and chills. Instead, Hui pursued an integrative vision of medicine, with an emphasis on health promotion, disease prevention, treatment, and rehabilitation. He founded the UCLA Center for East-West Medicine, one of the first integrative medicine centers in the United States, in 1993. In his Zócalo Public Square essay, Hui explains:

My method of integrative medicine . . . is not like an international buffet, where a provider picks randomly from a disjointed assortment of therapies, such as adding acupuncture or massage to a drug therapy. Instead, it is like a carefully curated dinner menu, with the most appropriate therapies working together to address the specific needs of each patient. We combine Western biomedicine's strengths in disease detection, acute condition management, and vital system stabilization with Traditional Chinese Medicine's concept of balance and emphasis on the body's innate ability to heal.[38]

During the early decades of his career, Hui encountered the perception of Chinese medicine as quackery. The possibility of integrating traditional Chinese medicine with Western biomedicine was also met with skepticism. Since then, hundreds of Western-trained doctors have referred their patients to the Center for East-West Medicine, thousands of students have joined its educational programs, and Hui has worked with many institutions, including the US Food and Drug Administration and the National Institutes of Health. Hui reminds us of the benefits of immigrants' innovative spirit: "Immigration, after all, is a risk, and we need to see more risk-taking to make health care safer, more effective, more affordable, and more accessible."[39]

Platforms that publicize immigrants' innovations and contributions are of the utmost importance because even though immigrants have transformed virtually every aspect of American life for the better, xenophobia continues to be an American tradition.[40] Anti-immigrant sentiment dehumanizes immigrants by stereotyping them as diseased, lazy, or criminal. Do you know any of the faces of post-1965 Asian America? Might they belong to you, your family, or members of your community?

I do. I am the daughter of Filipino immigrants who settled in New York City during this time. I grew up among many Filipino immigrant nurses who lived in my neighborhood and worked in the surrounding hospitals, a phenomenon that inspired my first book on the history of Filipino nurse migration.[41] For me, writing about post-1965 immigration is deeply personal as well as professional. I have many childhood memories of seeing the Statue of Liberty while walking in Battery Park or riding the Staten Island Ferry. The "golden door" that she represents had instilled hope in me.

During a family visit in the summer of 2018, seeing the Statue of Liberty stirred very different emotions. In the midst of yet another intense moment of anti-immigrant sentiment in the United States—earlier that year, US Citizenship and Immigration Services changed its mission statement to eliminate a passage describing the US as "a nation of immigrants"—the sight of Lady Liberty compelled me to reflect on how and why such contradictory narratives of the United States continue to exist.[42] Thus, I wonder if the 1965 Immigration and Nationality Act has not become common knowledge because of this dispiriting American choreography that we perform, embracing immigrants as foundational to US history when we need their labor, skills, or other resources, and pushing them back when we need a ready-made enemy.

Asian Americans are in sight, but unseen. And this must change. Placing a human face on the Asian immigrant experience is one way to contest this vicious cycle of nativism. If you are part of this post-1965 history, I hope you share your story.

INTERLUDE

1965 REPRISE:
THE FACES BEHIND THE FOOD

THIS IS FOR THE ASIAN AMERICAN FACES BEHIND THE FOOD THAT NOURISHES AMERICANS AND ENRICHES AMERICAN CUISINE. The general public knows so little about Asian American people, but our food is everywhere, at once exotic and mainstream. To appreciate the contributions of Asian Americans to food—its production, preservation, preparation, presentation, and consumption—we need to see the faces behind the food. The year 1965 compels a second look as an origin year of food histories.

THIS IS FOR LARRY ITLIONG AND THE FILIPINO AMERICAN FARMWORKERS WHO STARTED THE GRAPE STRIKE IN DELANO, CALIFORNIA, IN 1965. Under Itliong's leadership, the Agricultural Workers Organizing Committee (AWOC)—a group made up primarily of Filipino American laborers—gathered in Delano's Filipino Community Hall on September 7 and that evening voted to strike. On September 8, approximately 1,500 Filipino farmworkers walked out of the fields, leaving ripe grapes on the ground. They remained militant in the face of eviction from their homes and violent encounters with law enforcement.

To deter growers from hiring replacement workers, Itliong reached out to Cesar Chavez to ask if the National Farm Workers Association (NFWA)—a predominantly Mexican American group—would join the strike. The United Farm Workers (UFW) emerged from the joined forces of AWOC and NFWA. Chavez and Itliong were at its helm, serving as the UFW's director and assistant director, respectively, from 1966 to 1971.

The five-year Delano Grape Strike launched one of the most significant movements for social justice in the second half of the twentieth century.

The farmworkers' movement raised public consciousness about the harsh conditions in which they worked in the fields. These conditions included no work breaks during twelve-hour days under unrelenting sun or windy and dusty conditions, and no access to clean drinking water and toilets. Farmworkers also endured exposure to pesticides and lived in substandard housing. It is ironic that the laborers who nourished the masses by growing, tending, and harvesting fruits and vegetables were doing so in unsafe environments and for meager wages. Their demands for change resonated with consumers on regional, national, and international levels.

The UFW achieved many post-strike victories—not the least of which was the 1975 passage of the Agricultural Labor Relations Act, a landmark agreement recognizing the right of farmworkers in California to organize—but Filipinos were increasingly marginalized in the union that they had helped to create.[1] Distinct organizing philosophies and priorities began to pull the Filipino and Mexican American coalition apart. Cesar Chavez Day is a US federal commemorative holiday, but the struggle to remember Larry Itliong and the Filipino farmworkers continues.

Their legacy shines more brightly in large part thanks to the research and writing of scholar Dawn Bohulano Mabalon, the author of *Little Manila Is in the Heart*, which preserves the histories of the farmworkers who made Stockton, California, a vibrant Filipino community until its Little Manila neighborhood was decimated by urban redevelopment in the 1960s. In an interview for the *California Report*, she related that her grandparents were farmworkers. And her dad was a farmworker who knew Larry Itliong. However, Dawn did not even know who Larry Itliong was until she went to college. She reflected, "I think it's such a tragedy that so many young Filipino Americans grew up without knowing the central, pivotal, significant role that we've played in American history."[2]

THIS IS FOR DAWN BOHULANO MABALON AND THOSE WHO CHAMPION LABOR HISTORY. These advocates include California attorney general Rob Bonta, whose parents worked for the UFW. Before becoming attorney general,

Bonta was an assemblyman—the first Filipino American in California history to win election to the legislature—who shepherded Assembly Bill 123, which involved changes in the state school curriculum to cover the role of immigrants, including Filipino Americans, in the farm labor movement.

These bittersweet labor histories were a century in the making.

THIS IS FOR THE OVER THREE HUNDRED THOUSAND ASIAN MIGRANTS—CHINESE, JAPANESE, KOREAN, AND FILIPINO—WHOSE LABOR MADE SUGAR PRODUCTION HAWAI'I'S TOP INDUSTRY. Between 1850 and 1920, they were brought to the Hawai'ian Islands as "cheap labor." Women workers, most of them Japanese, were among them. They included scholar Ronald Takaki's grandmother Katsu Okawa, who was a cane cutter on Hana Plantation, and his aunt Yukino Takaki, who was an *hapaiko* worker, or cane loader, on the Puunene Plantation.[3] The grueling work of plantation labor imprinted their bodies with calloused hands and cauliflower ears. Writer Milton Murayama, the son of Japanese immigrants, grew up in a plantation camp in Pu'ukoli'i. His award-winning novel about plantation life is titled *All I Asking for Is My Body*.[4]

THIS IS FOR THE CHINESE WORKERS WHO TRANSFORMED TENS OF THOUSANDS OF ACRES OF CALIFORNIA SWAMPLAND INTO ARABLE LAND AND WHO APPLIED THEIR INGENUITY TO ORCHARDS FROM OREGON TO FLORIDA. Beginning in the late 1860s, they built more than a thousand miles of levees in the Sacramento–San Joaquin Delta, using only shovels and wheelbarrows and working in waist-deep water.[5] After arriving in the United States around 1855, Ah Bing worked as a foreman in the Lewelling family fruit orchards in Milwaukie, Oregon, for thirty-five years. He is credited as the cultivator and namesake of the popular Bing cherry.[6] In Florida, Lue Gim Gong experimented with cross-pollination to produce fruits that were more tolerant of cold weather after the state recorded some of the worst freezes in 1894 and 1895. In 1911, he successfully cross-pollinated a "Hart's Late" Valencia orange with a "Mediterranean Sweet" to produce a new orange named the "Lue Gim Gong," which was much more resistant to the cold. His many innovations also included a cold-tolerant grapefruit.[7]

THIS IS FOR THE CHINESE, JAPANESE, AND FILIPINO WORKERS IN THE CANNED SALMON INDUSTRY OF THE PACIFIC NORTHWEST. Between the 1870s and World War II, they made up the majority of laborers in the canneries that dotted the narrow coastal zone from Alaska to central California. While the fishing life has been celebrated in popular culture, the workers who processed and canned salmon have been overlooked. Yet their labor was a key element of the American West's economic development. Between 1880 and 1937, Alaska's canned salmon was more valuable than the minerals mined in the territory in the same period.[8]

THIS IS FOR THE JAPANESE FRUIT AND VEGETABLE FARMERS. By 1909, more than thirty thousand Japanese were tenant farmers or farm laborers in California.[9] They produced 70 percent of California's strawberries. They also grew the majority of the state's snap beans, tomatoes, spring and summer celery, onions, and green peas, fulfilling the increasing demands for fresh produce in the cities.[10] Issei—or first generation—Japanese women, many of them picture brides, worked in the farms with their husbands, sometimes bringing their children with them during harvest.[11] One of these women was Maju Sakaguchi, who was born in Kumamoto Prefecture in 1894 and arrived in the United States in 1915 to join her husband, Chokichi Sakaguchi. Her high expectations of her new life in San Jose, California, were immediately dashed. She spent her honeymoon working in a strawberry field. Furthermore, discriminatory California land laws restricted the Issei from owning land and limited their property leases to three years. Families typically cultivated new land, then had to leave it and begin again.[12]

THIS IS FOR THE ASIAN INDIAN AGRICULTURAL WORKERS, MANY OF WHOM FOUND WORK IN CALIFORNIA'S FIELDS IN THE EARLY TWENTIETH CENTURY. The Sacramento Valley reminded Puna Singh of the Punjab: "Fertile fields stretched across the flat valley to the foothills lying far in the distance."[13] These workers moved around the state in groups as contract workers. In the Sacramento Valley, they worked in the orchards and sugar beet fields, then moved on to the vineyards and citrus groves of the San Joaquin

Valley in central California until they reached the Imperial Valley's cantaloupe fields in the south.

THIS IS FOR THE RESTAURANT WORKERS, LIKE CHIN SHUCK WING, WHO STARTED WORKING AT AN AMERICANIZED CHINESE RESTAURANT IN 1936 IN NEW YORK CITY. The first Chinese restaurants in New York emerged in the 1870s, serving Chinese immigrants almost exclusively. By the 1920s, however, other New Yorkers became the majority of diners, and they especially loved chop suey—meaning "different pieces" in Cantonese—with its morsels of meat and vegetables in a brown gravy served over rice or noodles. These restaurants provided their American customers with a gateway to a seemingly exotic new world without traveling far from home. But this was hardly the case for many of its immigrant workers. As a line cook, Chin typically worked a grueling ten-hour day over hot ranges, preparing and cooking chop suey and other dishes. Line cooks sometimes worked back-to-back shifts and, like waiters, dealt with abusive managers and bosses. Chin lived in the United States for a little over fifty years, during which he sent letters and remittances to his wife and children who he left behind in China. But he was unable to return to China before his death in 1987.[14]

THIS IS FOR THE FOOD SERVICE WORKERS IN CAFETERIAS. These workers include the predominantly female Japanese, Okinawan, Korean, Chinese, and Filipino servers, cooks, and, later, managers in Hawai'i's public elementary school system in the twentieth century. Students' memories of these "cafeteria ladies" as they stood in line for lunch were among the most indelible. One cafeteria lady was Eleanor Kim Tyau, a Korean American who was born in 1915 in Kona on the island of Hawai'i. After her first job at Kalihi-waena Elementary School, she was reassigned to Saint Louis School during World War II. The cafeteria was utilized as a civilian defense canteen and a feeding station for war workers. After the war, Tyau resumed providing meals for students and school staff. During her thirty-seven-year career there, she made gallons of kimchi, the Korean spicy dish of pickled and fermented vegetables, and *taigu*, Korean seasoned codfish, for school fundraisers. Despite the prodigious amount she prepared year after year, Tyau recalled, "I just never seemed to make enough of it."[15]

THIS IS FOR THE WRITER AND MIGRANT WORKER CARLOS BULOSAN. He chronicled the plight of the Filipino agricultural migrant workers in his semi-autobiographical novel *America Is in the Heart*, published in 1946. America was in their hearts because, although their "stoop labor" contributed to the American West's health and prosperity, the unalienable rights of life, liberty, and the pursuit of happiness were not available to them. What life is this when you are compelled to live in segregated places full of desperation, when you are repeatedly demeaned as an animal—"Listen to the brown monkey talk"—and when you are brutalized by police without provocation?[16]

THIS IS FOR DALIP SINGH SAUND, WHO, IN 1956, BECAME THE FIRST PERSON OF ASIAN DESCENT ELECTED TO SERVE AS A US REPRESENTATIVE, AND CHAMPIONED THE FARMERS OF HIS SOUTHERN CALIFORNIA DISTRICT. Raised in Chhajjalwaddi in Punjab, India, Saund arrived in New York in 1920. He eventually moved to California's Imperial Valley, where a number of other Indians had settled, and worked in farming—growing lettuce and beets as well as cotton—over two decades. Although his race, ethnicity, and religious beliefs were consistently raised by the media and critics during the election, Saund credited his political victory to his commitment to small-scale farmers and small businesses.[17]

THIS IS FOR THAI AMERICANS WHO HAVE A COMPLICATED RELATIONSHIP WITH THAI FOOD BECAUSE THEY ARE OFTEN CONFLATED WITH IT. Scholar Mark Padoongpatt's groundbreaking research in his book on this subject, *Flavors of Empire*, provides a transnational historical context for the rise of Thai food's popularity in the United States.[18] During the Cold War, the presence of Americans in Thailand through cultural exchange programs, tourism, and military bases exposed them to the flavors of Thai cuisine that they sought to replicate in the United States. As Thai immigration increased beginning in the 1960s, some of them entered the food and restaurant industry for individual, but also historical, reasons. The US global presence in Thailand had created consumer demand for Thai flavors and dishes, such as pad thai.

THIS IS FOR THE MANONGS. *Manong* is a term that conveys respect for Filipino elders. It also refers to the generation of mostly Filipino men who came to the United States in the tens of thousands in the 1920s and 1930s, and who labored as migrant agricultural workers. They followed the crops from California to the Pacific Northwest, harvesting grapes, onions, tomatoes, asparagus, potatoes, peaches, lettuce, sugar beets, celery, and more. Their labor contributed to the wealth of growers, while they earned a dollar a day. From the 1920s to the 1940s, the manongs demonstrated their militancy, organizing a wildcat grape strike near Lodi in 1924, a celery strike in the San Joaquin and Sacramento Delta in 1936, and asparagus strikes in Stockton in 1948 and 1949.[19] In the 1950s, union members were accused of Communist Party membership, arrested by the INS (Immigration and Naturalization Service), and threatened with deportation.[20] But their belief in the power of organizing persisted. The 1965 Grape Strike was not an exception, but rather a singular point on a continuum.

As this brief history shows, the labor, innovations, and struggles of Asian Americans in food and foodways overlapped with the post-1965 period. In the age of COVID-19, Asian Americans continue to be the many faces behind the food, using their creativity and leadership to promote communal care during a critical time. This work includes the social entrepreneurship of Hannah Dehradunwala, who cofounded the nonprofit Transfernation and serves as its CEO. Transfernation is a technology platform that redistributes leftover prepared food from restaurants and companies to places that need them, such as homeless shelters, food pantries, and senior centers, thereby reducing edible food waste as well as responding to heightened food insecurity during crises, such as New York City's coronavirus-related lockdown.[21]

Another example of food-related communal care is Heart of Dinner, whose mission is to nourish New York City's Asian elders with love and food every week.[22] Founded by Yin Chang and Moonlynn Tsai as a supper club to create a sense of community around a shared meal, Chang and Tsai shifted their vision at the onset of the pandemic given the surge in anti-Asian violence. In April 2020, they cooked Heart of Dinner #LovingChinatown hot lunches for homebound elders in and around Manhattan's Chinatown area. Volunteers and partner businesses—such as chef-owner of Saigon Social, Helen Nguyen; baker and founder of Partybus Bakeshop, Jacqueline Russo Eng; and owner and executive chef of Bessou, Maiko Kyogoku and Emily Yuen—enabled Heart of Dinner's expansion to other parts of New York City, delivering over seventy thousand meals as of May 2021. One distinctive aspect of the volunteers' work is the handwritten notes they provide, composed in the elders' native languages of Chinese, Korean, Japanese, and Tagalog with English translations, to personalize their meal-based care packages. Volunteers are also encouraged to decorate the notes and brown bags to bring joy to elderly recipients.

The irony of Asian Americans producing America's food and enlivening the overall food experience in the context of hate and violence has not been lost on them, historically and in the present day. In March 2021, people gathered at North Dakota State University in Fargo to protest against anti-Asian hatred. One poster read, "Love us like you love our food."[23]

FIVE

1953: MIXED RACE LIVES

What would we glean if we placed mixed race experiences at the center of Asian American histories? This chapter spotlights three revelations. First, the American occupation of Japan and US involvement in the Korean War ushered the first mass wave of international and interracial adoptions in world history. Mixed race children, born of American servicemen and Japanese and Korean women, and subsequently adopted by American families, were among the pioneers of this distinctive form of family formation.[1] In 1953, the passage of Public Law 162 created five hundred non-quota immigration visas that facilitated the admission of adopted children. The Orphan Section of the Refugee Relief Act of 1953 provided an additional four thousand non-quota immigrant visas to orphans under the age of ten years. Since the 1950s, over two hundred thousand Korean children have been adopted by families in more than fifteen countries, with the vast majority living in the United States.[2] Although most of these children were fully Korean, mixed race children played a formative role in the phenomenon of international and transracial adoption, in which parents adopt children of a different racial background. It was, as writer Bettijane Levine observes, "the forerunner of all those that have since become commonplace."[3]

The second revelation is that multiracial Asian Americans have a history that is over 150 years old. They emerge from nineteenth-century port cultures in New York City and New Orleans and extend across to midwestern and western urban and rural areas. In the 1920s, a white

American woman provided an account of her marriages to a Chinese American man and, after his death, a Japanese American man. She met her first husband, Rev. Walter Ngon Fong, pastor of the Methodist Mission of San Jose, in an economics class at Stanford University. Although she noted that he was well liked by classmates and that her parents were "not narrow-minded," after Fong proposed to her in 1896, "it was then that the race question and popular prejudice against the Chinese" loomed before her. [4] Yet, she was convinced that "there was no reasonable ground for one member of the human family to regard himself as superior to another no matter what the race or the color of the skin that individual might be." [5] After they married, they settled in Berkeley, California, and had two sons. She described their first son as "a most precocious child, talking and carrying a tune at six months, and at nine forming short sentences and replying to questions." [6] Their younger son was a quiet, deep thinker. Her recollection of both their personalities and achievements brims with pride.

The third and final revelation is that our society today is increasingly multiracial. Mixed race Asian Americans are documenting their lived experiences, challenging social attitudes that dismiss them as incomplete, and charting holistic ways of seeing and being. In her essay "Rising Sun, Rising Soul: On Mixed Race Identity That Includes Blackness," writer Velina Hasu Houston juxtaposes a photo of her biological mother, Setsuko Okazaki Takechi, circa 1952, next to one of herself, circa 1990. Houston writes:

> It is likely that you have met someone who is an Asian of African descent. If, however, they are under the age of fifty-five, they may differ from me culturally. I am one of the last of my kind—a person of Japanese, Black, Native American Indian, and Cuban descent with a Japanese grandmother born in Japan's Meiji era, Japanese aunts born in the Taisho era, and a Showa-era Japanese mother. [7]

Houston reminds us that histories of people who are of multiple lines of minority descent deserve our attention.

INTERNATIONAL ADOPTION NATION

In the destructive and chaotic aftermath of World War II, Germany, Greece, and Italy, as well as Japan and Korea, were among the nations sending the highest number of adoptive children. Largely untouched by war damage, the United States became the top receiving country of these children. Why then is it important to study the history of Asian international adoption in the United States on its own terms? Histories of race informed early Asian international adoption history in ways that distinguished it from international adoption from Europe.

In the 1950s, interracial intimacy—both romance and marriage— was a central feature of US-Asian relations. A social outcome of the post–World War II US occupation of Japan (1945–52) and US Cold War involvement in the Korean War (1950–53) was a population of mixed race children of American servicemen and Japanese and Korean women. Although war had a devastating impact on all sectors of Japanese and Korean societies, the lives of these children were especially bleak. Japanese and Korean societies rejected them as "improper" children because many were conceived out of wedlock, and they embodied the unequal political relationship between the US and these nations. The distinctive racial features of these mixed Asian and American children made them visible targets for abuse. Separate orphanages for mixed race children in Japan, such as the Elizabeth Saunders Home in Oiso and Our Lady of Lourdes Baby Home in Yokohama, and special wings of orphanages in Korea, such as the Choong Hyun Baby Home near Seoul, offered better care for these children. Yet, the possibility of the children leaving institutional care was minimal.[8]

In the 1950s, popular culture presented utopian visions of interracial relationships. Hollywood films such as *Sayonara* popularized these relationships to the American masses with hopeful messages about the peaceful integration of East and West. These messages enabled current and future generations to imagine an interracial world. However, the plight of children born to US servicemen and Japanese or Korean women, also referred to as "occupation babies" and "GI babies," received little attention or support. An American military presence in Japan and Korea was responsible for these children's births, but the US government bore no official responsibility for the children's or their mothers' welfare. The US military actively discouraged marriages between American servicemen and Japanese and Korean women. Thus, discrimination against these children in Japan and Korea, the lack of US governmental support, and desertion by their American fathers influenced their mothers' decisions to abandon them, creating a group of children in need of rescue and available for adoption.[9]

Non-governmental organizations and concerned individuals stepped in to provide some relief and to arrange international adoptions. Given restrictive quotas, they were dependent upon ad hoc government actions.[10] For example, in the early 1950s, American military families stationed in Japan who had adopted children there were able to bring these children to the United States only after the passage of private bills that authorized the immigration of each child.[11] The most important piece of legislation to enable the immigration of internationally adopted children, the Orphan Section of the 1953 Refugee Relief Act, was set to expire on December 31, 1956. These short temporal windows of opportunity intensified the link between international adoption and humanitarian rescue.

In the broader history of US expansionism in Asia, mixed race children were not a new people. US colonization of the Philippines resulted in a population of mixed race children of US servicemen and Filipino women. By 1925, there were an estimated eighteen thousand Filipino and American mestizo, or mixed, children in the Philippines. US governor-general Leonard Wood formed a charity, the American Guardian Association, which aimed to protect these children. According to scholar Gladys Nubla, association members believed that the Caucasian roots of the American mestizo children endowed them with the potential to lead the Philippines with American interests in mind, unlike the "inferior" Filipino natives.[12]

In the early twentieth century, there was also a small population of African American and Filipino children in the Philippines. In her memoir, Evangeline Canonizado Buell recounts how her grandfather, Ernest Stokes, was among six thousand African American soldiers, known as

"Buffalo Soldiers," who were sent to the Philippines in 1898 to fight in the Spanish-American War. A group of these men, including her grandfather, remained in the Philippines, married Filipino women, and had children. After the death of his Filipina wife, Maria, Buell's grandfather had his three daughters stay with his wife's relatives while he completed his army service. While one daughter found love and acceptance in her new home, a different set of relatives treated the other two daughters "like servants because they were half black and did not look like their cousins with straight hair and fairer skin."[13] Although these children did not fare well, there was no outcry from the American public, and the US colonial government did not assume responsibility for these children. In addition to the overt American racism against both African Americans and Filipinos during this period, the US colonial government's major objective of preparing Filipinos and the Philippines for gradual independence involved American tutelage but no commitment to integrate these children with families in the United States.

By the 1950s, however, the escalation of the Cold War posed fundamental challenges to American racism. Communist governments challenged US claims of democracy and freedom by pointing to the social realities of racial segregation, violence, and protest in the United States. Although the Soviet Union led the communist world, the role of Asian nations in the Cold War was a major concern of the US government, especially after the victory of the Chinese Communist Party in the Chinese Revolution of 1949. The international politics of race heightened debates about US accountability for the population of mixed race Asian and American children and informed the moral urgency to rescue them.

News articles popularized international adoption by publicizing the arrivals of the adopted children and their new life-altering circumstances. A January 1955 article in the *New York Times* announced that five children from Japan—"all are children of American fathers and Japanese mothers"—were getting homes in the United States. One adoptive family "welcomed their new sister with an armful of dolls."[14] A 1956 *Kansas City Times* news article featured the excitement of adoptive parents of five Korean African American children who had just arrived from Seoul.

One mother commented that when the children arrived in Chicago, they lacked warm clothes, but, upon arrival, were wrapped in blankets and later had sufficient clothes purchased for them.[15]

Television also spread the idea of Asian international adoption as a benevolent one. A 1957 episode, "Have Jacket, Will Travel," of the long-running series *Armstrong Circle Theatre* featured the international adoption stories of a mixed race Korean American boy as well as a Greek boy and an Italian girl. In the closing "real life" segment of the episode, *Armstrong Circle Theatre* host Douglas Edwards explains that, for the last three years, an adoption division of the International Social Service-USA (ISS-USA) branch, called World Adoption International Fund (WAIF), played a part in more than four thousand adoptions by families in the United States. He introduces two Korean children, Deborah and Johnny, who were adopted by a couple in New York. Edwards tells the audience viewers that Johnny—a kindergartner dressed smartly in a blazer and tie—spoke only Korean when he came to the United States but says he now speaks "American." Edwards describes the younger Deborah—who wears a poofy ball gown—as "a doll" who "doesn't speak very much yet." Noting that these were two of the many children who find families through ISS-USA and WAIF, he concludes, "Every child in this world is entitled to a home and loving parents."[16]

These stories created a simplistic narrative about the rescue of mixed race children and their successful Americanization. However, the realities in Asian countries as well as in the United States were more nuanced and complex. Japan's Ministry of Education supported integrated schooling by 1952. In 1953, the Ministry of Welfare issued a statement claiming that various government agencies would pay special attention to mixed race children who remained in Japan, supporting them to become respectable Japanese citizens.[17] The Korean government admitted mixed race children in middle and upper schools in the 1960s.[18] Such improvements toward the treatment of these children raised questions about whether their widespread adoption was necessary.

In the United States, the shared desire of adoption advocates and adoptive families for less oversight, bureaucracy, and waiting periods resulted in tragic cases that moved children from one abusive situation in

Asia to another in the United States. Individual advocates, such as Harry and Bertha Holt; social service organizations, such as the US branch of the International Social Service; and the Pearl S. Buck Foundation espoused different philosophies about adoption and often criticized each other's tactics regarding what was best for the mixed race child. Sometimes these disagreements resulted in competition for children and their commodification for a nascent international adoption market.

Potential adoptive parents underwent extensive social service investigations and experienced the emotional and financial stress of having to conform to the nuclear-family and middle-class ideals of the period. They also learned that the simple joys of adoptive family life that had been publicized in news stories were far from simple. The profound sorrow (sometimes expressed through incessant crying) that adopted children felt because they missed their birth mothers or foster mothers challenged idealized notions of adoptive family life and signaled the significance of their birth families and countries of origin. Although the plight of "GI babies" persisted in the 1970s in the context of the Vietnam War, by that time more American families had turned to international adoption not as an expression of cultural superiority or humanitarianism but rather as a critique of the failure of US policy.[19]

Nevertheless, the international adoption of mixed race Asian and American children created a paradigm shift regarding the meaning and the making of a family. It contributed to making international and transracial adoption more of a social norm. By the late twentieth century, the United States distinguished itself as an international adoption nation. According to the Evan B. Donaldson Adoption Institute, international adoptions in the United States more than doubled between 1991 and 2001. While Russia, Guatemala, Romania, and Ukraine have been among the top sending countries of adoptive children, Asian children have constituted the majority of children internationally adopted by US citizens.

OUR MULTIRACIAL HERITAGE

Asian American interracial intimacies—romance, marriage, and family and community formation—have a history that is over 150 years old.

One of the developments behind their origins was the flourishing of international port cultures in places such as nineteenth-century New York City. The centuries-long seafaring traditions of Chinese traders and adventurers, European participation in Asian markets, and Western fascination with export luxury goods shaped an international diaspora of Chinese seamen. Scholar John Kuo Wei Tchen's research documents the history of a Chinese community in New York City before the advent of its Chinatown in the 1870s. It was a community that included Chinese-Irish families.[20]

In the mid-1850s, a census official who walked the streets of lower New York encountered John Huston and his Irish wife, Margaret, at home with their two young daughters, Kate and Mary. Although Huston was a common Anglo-American name, John was born in China. He arrived in New York in 1829 and worked as a seaman.[21] The Hustons were part of a pattern. The census taker found five apartments in one building, each occupied by a Chinese man married to an Irish woman. They included William Brown, a Chinese ship steward, who was married to Irishwoman Rebecca Brown. They had a six-year-old son, William, who, like Kate and Mary, was a native New Yorker.[22]

Why did these Chinese men take on Western names? Tchen presents multiple possibilities. Their Anglo-Christian names may have stemmed from British influence after Hong Kong became a British colony in 1842. A British or American shipmaster might have given them these names as they sometimes did to Chinese crew members. Or, the men could have taken on these names as the result of the influence of Bible and English-language classes they took in American churches, such as the Fourth Avenue Presbyterian Church, which had a Chinese Mission.[23] Furthermore, in Chinese culture, it was traditional to take on various names. Taking on a new Western name suggested a willingness to live and work with non-Chinese workers and neighbors. It performed the same function as intermarriage in that it signaled that they had intended to stay.[24]

In the 1910s, the maritime trade brought hundreds of Indian seamen to the waterfronts of New York, Philadelphia, and Baltimore. Most of these men were Muslims, coming primarily from rural villages in East

Bengal—which would later become the nation of Bangladesh—but also from regions that are part of present-day Pakistan, such as Punjab, Kashmir, and the Northwest Frontier. They formed networks that inspired them to jump ship and escape the harsh working conditions onboard. And they helped each other to find work in the expanding US steel, shipbuilding, and munitions industries.

While the majority returned to the subcontinent, scholar and filmmaker Vivek Bald found that some remained in the United States for good, with the majority settling in Harlem.[25] They married local women, had children, and developed new networks that included Puerto Rican, African American, and West Indian extended families and friends. Living on the same neighborhood block forged a communal identity that superseded other kinds of difference. At the same time, these Bengali Muslim men kept in touch with one another. They gathered at one another's homes and at restaurants and other businesses that they had opened. They prayed together and celebrated Eid. Their multicultural worlds were distinct from the ethnic enclaves that had more recently emerged, such as the Little Indias of post-1965 Asian America. Still, their presence was an integral part of New York City's multiracial community in Harlem and beyond during the 1930s through the 1960s.

Firsthand accounts by community members, such as Noor Chowdry, offer a glimpse into this history. During his early childhood, Chowdry lived with his mother and maternal grandmother in East Harlem, speaking only Spanish until the age of six. Later he lived with his Bengali uncle, African American aunt, and his aunt's son in Belleville, New Jersey. During Thanksgiving and Christmas holidays, the extended family gathered in an African American section of Montclair, New Jersey. It included more than a dozen American-born cousins who were Bengali and Puerto Rican, Bengali and African American, and Bengali and white. They shared different kinds of traditional food and conversed in multiple languages.[26]

New Orleans's Tremé neighborhood was also the site of a mixed Bengali Muslim, African American, and Creole community. According to Bald, these Bengali Muslims were not seamen, but rather groups of peddlers from the present-day Indian state of West Bengal who came to the

United States as early as the 1880s. They brought exotic goods, such as embroidered silk, to sell to an American public fascinated by "Oriental" items.[27]

New Orleans's international port culture also gave birth to a multi-racial Filipino Irish American community in the nineteenth century. Seaman Felipe Madrigal hailed from the Philippines and arrived in New Orleans in the early 1800s. While working on a passenger ship between Europe and the United States, he met Bridgett Nugent, an Irish woman. After getting to know one another during the three-month journey, they married upon their arrival in New Orleans. Bridgett's parents were disappointed. They had hoped their daughter would marry a rich American and, after proceeding north, they never contacted her again.[28]

Undeterred by their disapproval, Felipe and Bridgett settled in New Orleans's Westbank. Felipe quit seafaring and engaged in business, opening his own restaurant. During the Civil War, when Confederate money replaced US dollars in the region, he hid two hundred Yankee dollars. His prescience paid off. After the war, he became a rich Filipino in a land of Confederate money. Librarian Marina Espina's research traces the multiple generations of their Filipino Irish American family. Felipe and Bridgett had three daughters, Helen, Mary Ellen, and Elizabeth, all of whom married Filipinos: Teodoro Victoriano, Daniel Reyes, and Baltic Borabod. Elizabeth became a fluent speaker of French, Spanish, English, and Tagalog. She and Baltic had five children, Mathilda, Othelia, Sidonia, Rosalie, and Peter. Espina writes that the descendants return to New Orleans for regular reunions, fulfilling Elizabeth's wish that they keep in touch "no matter how far they might be apart and no matter how many years might intervene."[29]

Ideas of racial purity and white supremacy ran counter to this vibrant multiracial heritage. As the numbers of Asians increased in the second half of the nineteenth century, attempts to define Americanness as whiteness included the passage of anti-miscegenation laws that prohibited Asian-white marriages. Thirty-eight states adopted laws that regulated interracial sex and marriage. All of these laws banned Black-white relationships; seven states prohibited Native American-white unions, and fourteen states prohibited Asian-white marriages.[30] Many of the states prohibiting Asian-white marriages were in the American West.[31] They included the state of California, which forbade the issuance of marriage licenses to Mongolian-white couples beginning in 1880, until the California Supreme Court declared the anti-miscegenation law unconstitutional in the 1948 case of *Perez v. Sharp*. While there were Asian-white married couples in California during this period, they typically faced the threat of violence and strong prejudice against their unions.

Thus, the marriage of the white American woman (whose story appears in this chapter's introduction) and Rev. Walter Ngon Fong in June 1897, took place in Denver, Colorado, instead of San Francisco. Their marriage was the subject of cruel gossip. The woman had heard that she had disgraced her family by marrying a Chinese man. When they relocated to Berkeley, she recounted that "women in their clubs and various chit-chat societies raked me over unmercifully."[32] These discriminatory attitudes contributed to why, she explained, "many American girls married to Orientals . . . have tried to conceal, from all but their immediate associates, the fact that the head of the house was Oriental."[33]

Such prejudice extended beyond Berkeley to Chicago. After historian Barbara Posadas's Filipino father and Polish mother met in Chicago and eloped in 1931, their marriage sent a "shock wave" in her family that lasted for years.[34] By 1945, when Barbara was born, her mother's family had been mostly reconciled to her choice of a husband but continued to exclude them from celebrations that involved the broader Polish community. This exclusion contributed to Posadas's reflection that she never thought of herself as Polish despite some cultural exposure to her heritage. She heard polkas played on records but did not learn the polka dance. She enjoyed eating pierogis with plums, but rarely ate them after the death of her step-grandmother, who prepared the dish this way. Her mother spoke Polish to her father and her sisters, but Posadas suspected that she did not want her to hear their conversations.

Although Posadas did not experience overt racial discrimination at school or in her neighborhood, having a non-white father and a white mother profoundly shaped her identity. She keenly observed how "race constantly defined how my parents dealt with the world around them."[35] It restricted their lives in public spaces. To reduce the likelihood of racial confrontations, they avoided being seen together as a couple. Either her mother took her shopping, or her father did. On those rare occasions when they did go out, they dined at Chinese restaurants, which seemed relatively safer. Posadas recollected a one-time family outing to a neighborhood theater to see the 1957 movie *Sayonara*, about interracial love and racial prejudice in postwar Japan, starring Marlon Brando and Miiko Taka. The constant physical and social maneuvering to avoid harm could not fully protect their mixed race family, however. It also took an emotional toll. Posadas recalls:

> Most traumatically, when they tried to buy a single-family home in the newly developed area on the far Northwest side to which my mother's sister, her husband, and their daughter had recently moved, neighbors on the block made clear that my father was not welcome, and the seller backed out.[36]

The social and spatial impacts of racism contributed to the formation of mixed race families among non-whites in California in the first half of the twentieth century. In her study of "romantic crossings," scholar Allison Varzally argues that "non-whites mixed in churches, farms, schools, working districts, and neighborhoods because it was difficult not to."[37] Restrictive housing covenants, alien land laws, employment discrimination, and school segregation circumscribed their mobility, often compelling them to interact in the same places.

Restrictive immigration laws prevented the approximately 6,800 Indian men who came to the American West between 1899 and 1914 from bringing wives. Most of these men hailed from the Punjab province. Collectively—though incorrectly—labeled as "Hindus" during this period, the vast majority of them were Sikh and a smaller percentage were Muslim. They faced intense prejudice from their relationships with white women. When one Punjabi man mentioned a romance he had had with a white woman, his Anglo neighbor threatened him with a shotgun and had him arrested.[38]

Although Mexican Americans were "white" by law, their relationships with non-white men, including romantic ones, were generally more acceptable in county clerk offices and in everyday life. If a clerk decided not to issue a marriage license, couples went to another county, state, or even on the high seas for a ship captain's ceremony.[39] In her study of California's Punjabi Mexican American community, scholar Karen Leonard traces a pattern of intermarriage that extended from El Paso and Canutillo in Texas to Las Cruces, New Mexico, to California's Imperial Valley, where most of the Punjabi Mexican couples lived. Their labor in cotton fields as well as racial segregation brought them together. Mexican women played a major role in growing this community by arranging matches between relatives and friends and Punjabis.

These marriages produced many children, including stepchildren, and a multigenerational Punjabi Mexican American community emerged. Their histories are reflected in their children's names, such as Maria Jesusita Singh, Jose Akbar Khan, and Armando Chand.[40] A strong Mexican cultural influence came from mothers, aunts and grandmothers, godmothers, and other children, including older Spanish-speaking stepchildren who helped take care of the younger ones, and classmates, many of whom were Spanish speakers. According to Leonard, even in the present day, some in the Imperial Valley think of Singh as a Mexican American surname.[41]

Although Punjabi culture may not have been as prominent in the children's upbringing, it still mattered. The men taught their wives how to prepare Punjabi-style vegetables and chicken curry. Some took off their traditional turbans but kept the iron wrist bangles that symbolized their Sikh faith.[42] Many did not teach their children Punjabi language in part because they considered their children to be American, but also because of their own intense work schedules in the agricultural fields. As they aged and became grandfathers, they had more time to share stories about the Punjab. Some of their descendants relished this time, such as John Diwan's daughter, Janie, who felt a sense of loss when her father suddenly stopped their evening story sessions about Punjabi culture.[43] Overall, Leonard found that Punjabi Mexican children grew up taking great pride in their Indian heritage.[44]

Like Punjabi Mexican couples, Filipino Mexican couples did not face the harsh social ostracism and violence that Filipino-white couples endured in California and beyond. In 1933, an amendment to California's anti-miscegenation law prohibited Filipino-white intermarriage. Scholar Rudy P. Guevarra Jr.'s research shows that multiracial areas in San Diego brought Filipino men and Mexican women together.[45] These places included the Southeast, the South Bay, and along the waterfront, such as Logan Heights and National City. The labor needs of the agricultural, fish canning, defense, and service industries attracted Mexican and Filipino workers to these areas. While San Diego's proximity to the Mexican border contributed to continual migration flows, the US Navy's recruitment of Filipinos beginning in the early twentieth century facilitated Filipino migration to San Diego. Until 1998, San Diego was the site of the largest US naval base and the Naval Training Center. Approximately half of San Diego's Filipino population has ties to the US Navy.[46]

A shared Spanish colonial past that intertwined Mexico and the Philippines through the Acapulco-Manila Galleon Trade (1565–1815) and its cultural legacies—most notably Catholicism, Spanish language, cuisine, and practices such as *compadrazgo*, or "godparenthood"—created common ground. Beginning in the 1930s, marriages between Filipino men and Mexican women produced generations of Mexipino children. Their mothers' influence as well as the geographic proximity to Mexico contributed to the strong Mexican cultural influence in Mexipino lives. In spite of the vast ocean that separated San Diego from the Philippine Islands, Filipino traditions were also maintained. The sound of conversations in Tagalog and Ilocano, the sight of Filipino elders, and the tastes of traditional food at Filipino community events and family gatherings enabled the transmission of Filipino culture. Like Mexican cuisine, Filipino dishes, such as menudo, empanadas, adobo, and *caldo de arroz*, displayed Spanish influences, but were also uniquely Filipino in their preparation, presentation, and flavor.[47]

Sometimes a sense of belonging was a challenge for Mexipinos even in these multiracial spaces. Suzanna Balino Fernandez explained: "The Mexicans thought you were too 'Oriental' and the Filipinos thought you were too Mexican. If you didn't know Spanish, they [the Mexicans] would make fun of you, and if you didn't know Tagalog, they [the Filipinos] would make fun of you too."[48]

Rituals surrounding the preparation and consumption of food were among the strongest factors in a holistic formation of Mexipinos' mixed identity. Rashaan Meneses related that both of her parents prepared Mexican and Filipino dishes: "They would both cook adobo. . . . They definitely mixed it. We'd have lumpia and homemade enchiladas together."[49] Sophia Limjoco shared: "When we have parties, both the Mexican and Filipino sides of our family get together. There are a lot of people there! Our food is a combination of Mexican and Filipino. We have tortillas, beans, salsa, *nopales*, as well as lumpia, rice, *pan de sal*, and sandwiches. It's great!" People's eagerness to participate in everyday activities and special occasions created belonging and sustained community.

Guevarra concludes that the Mexipino experience presents a new perspective, one forged out of multiracial spaces and comparative and relational histories.[50] This perspective is needed because our future is becoming more multiracial.

OUR MULTIRACIAL FUTURE

According to the first racial and ethnic breakdown from the 2020 census, the biggest population increase was among people who identified as more than one race. Americans who identified as non-Hispanic and more than one race rose from 6 million to 13.5 million. For people who identified as Hispanic and multiracial, the increase was even higher, from 3 million to 20.3 million. The 2000 census was the first time Americans were able to choose more than one race to describe themselves.[51]

Public figures, such as Vice President Kamala Harris, who is the daughter of Indian and Jamaican parents, and the first female, first Black, and first Asian American US vice president, are bringing more attention to multiracial individuals and families. Harris has spoken openly and positively about her multiracial background. Her mother, Shyamala Gopalan, immigrated to the US to pursue a doctorate in nutrition and endocrinology at the University of California, Berkeley, and became a civil rights activist and a breast cancer researcher. On the campaign trail, Harris described her mother as a proud woman: "She was a brown woman. She was a woman with a heavy accent. She was a woman who, many times, people would overlook her or not take her seriously."[52] After Harris's parents' divorce, Gopalan raised Harris and her younger sister as a single mother. She exposed them to their Indian heritage, while being equally committed to having them grow into confident Black women.

Many factors contributed to the growing multiracial Asian American population of our present day. Changing laws and judicial precedents, most notably with the Supreme Court decision of *Loving v. Virginia* in 1967, made anti-miscegenation laws unconstitutional, enabling a rise in intermarriage from 7 percent in 1980 to 17 percent in 2015.[53] The pioneering research of scholars such as Paul Spickard and Maria P. P. Root, featuring multiracial Asian American histories and contemporary experiences, expanded both the Black-white paradigm of mixed race studies and the monoracial approaches of Asian American studies.[54] Root's Filipino American background and work as a clinical psychologist influenced her research and advocacy. She explained that "because most Filipinos have racially diverse family roots—like Spanish, Malay and Chinese—they often struggle to find a place within the Asian-American community."[55]

Root authored the 1993 Bill of Rights for People of Mixed Heritage, a groundbreaking and generative text. The bill opens with "I have the right . . ." and includes the following phrases: "Not to justify my existence in the world"; "To identify myself differently than strangers expect me to identify"; and "To create a vocabulary to communicate about being multiracial or multiethnic." It concludes with the right "to freely choose whom I befriend and love."[56]

In 2006, artist Kip Fulbeck's landmark project, *Part Asian, 100% Hapa*, became the first museum exhibition to explicitly explore multiracial Asian identity. *Hapa*, the Hawai'ian word for "half," has been used by many multiracial Asian Americans to describe themselves, although some have become more critical of this use of the Hawai'ian word and no longer use it.[57] The project showcases individual photographic portraits of multiracial Asian people accompanied by their own answers to the ubiquitous question: "What are you?"

Alongside their portrait, one person responds, "African American, Japanese," and in their own handwriting writes, "I am 100% Black and

100% Japanese."[58] Another replies, "Vietnamese, Spanish, French," and "No. Spain never colonized Viet Nam. But, thanks for asking. I am a scholar, organizer & adventurer. I strive for unique thoughts with universal understandings—precisely because it is expected of me & not expected of me."[59] The exhibition was first displayed at the Japanese American National Museum (JANM) before traveling throughout the United States and abroad. It was one of the most popular exhibitions in JANM's history.

In 2018, a new exhibition, *hapa.me: 15 years of the hapa project*, paired the original photographs and statements from the 2006 exhibition with contemporary portraits of the same individuals and new statements, showing not only their physical changes over fifteen years, but also their changes in perspective and outlook on the world.[60] The person who responded "African American, Japanese" to the question "What are you?" expanded on the answer to include "son, husband, father." The other person replied, "Being mixed-race means having the gift of empathy and knowing that differing ideas, beliefs, backgrounds . . . can, and have, come together for love, peace, and understanding."[61]

Fulbeck, who is of Chinese, English, and Irish descent, shares that, like many Hapa children, he felt like he was "the only one." The project produced two companion volumes, the kind of books Fulbeck wishes he had when he was growing up. He writes that the project started with a simple idea: "To photograph a couple hundred Hapas and have them write about themselves. Give them the opportunity to show their image and respond in their own words to the question that accompanies the lives of us in-betweens like a second skin."[62]

New multiracial histories are emerging. After his mother was killed in the Atlanta spa shootings on March 16, 2021, Robert Peterson took up an offer to receive a free tattoo from celebrity tattoo artist Young Bae to memorialize his mother. Like Bae, Robert is Black and Korean. His tattoo features his mother's name, Yong Ae Yue, and a boiling stone pot of *kimchi jjigae*, the first dish that she taught him to make and his favorite.

In an insightful and moving story for the *Washington Post*, Michelle Ye Hee Lee reports that Yue was born in 1957 and grew up in South Korea. She married an American soldier who she met there, and they moved to Fort Benning, Georgia, around 1980. Yue taught herself to read and write in English and became a US citizen. After she and her husband divorced around 1984, she gave him full custody of their sons, Elliott and Robert. It was a difficult choice for her, but she was mindful that her sons looked more Black than Asian, and she believed that they could better understand their experiences as Black men in America with their father.

After Elliott joined the army, Yue eventually moved back to Georgia where Robert was still in high school. She loved to cook Korean food for her sons, once bringing a large amount of kimchi for Robert in his dormitory at Morehouse College, a historically Black men's liberal arts college. Yue also loved working. She had worked at a grocery store before cooking and cleaning for a spa. When she lost that job during the pandemic, she found a similar one at another spa, where she monitored the security cameras and opened the door for customers. The shooter took Yue's life with a single gunshot to her head. The Atlanta spa shootings took place at three spas and claimed the lives of eight people, six of whom were Asian women.

In the midst of their grief, Elliott and Robert have pondered over their mother's life history in relation to their own. Elliott said, "I'm very proud to be mixed. I'm very proud that when she was young, in Korea, that she gave my father a chance." After receiving support from both Black and Asian communities, Robert, who has a doctorate in medical sociology, has been working toward bringing both communities together to fight for greater equity. The Congressional Asian Pacific American and Black Caucuses have invited him to speak about his experience. Robert believes that, had his mother been alive to see him and his brother "embraced" by both communities, "she would have loved that."[63]

By placing mixed race lives at the center of Asian American histories, we are able to glean distinctive viewpoints and voices. They offer new perspectives about our past and present. And they present new possibilities for making and re-making a family, a community, a nation.

SIX

1941 AND 1942: THE DAYS
THAT YOU REMEMBER

What are the days that you remember? Birthdays, weddings, and graduations may immediately come to mind—days that are associated with the most joyous occasions. At other times, the most memorable days might be ones that evoked fear, anguish, and sorrow.

Reflecting upon this question in the context of Asian American history, I think about the Japanese American students who had to leave their colleges and universities soon after Japan bombed Pearl Harbor on December 7, 1941. This is a day that many Americans know as the "date which will live in infamy," as President Franklin D. Roosevelt called it in a speech.

February 19, 1942, is a day we should also remember. On this day President Roosevelt issued Executive Order 9066. It set in motion the forced removal of Japanese Americans on the West Coast to assembly centers and subsequently internment camps in remote areas of California, Arizona, Colorado, Utah, Arkansas, Wyoming, and Idaho. The incarceration of 120,000 Japanese Americans, two-thirds of whom were US-born, took place without due process. Long-standing anti-Japanese hostility, racism, and wartime hysteria enabled this denial of justice.

World War II alliances also dramatically changed the status of Chinese, Filipino, Korean, and Asian Indians in the United States. The repeal of discriminatory legislation, such as the Chinese Exclusion Act, and participation in US military service provided pathways to naturalization.

Wartime needs provided new employment opportunities for Asian Americans. These, too, are days we should remember.

At the same time, anti-Asian violence and erasure persisted. Wartime alliances with specific Asian nations did not protect Asian Americans from racism. The impounding of over one hundred of Dorothea Lange's photographs of the Japanese American evacuation and the internment camps, photographs that portrayed Japanese Americans as Americans and as human beings, concealed this injustice. In the 1980s, internees demanded an apology and redress. They wanted us to listen to their experiences and to learn from them so that this history would never happen again.

JUSTICE DENIED

After Japan's attack on Pearl Harbor, if you are a Japanese language teacher, Buddhist priest, newspaper editor, or business leader, you are swiftly targeted as an "enemy alien." You may be among the 1,300 men who are arrested in Hawai'i and the US mainland within forty-eight hours of the Pearl Harbor attack.[1] If you are Yoshiaki Fukuda, who was born in Japan, studied the Konko faith that emphasizes interdependence at a seminary in Okayama Prefecture, and founded the Konko Church in San Francisco in the 1930s, you are apprehended and you are forced on board a train without knowing your destination. The view outside is blocked by shades on the windows. You are "watched constantly by sentries with bayoneted rifles."[2]

You try to protect your family's resources in order to survive what may happen next. In Oakland, a Japanese American store owner places a large "I AM AN AMERICAN" banner on the storefront.[3] Japanese banks close and the bank accounts of Issei, the immigrant generation, are frozen.

If you are twelve-year-old Donald Nakahara, you walk with your father, a newspaperman, to a bus stop in San Francisco. Your father is on his way to help Japanese Americans in San Jose. This will be the last time you see him. Your father is arrested, held at a local detention center, and then sent to several camps with other Japanese American community leaders. You will hear from him through a few letters. From these letters, you will learn some things, but not others. You know that your father suffered several strokes in various detention facilities. That he was in Fort Sill, Oklahoma, and Camp Livingstone, Louisiana. You think he died in Bismarck, North Dakota, but you are uncertain. Not knowing compounds your grief.[4]

If you are Japanese in Hawai'i, you are not forcibly relocated on a mass scale because, unlike the Japanese on the US mainland, you have a history of close connections with local leaders. There are also practical and logistical impediments, as your community makes up 37 percent of the local population.[5] You live under martial law, however, and you are required to carry a registration card at all times and comply with travel and work restrictions.

If you are Japanese on the US West Coast, even if you are second- or third-generation, General John L. DeWitt of the Western Defense Command recommends your removal, declaring that "the Japanese race is an enemy race" and "racial strains are undiluted."[6] In San Francisco, you observe that the text of Executive Order 9066 does not name the Japanese American community. However, the April 1, 1942, notice posted at First and Front Streets makes clear in large, bold, and capitalized letters that these are "INSTRUCTIONS TO ALL PERSONS OF JAPANESE ANCESTRY." In this title phrase, the word "JAPANESE" is highlighted in even larger-sized font. In the fine print it says that "all Japanese persons, alien and non-alien, will be evacuated from the above designated area by 12:00 o'clock noon Tuesday, April 7, 1942."[7] You might be an orphan or mixed race. So long as you have Japanese blood, these instructions apply to you.

You are forced to go to one of seventeen assembly centers or "reception centers" located in fairgrounds or horse racing tracks. You are instructed to bring only what you can carry and what has been authorized by the US Army, such as bedding, linens, toiletries, enamel plates, and eating utensils. You cannot bring all your clothes, let alone furniture and other household items. Knowing this, some people come to your home looking for bargains. Jeanne Wakatsuki Houston watches her mother break her heirloom china before giving it away to a bargain hunter.[8] Her mother's actions speak volumes: *They cannot take everything away from me, from my family.*

If you are a Japanese American undergraduate student at the University of California, Berkeley, like Yoshiko Uchida, who was born and raised in Berkeley, you must leave your campus as well as your childhood home. Uchida cannot bring her pet collie, Laddie, to the horse stall that is the makeshift housing for her and her family at Tanforan Racetrack, which has been repurposed as an assembly center. In desperation, she sends a letter to the student newspaper, the *Daily Californian*, pleading: "I am one of the Japanese American students soon to be evacuated and have a male Scotch collie that can't come with me. Can anyone give him a home? If interested, please call me immediately."[9] If you are a Japanese American college senior, like Uchida, you miss your commencement by two weeks. Her undergraduate education ends unceremoniously with the Tanforan mailman handing her diploma, rolled in a cardboard container, to her in a horse stall.[10]

The process of your dehumanization has begun. Your name is replaced by a number. For Miné Okubo, that number is 13660. The number is supposed to identify her, but it conceals more than it reveals. It belies her family's immigration story of her father having been a scholar and her mother, a calligrapher.[11] In the United States, her mother became a housewife while her father worked in a candy shop, and later as a gardener and landscaper. Her mother encouraged her to pursue her interest in art. Okubo completed her undergraduate degree in art and her master's degree in art and anthropology at the University of California, Berkeley, while working as a seamstress, maid, farm laborer, and tutor. She received an incredible honor, a fellowship to study in Paris under artist Fernand Léger. Upon her return to the United States, she worked with the Works Progress Administration's Federal Art Project on mural projects, including those at the Oakland Hospitality House and Fort Ord. From 1940 to 1941, she curated two exhibitions at the San Francisco Museum of Modern Art. In 1942, Okubo is given tags to wear that bear the number 13660.

There are guards surrounding the assembly centers and barbed wire all around you. The stench is awful. The heat can soar to 120 degrees.

You have no privacy whatsoever. The walls are flimsy, if there are any walls at all. The toilets have no partitions. You spend your time worrying, getting angry, feeling melancholy. Humor, imagination, play, and beauty remind you that you are human. Internees hold a fly-catching contest and the winner "proudly" displays a gallon jug filled with 2,426 dead flies.[12] They vie for the "honor" of being assigned to the stall once occupied by the legendary racing horse Seabiscuit. There is so much dust in this place that a young internee imagines "a mole digging his burrow" that is "ten feet up in the air."[13]

Some non-Japanese Asian Americans help you by looking out for your homes and your businesses. They include Filipino American Johnny Ibarra, who took over the farm of his former boss, Yoshio Ando, in the Santa Clara Valley near San Jose, California, charging a token sum to cover the property tax bill.[14] In Whittier, California, the family of Korean American Mary Paik Lee looked after the property of a Japanese American family who were their neighbors.[15] On Bainbridge Island, Washington, Filipino American employees Felix Narte and Elaulio Aquino did the same for the Kitamoto family farm until the family could reclaim it.[16] However, others direct their hatred of Japan toward you and take advantage of your forced eviction and removal.

If you are married to a non-Japanese American, you may be anxious like Mary Ventura, née Chiyo Asaba, who is a native of Washington State. She and her Filipino American husband, Mamerto Ventura, have built a life together in Seattle's International District. At first, they politely request exemption for mixed race couples. When their requests are denied, they hire a lawyer and file the first known courtroom challenge in the United States to Japanese internment. Mary Ventura insists on her loyalty and devotion to the Constitution and its laws. Federal district court judge Lloyd Black rejects her claim, setting a dangerous precedent.[17]

Judge Black cites his ruling in *Ex parte Ventura* to dismiss the case of University of Washington student Gordon Hirabayashi, who challenged the War Department's curfew for violating the Fourteenth Amendment's equal protection clause. Lawyer Minoru Yasui also believes that these military orders are unconstitutional, and he violates the curfew order in order to challenge it in court. Fred Korematsu is arrested for defying evacuation orders and not reporting to a relocation center. All three convictions will be upheld by the US Supreme Court in 1943 and 1944.

A newly created War Relocation Authority builds ten internment camps: Tule Lake, California; Minidoka, Idaho; Manzanar, California; Topaz, Utah; Jerome, Arkansas; Heart Mountain, Wyoming; Poston, Arizona; Granada, Colorado; Gila River, Arizona; and Rohwer, Arkansas. They are located in desert and swamp areas with extreme conditions of heat, dust, wind, and cold. A young George Takei is not yet famous for portraying helmsman Hikaru Sulu of the USS *Enterprise* on *Star Trek*. He and his family are interned at Camp Rohwer in the swamps of Arkansas. His father is able to convince camp commanders to let the teenagers hold dances with a record player brought in by the guards. Takei is too young to attend the dances, but he listens to the music through the wall. The bayou seeps under the barbed wire fence, and cypress trees grow out of this water. He watches his father carve a sculpture from the root of a cypress tree and learns an important lesson about the meaning of resilience, that it is "the ability to find beauty in an ugly situation."[18]

There are times that violence erupts among internees, such as in the Poston and Manzanar camps. This violence stems from fear, tensions, and suspicions regarding the presence of *inu*, or spies. There are guards in towers with guns. You have been told that you were put in these camps for your own protection. *Then why*, you wonder, *are these guns pointing inward instead of outward?*[19]

After all this, Nisei (second-generation Japanese American) men who are seventeen or older are given an "opportunity" to demonstrate their patriotism by serving in the US armed forces. You are asked to fill out a form also known as the "loyalty" questionnaire. Question 27 asks if you are willing to serve in combat duty wherever ordered. Question 28 asks if you are willing to swear allegiance to the United States and to renounce your allegiance to the Japanese emperor. What does "willingness" mean when you are incarcerated without due process?

Some of you become part of the 442nd Regimental Combat Team, a Japanese American segregated unit. The segregated 100th Infantry Battalion from Hawai'i joins you. You are on the front lines of some of the bloodiest battles in Europe, such as the rescue of the Texas "Lost Battalion" in France. You are one of the recipients of over 4,000 Purple Hearts, 29 Distinguished Service Crosses, 588 Silver Stars, and more than 4,000 Bronze Stars. Your segregated unit is among the most decorated units in the war.[20]

An estimated six thousand Nisei also serve as linguists as part of the Military Intelligence Service. They include John Okada, who is interned at Minidoka camp in Idaho, and subsequently trains to become a Japanese language translator at the Military Intelligence Service Language School in Minnesota. Okada earns the rank of sergeant as a translator and interpreter. About a decade later, his writing will immortalize the experience of the conscientious objectors who answered "no" to questions 27 and 28 in the loyalty questionnaire. His novel will be titled *No-No Boy*.[21]

During the war, there are other ways to leave the internment camps. You may leave to do much-needed agricultural labor in Idaho, Colorado, and Utah. Or you might attend college in the East or Midwest. The beginning of the end of internment and the closure of the camps is what results from Mitsuye Endo's successful challenge to this injustice in a December 1944 Supreme Court decision.[22] Endo, the chief plaintiff, was born in Sacramento. At the beginning of the war, she was a twenty-two-year-old typist for California's Department of Motor Vehicles when she was fired because of her Japanese ancestry. She and her family were then interned at Tule Lake camp in California. In July 1942, she petitioned Judge Michael J. Roche of the United States District Court in Northern California for a writ of habeas corpus to obtain her release. She was an American citizen who was interned without charge for any law violation and without a hearing. Judge Roche denied her freedom, but a lawyer from the War Relocation Authority met with Endo in camp, offering her freedom on the condition that she not return to the West Coast. Endo refused and continued to be incarcerated while her case was under appeal. On December 18, 1944, in *Ex parte Mitsuye Endo*, the US Supreme Court unanimously rules that the government cannot detain citizens who are loyal to the United States.

The announcement that internment camps will close within a year creates panic, anger, confusion, and anxiety at Tule Lake. Initially, less than two dozen internees apply to renounce their US citizenship. In the subsequent weeks, you may be one of the thousands who join them. The injustice of internment, coercion by Japanese nationalists, and parental pressure to keep families together create complex and divided loyalties that motivate renunciation. You had thought that renunciation of your US citizenship would give you and your family members more options for resettlement. But then you learn that Japan is losing the war. Now you and your family face the prospect of deportation to a devastated Japan.[23] You did not fully understand the implications of your actions. You realize that you have made a grave mistake. The herculean efforts of lawyer Wayne Collins, who dedicates most of his career to defending Japanese Americans affected by the war, helps the majority get their citizenships restored. In some cases, this process takes over two decades.

By the war's end, you are afraid of what awaits you outside the camps. If you are among those still left because you are elderly, have young children, or are unsure of how you will support yourself, you are forced out and issued twenty-five dollars. The West Coast has changed. Its population has grown. You may have no choice but to live in surplus army barracks supplied by the War Relocation Authority. They bear an eerie resemblance to the camps you had just left.[24]

REVOLUTIONARY CHANGES

If you were not of Japanese ancestry, the days that you remember varied greatly, depending on who you were. In the 1930s, Japanese invasions mobilized Chinese American communities to aid their Asian homeland even before US entry in the war. The outbreak of the Second Sino-Japanese War in 1937 inspired "Bowl of Rice" fundraisers from New York to Portland, San Francisco, and Santa Barbara that raised millions of dollars for China war relief. The son of Chinese immigrants, John Fong, was born and raised in San Francisco's Chinatown, where his family owned a bakery and grocery store. He was twelve years old when his Boy Scout troop participated in a fundraising festival and parade in San Francisco. Parade-goers threw money in large receptacles built in the shape of rice bowls resting on platforms with wheels. Fong remembers:

"We were assigned four scouts to each rice bowl, and we pushed that thing from City Hall on Van Ness to Market, and down Market to Grant and then up Grant until . . . Broadway."[25]

Chinese Americans also organized protests against the sale of scrap metal to Japan, where it was being recycled into war matériel. Fong recalls his parents participating in this effort: "Well, they went down to the docks one time because they were loading scrap metal. They were selling scrap metal to Japan. . . . So of course a lot of scrap metal came back as bombs. . . . My mother and father a couple of times went down there to demonstrate."[26] Similar demonstrations took place in Oregon. In February 1939, several dozen Chinese American men, women, and children carried signs denouncing the loading of scrap iron onto the *Norway Maru*, a large Japanese freighter, at the Port of Astoria. Some of the signs read "This Iron Is For Bullets" and "Help Us Stop Slaughtering Innocents."[27]

Within hours of the bombing of Pearl Harbor, Japan bombed and invaded the Philippines. Seattle native and Filipino American Dorothy Cordova was nine years old on that day. She remembers December 8th:

> They started to bomb the Philippines. In fact, they bombed my mother's hometown because they have an airfield there. I remember my cousin and I walking up Denny to go to the drugstore on the top on Twenty-Third, and all the time we were watching the sky . . . we were kids. We didn't know what was going to happen.[28]

The city's preparation for possible future attacks also made an impression on her. In Seattle, if you wanted to turn on the lights at night, the windows of your homes had to have heavy curtains. Air raid wardens patrolled Cordova's neighborhood to make sure their windows were fully covered.

After people started shaking their fists at both the Japanese and Filipino American children who rode the school bus, Cordova and other Filipino children were given buttons that said, "I'm a Filipino." Her sentiments about Japanese American internment contrasted dramatically with those of her family members, who resented the attack by Japan that had "leveled" her mother's hometown. Since she attended an elementary school with Japanese American classmates, she remembers feeling differently:

> I didn't think it was right; see, they were sending away my friends. I didn't know their parents, but then my friends, the children, were going. I'll tell you what was bad was listening to comments by my relatives who I really loved—always having to defend—I remember as a little girl the times that I would leave the room yelling, "That's not fair. That's not fair. They're just kids."[29]

Enlistment figured prominently in Asian American memories of the war. Twelve thousand to fifteen thousand Chinese Americans served in the armed forces, in segregated and non-segregated units.[30] In May 1942, the US Navy allowed Chinese Americans to enlist as apprentice seamen. Previously, they had been restricted to work as mess stewards or cabin boys.[31] Chinese Americans also enlisted in the Chinese American Composite Wing, created in 1943 as part of a joint US-China air effort. It involved sending planes and supplies to the Chinese Air Force and having their pilots trained by American aviators.[32]

The largest concentration of Chinese Americans was in the 14th Air Service Group. Formed in Venice, Florida, in 1944, it consisted of nine units made up of Chinese American personnel. Of its fifty-four officers, twenty-one were Chinese American, two Korean American, and the rest white.[33] Chinese Americans enlisted for various reasons including enmity against Japan, the chance to be close to family in China, and the opportunity to be "accepted as equals of all other Americans."[34] In 1944, Charles Leong wrote: "To GI Joe Wong, in the army a 'Chinaman's chance' means a fair chance, one based not on race or creed, but on the stuff of the man who wears the uniform of the U.S. Army." Many veterans similarly remember their enlistment as a way of giving Chinese Americans "a regular break" and a sense of "belongingness."[35]

In 1941, third-generation Chinese American Maggie Gee withdrew from her studies at the University of California, Berkeley to work as an electrical draftswoman at the Mare Island Naval Shipyard, where she charted the electrical wiring for the repair of damaged submarines. The war provided her with an opportunity of fulfilling her childhood dream of becoming a pilot like Amelia Earhart. She enrolled in flight school in Minden, Nevada, and became one of two Chinese American women in the Women Airforce Service Pilots. WASP transported military aircraft from one base to another within the United States and flew mock missions to train men about to go overseas for combat. Gee recalls that their passion for flying planes bonded the approximately 1,100 women pilots: "All we wanted to do is fly. That's what made the organization so good, because everyone loved flying so much and they wanted to do it."[36]

Thousands of Filipino Americans rushed to their local recruiting offices but were initially turned away because they were aliens ineligible for citizenship. On December 20, 1941, President Roosevelt signed the Selective Training and Service Act, which allowed Filipinos in the United States to enlist in the armed forces. The initial plan to organize a "Filipino Battalion" had to expand to two regiments in order to accommodate the large number of enlistees. Regiment member Toribio Rosal explained that many of these Filipino men came to the United States when they were young, leaving their relatives behind. They felt that "it was their duty" and that it "was in their hearts" to go back to the Philippines and fight the Japanese.[37] Approximately seven thousand Filipinos joined the First and Second Filipino Infantry Regiments in 1942. The first regiment trained at Camp San Luis Obispo and then the Salinas Rodeo Grounds near Watsonville, California, where many Filipinos worked in agriculture. The second trained at Lompoc's Camp Cooke.[38]

Alex Aguinid recollected wanting to join the regiment because "when they were having meals, they always had rice," and he needed to eat rice to maintain his stamina.[39] When Dixon Campos volunteered for the First Filipino Infantry Regiment, he didn't see many soldiers his age. Many were in their mid-thirties and even their forties. Some lied about their age to stay in the army. Yet, he remembers their excellent physical condition: "I had a hell of a time trying to keep up with them. They were strong as an ox because, I guess, of their fieldwork. They could go on a twenty-mile hike. I'd be dying at the end of the twenty-mile hike. And they'd say, 'Let's go another twenty.'"[40] In their missions to the Philippines, they played an important role given their familiarity with the difficult terrain. They were also able to work behind enemy lines, collecting intelligence and engaging in sabotage.

Filipinos in the Philippines also served in the US armed forces. Although the Philippines was a commonwealth by 1941, it was not fully independent from US rule. After observers in the Philippines and the United States concluded that war in the Pacific was inevitable, President Roosevelt recalled Douglas MacArthur in July 1941, and asked him to lead the United States Armed Forces in the Far East (USAFFE). USAFFE combined the US Army, Philippine Scouts, Philippine Army, Constabulary, and the Air Corps and placed them under US command. Filipino soldiers swore oaths to "bear true faith and allegiance to the United States of America."[41] One of the USAFFE soldiers was my *Lolo*, or grandfather, Braulio Ceniza. In a letter, he shared the following memory about his service:

> My role was a hit and run tactic, a guerrilla warfare. We did not have sufficient arms and weapons to face the enemy. The [Japanese] were after us all the time and we tried to evade. Many of my fellow officers and enlisted men were caught by surprise and they were killed. . . . I was able to survive in spite of all those sacrifices, thank God.[42]

After Japan colonized Korea in 1910, military service provided Korean Americans an opportunity to showcase their dedication to Korea as well as the United States. On December 7, a Korean Night program rehearsal took place in Los Angeles. The program's purpose was to raise funds for war relief for Korean refugee families and volunteers in China. After someone shouted that Japan had attacked Pearl Harbor and then called for war against Japan, everyone in the play cried out, "Teahan Toknip Mansee! (Long Live Korean Independence!)."[43]

Korean American men served in the US armed forces, volunteered as emergency fire wardens, and worked in military construction. Women served in the Red Cross and the USO, and sold war bonds. Those who were able to speak the Japanese language worked in government agencies as well as on the Pacific War's front lines as interpreters, translators, and intelligence officers. In 1941, Korean Americans organized the Tiger Brigade of the California National Guard in Los Angeles. Scholar Bong-Youn Choy participated in this Korean unit and observed that although many of the men were past the age of military duty, they still volunteered: "Every Saturday and Sunday afternoon, the Korean unit exercised for three to four hours in Exposition Park, Los Angeles. A similar unit was established in San Francisco and drilled at the War Memorial Auditorium every Sunday afternoon." On April 26, 1942, the Tiger Brigade hosted a gala with representatives from Korean and American communities. Choy writes: "For many Koreans it was their first opportunity to see their countrymen in army uniforms since the Korean national armed forces had been forced to disband by the Japanese authorities in 1907."[44]

Korean American individuals distinguished themselves through their valor. Colonel Young Oak Kim was a highly decorated US Army veteran of World War II and the Korean War. During World War II, he served with Japanese Americans in the 442nd Regimental Combat Team and as a combat leader in Italy and France. He received his first Purple Heart after being wounded in action while working to destroy several enemy machine-gun nests near Santa Maria Oliveto, Italy, in September 1943. In 1944, Kim and Private First Class Irving Akahoshi volunteered to cross a German field and capture German POWs in order to gather information for the Liberation of Rome, actions for which they received the Distinguished Service Cross.[45]

The daughter of Korean independence leader Ahn Chang Ho, Susan Ahn Cuddy, viewed her enlistment in the US Navy as an opportunity to honor her father's legacy. Reflecting upon her motivations, she emphasized that "when you're a Korean, and you have no country, and the Japanese are the predators, and you have a father who gave up his life for it, you go fight."[46] She became the first Asian woman to enlist in the navy and serve as its first female gunnery officer.

Another watershed for Asian Americans was in the realm of employment. In 1941, President Franklin D. Roosevelt's Executive Order 8802 prohibited racial discrimination in employment. Given the labor shortages from so many men entering the armed forces, new work opportunities abounded, especially in war-related industries. The six major shipyards of the San Francisco Bay Area—the Kaiser Shipyards in Richmond, Mare Island Navy Yard in Vallejo, Naval Drydocks in San Francisco, Marinship in Sausalito, Moore Dry Dock Company in Oakland, and Bethlehem Steel in Alameda and South San Francisco—offered jobs that were previously unavailable to Asian Americans.[47] After graduating from Mills College in 1942, Jade Snow Wong was advised to look for work only among Chinese firms because of racial prejudice. However, Wong was able to find work as a clerk typist in the shipyards, summarizing and typing reports based on suggestions made by workers to management. Her work resulted in the shipyard supplying vitamins to ward off colds.[48]

While the iconic image of "Rosie the Riveter" features a white woman wearing a red bandanna and blue work shirt and flexing her muscle, Asian American women were among the millions of women who worked in war-related industries during World War II. These work opportunities expanded Asian Americans' sense of community. Maggie Gee's forty-six-year-old mother, An Yoke Gee, worked at Kaiser Shipyards as a burner, cutting steel plate with a blowtorch. Maggie Gee characterized it as a "positive experience" for her mother: "She made non-Chinese friends for the first time, and it broadened her outlook on life. She was satisfied with being part of a Chinese community where she lived, but this allowed her to become part of a whole."[49] Dorothy Eng remembered seeing many women from Oakland's Chinatown going to and from work in the shipbuilding industry: "Matronly women who had never worked outside of their homes before got jobs as sweepers aboard ships. . . . I remember seeing them get off the bus, going home to Chinatown carrying their broom and having their hair tied."[50]

Asian American women recruited workers from their own families and communities. Such was the case with Manang Nene, a Filipino American friend of Evangeline Canonizado Buell's step-grandmother, Grandma Roberta. She encouraged Roberta to find work at the Richmond Shipyards. This was the first time in her life that Roberta joined the workforce. After experiencing so much overt racial discrimination, this meaningful work gave her a "renewed energy and outlook on life in America."[51] Buell elaborated:

Grandma loved going to work in the shipyard. Not only did it give her something to do outside the home, she also felt gratified to be able to contribute to household expenses. Once I heard her say to Uncle, "Now we can afford to buy a new stove and a new phonograph." She also felt proud that she was contributing toward the war effort, further boosting her self-confidence.[52]

In the context of US wartime alliances with China, the Philippines, and India, and Asian American participation in the war effort, the public's perception of specific Asian American groups dramatically shifted. The characterization of Chinese Americans as a yellow peril personified by popular villains Fu Manchu and Ming the Merciless shifted to that of "good Asians" in a "good war." Filipinos, once represented as uncivilized savages, had become brothers in arms. During the Bataan Death March in April 1942, some seventy thousand Filipino and American POWs marched to their incarceration after their surrender to Japanese forces in the Philippines, and thousands died en route.

These changes contributed to the passage of landmark legislation. Chinese Exclusion Acts were repealed and US naturalization rights to Chinese granted. The passage of the Luce-Celler Act in 1946 allowed Filipinos and Asian Indians to become US citizens. The War Brides Act of 1945 and the Alien Fiancées and Fiancés Act of 1946 facilitated thousands of Chinese and Filipino women to enter the United States as new brides. Their migration resulted in the growth of Asian American families and more balanced gender ratios.

Yet, anti-Asian violence and racism persisted. Korean American Mary Paik Lee recalled that even after Japanese Americans were interned, other Asian Americans feared going outside. Some endured beatings even in broad daylight. Acts of vandalism destroyed their cars and other belongings. Segregation continued for Filipinos in Stockton's movie theaters.[53] When their employment in war-related industries ended, Filipinos returning to the San Joaquin Delta found that the only jobs available to them continued to be in the fields and domestic work.

While enlistment demonstrated Asian American loyalty to the United States, Chinese and Filipino soldiers encountered great suspicion. When a group of Chinese American soldiers entered the town of Fayetteville, Arkansas, they were immediately surrounded by police, questioned, and detained until a white officer verified their documentation.[54] Soldiers from the Second Filipino Infantry Regiment were refused service at a restaurant in Marysville located near their training camp in Northern California.[55]

Filipinos in the United States who had joined the US military were eligible for GI Bill benefits, but like other veterans of color, they were barred by restrictive housing covenants from purchasing homes in white neighborhoods. As scholar Dawn Bohulano Mabalon points out, receiving the "worst postwar benefit package" were the more than 250,000 Filipino veterans who had joined the USAFFE in the Philippines, including her father, Ernesto Mabalon. The Rescission Act of 1946 declared that their service "shall not be deemed to be or to have been service in the military or national forces of the United States or any component thereof for the purposes of any law of the United States conferring rights, privileges or benefits," even though President Roosevelt had promised them full equity with other veterans. Mabalon's father considered the Rescission Act a deep insult, and my Lolo characterized it as a "cruel law."[56]

HISTORIES THAT WILL LIVE

In 1981, the Commission on Wartime Relocation and Internment of Civilians held eleven hearings across the country. More than 750 witnesses gave testimonies. Among them was Mary Kurihara, who delivered her husband's, Albert Kurihara's, testimony on his behalf because he had recently suffered a stroke. In it, he condemned the treatment of Japanese Americans:

> Sometimes I want to tell this government to go to hell. This government can never repay all the people who suffered. But, this should not be an excuse for token apologies, I hope this country will never forget what happened . . . and do what it can to make sure that future generations will never forget.[57]

The commission concluded that internment was a grave injustice and that Executive Order 9066 resulted from race prejudice, war hysteria, and a failure of political leadership. In August 1988, President Reagan signed the Civil Liberties Act, apologizing to the Japanese American internees and offering $20,000 to survivors of the camps. In 1998, Fred Korematsu received the Presidential Medal of Freedom from President Bill Clinton. Gordon Hirabayashi and Minoru Yasui received this honor posthumously in 2012 and 2015.

Nevertheless, these histories have been and continue to be vulnerable to erasure. The photography of Depression-era migrant farmworkers and sharecroppers by Dorothea Lange, one of the great documentary photographers, is well known, but her photographs of the Japanese internment during World War II are not. Although the federal government commissioned these photographs, almost all, approximately 97 percent, were never published. Instead they were suppressed during World War II, with a US Army major writing "Impounded" across some of the prints. At the end of the war, the army kept the internment photographs in the National Archives, out of public view. How can you see, study, and reflect upon histories that you didn't know were there?

In 2006, Lange's photographs were finally published in the book *Impounded: Dorothea Lange and the Censored Images of Japanese American Internment*, edited by historians Linda Gordon and Gary Y. Okihiro. Many of these photographs were in print for the first time. Gordon writes that these photographs "unequivocally denounce an unjustified, unnecessary, racist policy," in addition to showcasing Lange's skillful use of photography to express "human feelings and relationships."[58] What might have, and probably could have, shared the humanity of Japanese Americans, was kept out of view.

Numerous testimonies, creative nonfiction works, and scholarly resources exist so that we may remember and learn from internees' experiences. These include Miné Okubo's 1946 graphic memoir *Citizen 13660*, Jeanne Wakatsuki Houston's 1973 memoir *Farewell to Manzanar: A True Story of Japanese American Experience During and After the World War II Internment*, Yoshiko Uchida's 1982 autobiographical account *Desert Exile: The Uprooting of a Japanese American Family*, and George Takei's 2019 graphic memoir *They Called Us Enemy.*[59] In her introduction to the second edition of *Desert Exile*, scholar Traise Yamamoto emphasizes that Uchida wanted to use her writing to educate people, especially young people, and that she frequently gave talks to primary and secondary school groups.[60]

These efforts challenge contemporary attempts to rewrite the historical narrative. In 1990, Assemblyman Gil Ferguson from Orange County, California, introduced a controversial and ultimately unsuccessful resolution that said "it is simply untrue that Japanese-Americans were interned in concentration camps during World War II."[61] He had previously opposed a resolution asking California schools to teach that the Japanese internment resulted from racism, wartime hysteria, and political failure, and not for military reasons.

In 2016, Carl Higbie, a prominent supporter of President Donald Trump, cited the World War II incarceration of Japanese Americans as a precedent for an immigrant registry, using it as a justification for Trump's proposal of a ban on Muslim immigrants to the United States. Since the terrorist attacks on September 11, 2001, hate crimes and incidents against South Asian, Sikh, Muslim, and Arab Americans have spiked. Although these groups have unique identities and a long-standing presence in the United States, similar to Japanese Americans during World War II, their communities have experienced the dangerous impacts of being stereotyped as the enemy. Surviving Japanese American internees remain vigilant in the face of attempts to use their histories to justify further racial and religious profiling. And so should we.

The connection between these histories and the surge in anti-Asian hate and violence during the COVID-19 pandemic is striking to John Tateishi, a former internee at Manzanar camp and the author of a 2020 book about the Japanese American redress movement. He notes a "feeling of déjà vu": "People who attack Asians in the United States always target women, elders, or children, going after the most vulnerable most often, built out of so much ignorance."[62]

.   .   .

There are two days that I remember in relation to these histories. The first was in October 2017, the day my Lolo joined the over 250,000 Filipino veterans of World War II who have received the Congressional Gold Medal of Honor, the highest civilian honor bestowed by the US Congress. I was able to attend the ceremony held in the US Capitol Visitor Center together with my mother, Patria Ceniza, and aunt Lucita Ceniza. I brought with me a copy of my Lolo's photo in his military uniform. He passed away in 2009.[63]

Sadly, multiple attempts to pass Filipino veterans equity bills in Congress in the 1990s and early 2000s were unsuccessful. These bills would have revised the Rescission Act to recognize Filipino veterans' World War II service for the purposes of military benefits.[64] However, a 1990 immigration law enabled Filipino veterans to naturalize and become US citizens. A 2003 act provided VA (Veterans Administration) healthcare. And a 2009 stimulus package gave a lump sum benefit of $15,000 to Filipino veterans who were US citizens, and $9,000 to non-citizens. These gestures of recognition have been controversial. Some Filipino veterans have been mired in bureaucratic red tape in their applications for the lump sum benefit, already a puny amount in contrast to what had been promised.

When the news broke about the Congressional Gold Medal of Honor, some observers remarked that the "honor" had come too late. Only sixteen thousand to seventeen thousand Filipino veterans were alive by the time of the ceremony. I understood this criticism all too well. The Rescission Act and its legacies broke my Lolo's as well as my own heart. My Lolo would have had to have lived until 105 in order to attend this celebratory event. Why did it have to take this long?

Nevertheless, our attendance at the ceremony was hardly in vain. I witnessed the beautiful diversity and strength of the Filipino veteran community, a community primarily composed of Filipinos but also our non-Filipino allies. I observed the tireless advocacy of Major General Antonio Taguba (retired) and other leaders of the Filipino Veterans Recognition and Education Project. I was overjoyed to see my mother receive a bronze replica of the Congressional Gold Medal of Honor on behalf of her father. And we congratulated the living Filipino veterans and their family members.

On that day I learned that it is never too late to honor the sacrifices and achievements of those who have come before us. It is never too late to remember those who have made history. And it is never too late to pick up the broken pieces of ourselves and to do what we can to right a wrong.

A second memory is more recent. In 2021, my husband Greg, our son Louis, and I visited the site of what was once the Tanforan Assembly Center. In the 1970s, the site transformed again into a shopping mall. Just outside the mall's entrance is the Tanforan Assembly Center Commemorative Garden, which was dedicated in 2007 and funded by many former internees of Tanforan and their descendants.

A plaque explains that the garden memorializes a time when this site served as a temporary assembly center for 7,800 persons of Japanese ancestry who were forcibly removed and confined in the absence of criminal charges and due process of law. It reads: "May we honor this period of history by our remembrance and just action."

Thus, Asian American histories of World War II intertwine with our present moment, and the days that we remember will live on.

SEVEN

1919: DECLARATION OF INDEPENDENCE

In April 1919, a Korean Congress, composed of delegates from the United States, Korea, and other parts of the world, gathered in Philadelphia, the "Cradle of Liberty." They wanted Americans to know that on March 1st, Korean protestors in Seoul had declared their independence from Japan. That demonstration involved more than one million protestors shouting "Mansei!" (Long live Korea!) and sparked the March First Movement that spread throughout their country. Japan responded with a violent crackdown. Through news dispatches and private telegrams, delegates learned that tens of thousands of Korean revolutionists were arrested, and that thousands, including women and children, were killed or wounded. The Korean Congress in Philadelphia appealed to the American people for their support and sympathy: "We know you love justice; you also fought for liberty and democracy, and you stand for Christianity and humanity."[1]

In June 1919, the Honorable Manuel Quezon, president of the Philippine Senate and chairman of the Philippine Commission, extended "good will, respect, and gratitude" from the Filipino people before a congressional hearing on Philippine independence. Then he stated forcefully and clearly: "The Filipino people feel that the time has come when steps should be taken immediately by the Government of the United States for the recognition of the sovereignty of the Filipino people over their own country."[2] By 1919, the United States had colonized the Philippines for two decades. Although Filipinos had declared the independence of the

Philippines on June 12, 1898, after years of fighting against Spanish rule, the United States did not recognize the new republic. American colonizers replaced Spanish ones.

In April 1919, General Reginald Dyer led a group of British soldiers to Jallianwala Bagh, a public garden, in the Sikh holy city of Amritsar, in India. Several thousand civilians had gathered to celebrate the Sikh New Year. General Dyer ordered his troops to fire without warning. Women and children were among the 379 dead and more than a thousand injured.[3] Mohan Singh was present and saved himself by lying flat on the ground. The massacre deepened Singh's resentment toward British rule and motivated him to pursue his college education in the United States in the 1920s.[4] Indian students began coming to the United States in the late nineteenth century to further their education. Among a group holding wide-ranging political views, one contingent stood out for its fervent nationalism and organizing efforts to end British rule.

Imperialism and anti-imperialism shaped the early twentieth-century experiences of Korean, Filipino, and Asian Indians in the United States. However, like so much of Asian American history, these histories are not well known. It is not solely because more research and writing about them are necessary. It is also because these histories are erased and forgotten in multiple ways. Relevant historic places have been redeveloped for commercial use and subsequently bear no trace of what was once there. Plaques and monuments that pay tribute to US victories in war gloss over suffering and attempts at self-determination. The commemorations of related historical milestones are overshadowed by contemporary violence.

This chapter juxtaposes the presence and absence of these histories, and highlights community-driven ways of preserving them.

DREAMS OF INDEPENDENCE

The news of Japan's colonization of Korea in 1910 devastated Koreans who were living and working in Hawai'i and the US mainland. One man recalled that they had left their home country to make money in America, "the land of prosperity," but they had hoped to return. Now there was no going back:

The news of the fall of our country tore our hearts apart! Just thinking about it now gives me warm tears in my eyes. How we cried in our plantation fields and mining stations. And how we could not help running around like we had lost our minds.[5]

Before 1910, Japan had encroached on Korean sovereignty through a series of unequal treaties. The 1876 Treaty of Kanghwa gave Japan special trading privileges in Korea that were not reciprocated for Koreans in Japan. Japan forced Korea to sign a treaty that gave Japan the right to use Korea for military purposes in the Russo-Japanese War (1904–5) despite Korea's declaration of neutrality.[6] After Japan's victory in the war, it established a protectorate over Korea in 1905.

Koreans in Hawai'i and the US mainland responded to the growing threat on Korea's autonomy by organizing. In Hawai'i, Koreans created the Kongniphoe (Mutual Aid Society) and the Changanhoe (Self-Strengthening Society) in 1905, and the Noso Tongmaenghoe (Young and Old Alliance) in 1907. On the US mainland, they formed the Gongnip Hyeophoe (Cooperative Association) in Riverside, California, in 1905, and the Kongjehoe (Mutual Salvation Society) in New York, the Tongmaeng Sinhunghoe (Newly Rising Alliance) in Seattle, and Taedong Pokukhoe (All-Together Protecting the Nation Society) in San Francisco in 1907.[7] Scholar Lili Kim has found that no fewer than twenty-four political organizations existed by 1907.

The early twentieth-century presence of Koreans in Hawai'i emerged from the interplay of sugar plantations' recruitment of their labor, their own dreams of socioeconomic mobility, and their practice of Christianity as well as Japanese subjugation. Although a small group of approximately fifty Koreans had entered the United States as diplomats, merchants, and students between 1880 and 1902, larger migrations began in 1903. Approximately 7,400 Koreans migrated to Hawai'i between 1903 and 1905.[8] They endured ten-hour days of backbreaking labor on sugar plantations, earning less than a dollar a day.

An estimated one thousand Koreans from Hawai'i moved to the US mainland between 1905 and 1907. Migration offered work opportunities in small shops, construction, and mining as well as agricultural work.

Between 1906 to 1924, six hundred political refugees and a thousand "picture brides," who had arranged marriages with earlier Korean migrants through photos and correspondence, entered the United States.[9] Although relatively small in number, Koreans on the mainland encountered the anti-Asian violence experienced by other Asian groups, including Japanese.

In June 1913, eleven Koreans from Riverside arrived in the small rural town of Hemet, California. Two ranchers had hired them to pick apricots in their orchard after they were unable to find enough workers locally. When the Koreans arrived in Hemet by train, an angry mob of over a hundred white men surrounded them, threatened them with physical violence, and ordered them to leave the town. They assumed the laborers were Japanese. When the ranchers later explained that the workers were Korean, it did not make a difference to the mob, who claimed that Hemet was "a white man's valley."[10]

The 1913 incident in Hemet was part of a well-established pattern of the racial lumping together of "Asiatics," but Koreans organized to resist this homogenization. They rejected a Japanese vice consul's and the Japanese Association of Southern California's attempts to intervene on their behalf and insisted on relying on their own Korean-led organizations and spokespeople to communicate with the US government. This nuance supports scholar Richard Kim's argument that, while their economic independence was important, "Korea's loss of national sovereignty to Japan between 1905 and 1910 would become the single most important issue for Korean immigrants."[11]

The numerous political organizations that emerged in the wake of Korea becoming a protectorate reflected the overseas Korean community's fragmentation as well as nationalism. Their efforts to unify resulted in the formation of an umbrella organization called Hanin Hapsonghoe (United Korean Society), headquartered in Honolulu, and the establishment of the Korean National Association in San Francisco to provide social services as well as advocate for Korean independence. Nationalist leaders espoused distinct styles of leadership, and rivalries among them ensued. Pak Yong-man was a proponent of military training and established a small military training camp in Nebraska and a military school in Hawai'i.

Syngman Rhee, who received a doctorate from Princeton University in 1910, emphasized education and diplomacy. Rhee became president of the Korean Provisional Government in exile from 1919 to 1939. Ahn Chang Ho's philosophy stressed the cultivation of inner strength, communal consciousness, and ethical leadership. He served as president of the Korean National Association and founded the HeungSaDan (Young Korean Academy) in San Francisco in 1913 to develop Korean leaders.

Women dedicated themselves to the nationalist cause. Scholar Lili Kim's research spotlights the leadership of Maria Hwang in the Korean Women's Relief Society, which was founded in Hawai'i in 1919. Hwang immigrated to Hawai'i with her children, leaving her husband, who had a concubine, behind in Korea. She allegedly told her husband: "I can no longer live under these circumstances with you. I am taking our children to America and will shame you in the future. These children shall become educated and I shall become a wonderful person. You can remain as you are."[12] Society members fundraised for the nationalist cause by selling homemade Korean food and copies of the 1919 Declaration of Korean Independence. They sent money to families who had members who had been killed or injured in the March First Movement. They also contributed funds to the Korean Provisional Government in exile, the Korean Commission in Washington, DC, and the Korean Independence Army in China. Similar organizations formed on the US mainland. The Korean Women's Patriotic Society of California boycotted Japanese products and sold homemade soy sauce and bean paste.[13]

Lee Hee Kyung arrived in Honolulu as a picture bride in 1912, recognizing her husband through the photo she held in her hand. When she stepped into her new home, she realized that the new life she had imagined, including her dream of attending college, was not to be. However, she found community with other Korean immigrant women helping the poor and the sick through the Youngnam Puin Hoe, an extension of the Methodist Society. Before leaving Korea, Lee had encountered Methodist missionaries in her hometown of Taegu and was inspired by their ancestors' stories of fleeing from religious and political oppression in their home countries and coming to the United States. In the 1910s, Youngnam Puin Hoe members, like so many other Koreans in Hawai'i, became more involved in the Korean nationalist cause. They raised enough funds so that Lee could return to Korea and participate in the March 1 demonstration in Seoul. In a memoir about her parents, author Margaret K. Pai writes:

> How quickly and brutally the Japanese suppressed the revolutionists! During the parade in Seoul a young woman's hand, proudly waving the Korean flag, was cut off by a Japanese sword. But before the flag touched the ground, she caught it with her other hand. More than 2,500 Koreans were thrown in prison in Seoul alone that day. Among the women activists incarcerated was my mother, Lee Hee Kyung.[14]

Religion, most notably Christianity, was a distinctive feature of the Korean independence movement in the United States as well as Korea. Christianity became a major religion in Korea in the nineteenth century as a result of American missionary efforts there as well as Koreans' embrace of the religion and the educational mobility it offered to women and lower classes.[15] Mission schools were sites where people could exchange ideas and views. This social and political element would continue in the United States. Scholars Edward T. Chang and Woo Sung Han observe: "Korean immigrant churches not only provided spiritual salvation, but more importantly a place to discuss and strategize the independence of Korea."[16]

When the Korean Congress drafted "An Appeal to America" in Philadelphia in April 1919, they framed their appeal on behalf of their religious brethren who desired freedom:

> On March 1st of this year some three million men, mostly of the educated class composed of Christians, Heaven Worshipers, Confucians, Buddhists, students of mission schools, under the leadership of the pastors of native Christian churches, declared their independence from Japan and formed a provisional government on the border of Manchuria.[17]

They linked American values with their own moral cause: "Our aim is freedom from militaristic autocracy; our object is democracy for Asia; our hope is universal Christianity."[18]

The US Congress responded cautiously to the Korean declaration of independence. In October 1919, Senate and House resolutions expressed sympathy with the Korean people's aspirations. However, as scholar Richard Kim observes, they were primarily symbolic gestures that "fell far short of official recognition of the newly formed Korean government."[19] What many Koreans, Americans, and even Japanese did not know was that in the secret 1905 Taft-Katsura Agreement, the United States had agreed not to interfere with Japan's interests in Korea in exchange for Japan's recognition of US control of the Philippines.[20]

After the US victory in the 1898 Spanish-American War, the United States and Spain negotiated the Treaty of Paris, in which Spain ceded the Philippines, Guam, and Puerto Rico to the United States for twenty million dollars. Although the United States entered the Spanish-American War in support of Cuban independence from Spanish rule, the war took place in the Philippines as well as Cuba. It presented the United States an opportunity to build an overseas empire in the Pacific. Economic and military objectives—such as access to overseas markets, especially the China market, to sell American manufactured goods, and the strategic use of overseas colonies as refueling stations for the US Navy as well as sources for raw materials—intertwined with moral and racial justifications. The popular nineteenth-century ideology of Manifest Destiny, which emphasized the divine right of white Americans to expand westward, justified the violence of the Mexican-American War (1846–48), the Wounded Knee Massacre (1890), and the overthrow of the Hawai'ian monarchy (1893).

On December 21, 1898, President William McKinley issued the "Proclamation of Benevolent Assimilation," emphasizing that the United States came to the Philippines as friends and not as conquerors. In an 1899 speech, McKinley claimed that "there was nothing to do but to take them all, and to educate the Filipinos, and uplift and civilize and Christianize them, and by God's grace do the very best we could by them, as our fellow-men for whom Christ also died."[21] British poet Rudyard Kipling's 1899 poem "The White Man's Burden" infamously encouraged

Americans to colonize the Philippines and "your new-caught, sullen peoples, half-devil and half-child."[22] Like other Western nations, the United States became a world power by joining the race for empire.

US colonization of the Philippines belied Filipino dreams of independence from over three centuries of Spanish rule. Their dreams were born out of Spanish corruption and the abuses of the Spanish friars who ruled the colony. A nationalist consciousness also emerged from Filipino reformist demands for fair representation in the Cortes Españolas (Spanish Courts), and the literature written by Filipino educated elites, such as Jose Rizal, who imagined the archipelago as one nation. The Philippine Revolution against Spain began in 1896.

Initially confident of US support of the Filipino cause, nationalist leader Emilio Aguinaldo declared the independence of the Philippines on June 12, 1898, in Kawit, in the province of Cavite. In September 1898, a constitutional convention met in Malolos, the capital of the new republic. The Philippine Republic was officially inaugurated on January 23, 1899, with Emilio Aguinaldo as its new president. However, the United States did not recognize the new republic.

In February 1899, when Private William Grayson shot at a group of Filipino soldiers in Manila, it ignited the Philippine-American War. The war was brutal. Clashes between Americans and Filipinos on the island of Samar in the central region of the Philippines led to a Filipino guerrilla attack that killed forty-eight American soldiers. Brigadier General Jacob Smith ordered American soldiers to take no prisoners and to kill and burn, stating: "The interior of Samar must be made a howling wilderness."[23] US interrogation tactics included the "water cure," which is now known as waterboarding. The policy of concentrating civilians in camps led to malnutrition, overcrowding, and tainted water supplies. An estimated 4,200 American and over 20,000 Filipino combatants died, and several hundred thousand Filipino civilians died from famine and disease as well as violence.[24] A cruel irony is that the United States justified its possession of the Philippines through claims of bringing public health to the archipelago. Yet, the war resulted in a cholera epidemic that claimed 150,000 to 200,000 lives. The official years of the Philippine-American War are 1899–1902, but armed conflict continued between American forces and the Moro people in the southern Philippines in the early 1900s until the Battle of Bud Bagsak in 1913.[25]

In the United States, the subject of colonizing the Philippines was highly controversial. The Anti-Imperialist League formed in 1898 to oppose US annexation of the Philippines for moral, racial, legal, and economic reasons. Prominent anti-imperialists included writer Mark Twain, scholar W. E. B. Du Bois, activist Jane Addams, industrialist Andrew Carnegie, Senator George Frisbie Hoar, and writer and Presbyterian minister Henry Van Dyke. In 1905, Twain penned "The War Prayer" to protest US military intervention in the Philippines. The antiwar text (which some have called a short story or prose poem) criticizes the blind patriotism and religious fervor that accompanies war. It features a minister who leads the people in a passionate prayer to protect their noble young soldiers in battle, but then an aged stranger interrupts him and begins articulating the part that is prayed for "silently" and "unthinkingly."[26] That part consists of pleas for the violent deaths of their opponents, the destruction of their homes, the grief of their widows and children, and other devastating, often unacknowledged, impacts of war. However, Americans were unable to read "The War Prayer" until well after the Philippine-American War had ended. *Harper's Bazaar* rejected it for publication, and "The War Prayer" was not published until 1923, thirteen years after Twain's death.

Pro-imperialists employed multiple strategies to counter anti-colonial criticism. One was to promote benevolent assimilation policies through educational opportunities. In addition to establishing a system of Americanized education in the Philippines at the elementary, secondary, and postsecondary levels, the US-established Philippine Commission created the *pensionado* program in 1903. The program sponsored promising Filipino students, many of them from elite families, to further their education in the United States. While most of the students, known as *pensionados*, were men, they included the feminist historian Encarnacion Alzona, the first Filipino woman to receive a doctoral degree, which she earned in history at Columbia University.[27] Upon their return, the *pensionados* assumed positions in the colonial government, education, and business, exemplifying the benefits of American tutelage.

Another strategy was to celebrate America's new possessions through popular cultural forms, such as world's fairs, that integrated education, commerce, and entertainment.[28] At the 1904 St. Louis World's Fair, over a thousand people—Tinguians, Bagobos, Bontoc Igorots, Suyoc Igorots, Negritos, Mangyans, Visayans, and Moros, among other groups—were displayed in a "living exhibition."[29] The exposition celebrated US expansion westward and overseas. It rationalized US imperialism through its representation of Philippine indigenous peoples at the bottom of a racial hierarchy.

One of the fair's most popular exhibits was the "Igorot Village" in the forty-seven-acre "Philippine Reservation." In 2004, on the centennial of the St. Louis World's Fair, Mia Abeya, whose Igorot grandfather was among those on display, reflected on the fair's colonial narrative: "They brought them to the fair to show to the world that here are people who need our help. They need us to develop them. Look at how they dress themselves, look at how they dance, just look at how they live."[30] In this narrative, one of the key examples of native savagery was the Igorot practice of dog eating. Abeya noted that they did so occasionally for ceremonial purposes. However, Igorots were fed the animals daily to give fairgoers the opportunity to witness this practice. "They made them butcher dogs, which is really abusing the culture of the Igorots," Abeya said.[31]

The passage of the Immigration Act of 1924 abolished virtually all Asian immigration to the United States, with one exception: Filipinos. As a result of US annexation, they became "US nationals," which meant they could immigrate to the United States but were ineligible to become US citizens. Filipino immigration significantly increased after 1924. Agricultural industries sought cheap labor, but Filipinos had dreams of their own. These dreams were not necessarily of their own choosing. What choice do you have when faced with famine, disease, and increasing land dispossession? Yet, stories about Abraham Lincoln and other prominent Americans with humble beginnings, which Filipinos had read in their American schoolbooks, infused their imaginations. They observed the socioeconomic mobility of the returning *pensionados* who had studied in the United States and realized that the trajectories of colonialism were multidirectional. The geography of their own hopes expanded toward the United States.

By the 1920s, when Mohan Singh decided to leave India and further his education in the United States, Indian students had been attending US colleges and universities for several decades. They studied engineering, medicine, agriculture, and manufacturing in institutions across the United States, from Columbia and Harvard in the Northeast to midwestern universities in Illinois, Iowa, and Nebraska. However, most of them attended institutions on the West Coast, such as the University of Washington, Oregon Agricultural College, Stanford University, and the University of California, Berkeley.[32]

Although the students held a wide range of political views, some became fervent advocates of Indian independence from British rule. Revolutionary intellectual and student leaders included Har Dayal and Taraknath Das. Har Dayal worked as a lecturer of Indian philosophy at Stanford University and lived in one of the Indian student hostels in Berkeley. During a meeting with Indian students, he called on them to engage in ending British rule: "Anybody can be a Collector, or an Engineer, or a Barrister, or a Doctor. What Indian [sic] needs today is warriors of freedom."[33] Taraknath Das became involved in revolutionary activity while in college in Calcutta. He evaded police by fleeing to Japan, and subsequently studied in the United States and worked in Canada. Das completed BA and MA degrees at the University of Washington in Seattle. He helped found the Hindusthan Association of America to support Indian students, as well as its journal, the *Hindusthanee Student*, which documented their activities and gave advice regarding education and employment opportunities.[34]

Students' experiences of racial discrimination on the West Coast intensified their interest in Indian independence. Although some students came from middle-class families, their socioeconomic privilege did not protect them from racial discrimination. Restaurants refused to serve them. College student clubs denied them membership. Historian Joan Jensen notes that hotels and boardinghouses, including the YMCA, refused to take them in, and recounts the story of one student who spent a cold winter night in a Southern Pacific depot in Northern California after being turned away from a dozen hotels.[35]

Between 1912 and 1913, a coalition of Bengali and Punjabi intellectuals and students and Punjabi agricultural workers formed the Ghadar Party. They overcame linguistic, religious, and regional differences as they aimed to overthrow the British Empire through armed revolution. Scholar Seema Sohi writes that their shared experiences—from being pushed out of India because of colonialism to enduring humiliation as degraded colonial subjects around the world to encountering anti-Asian racism and discrimination in Canada as well as the United States—created an "anti-colonial consciousness" that was "inseparable from attaining racial equality abroad."[36]

On November 1, 1913, the Ghadar Party launched its first newspaper, *Ghadar*, declaring that "today there begins in foreign lands, but in our country's language, a war against the English Raj."[37] They printed several thousand issues in Urdu and Gurmukhi in their headquarters, the Yugantar Ashram (Advent of a New Age Ashram), on Hill Street in San Francisco. Members memorized over a thousand subscribers' names to avoid creating a paper trail that could be used by the British government against them. Indians who engaged in anti-colonial activity overseas were targets of British and North American political surveillance.[38]

While Dayal authored many of the initial articles, Kartar Singh Sarabha ran the printing operation. Sarabha arrived in San Francisco in 1912 intent on freeing India from British rule. After a relatively short detention of three days, he passed the inspection at the Angel Island Immigration Station, thanks to his English-language proficiency, some financial resources, and plans to study electrical engineering at the University of California, Berkeley. However, when whites called him a "damn Hindu," it shocked and humiliated him. Like many other Indian students during that time, Sarabha found that these experiences deepened his commitment to Indian independence, which he expressed through impassioned lectures and poetry. Sarabha helped build the Ghadar Party's coalition by traveling among Indian migrant laborers and farmers in rural areas to fundraise for the nationalist cause.[39]

Farmers Jawala Singh and Wasakha Singh were among those who donated generously to the Ghadar Party. In 1912, they founded the Stockton Gurdwara, the first Sikh temple in the United States. The Stockton Gurdwara became a hub for the spiritual, social, and political life of South Asian migrants. South Asians from across the West Coast visited the gurdwara to see one another a few times a year for special holidays and festivals. It also served as a center for the Ghadar Party's activities. Jawala Singh served as the first Granthi, or ceremonial reader, of the Guru Granth Sahib, or Holy Book. Also known as the "Potato King," because of his success in farming this crop, Jawala Singh used his financial resources to sponsor scholarships for students in India to attend the University of California, providing them with room and board in a house he purchased in Berkeley. In 1913, he became a vice president of the Ghadar Party and recruited Punjabi farmworkers in California to return to India to fight against the British government.

Between 1914 and 1918, the Ghadar Party mobilized nearly eight thousand Indians from North America and other parts of the world to return to India in order to join the struggle for independence. While they had some success with recruiting Indians in the diaspora to their cause, they were unable to build a broader coalition with their compatriots in India. Furthermore, British intelligence thwarted their revolutionary plans, arresting hundreds of independence fighters even before they arrived in India.[40] Kartar Singh Sarabha made it back to the Punjab to participate in an armed uprising on February 21, 1915. But government authorities arrested him and sentenced him to death. Before his hanging on November 16, 1915, he wrote one last poem, titled "On the Way to the Gallows." In it, he reaffirmed his devotion to India even if it meant sacrificing his own life. For even in death, he proclaimed, "I will attain / A life of eternity."[41]

British repression of Ghadarites subdued the party's activities. However, one of its legacies, the Stockton Gurdwara, continued to flourish as a social and political hub for South Asian Americans of different faiths, political views, and generations. While it was the first Sikh house of worship established in the United States, it also served Muslims, Hindus, and the Catholic wives of South Asian immigrant pioneers. Before Dalip

Singh Saund became the first Asian, Sikh, and Indian American elected to serve in the US Congress in 1956, he served as a secretary of the Stockton Gurdwara.

The gurdwara also created a sense of community among the second generation. As scholar Karen Leonard writes, "To most members of the second generation, however, the Stockton temple was where one met 'other Hindu kids.' Asked about it, one woman responded, 'The Stockton temple, that's where we met the Khan kids every year, coming over from Phoenix to pick peaches.'"[42] Since many members of the second generation were Punjabi Mexican, the gurdwara was also a touchstone of memories of their Punjabi fathers—for example, how they sent money regularly to support the temple even when their families were in need. When a descendant recalled an event held there in connection with her father's passing, she described it as a reunion.[43] It was a reunion on multiple levels, the coming together of family members, of rarely seen friends, and of a historic community.

ERASING, FORGETTING, OVERSHADOWING

Asian American histories of imperialism and anti-imperialism are erased and forgotten in multiple ways. One way relates to the difference that historical perspective makes, specifically the power that comes from who gets to tell the story. If you read that the surrender of Japan in World War II led to the "liberation of Korea" in 1945; that the United States "granted Philippine independence" in 1946; and that the British passage of the 1947 Indian Independence Act "granted Indian independence" and "partitioned British India" into the dominions of India and Pakistan, consider this question: Who are the major actors in these stories? Imperial nations can continue to occupy center stage even in the histories of decolonization. These narratives can be found in memorials and plaques such as the one installed in the Minnesota State Capitol Rotunda in 1948, which commemorated the service of soldiers who "battled to free the oppressed peoples of the Philippine Islands, who suffered under the despotic rule of Spain."[44]

The erasing and forgetting of these histories are also a consequence of the inaccessibility of historical evidence. Who gets to write history, and which primary source materials are collected, preserved, and made accessible, are often intertwined. Hence, activists and scholars Abe Ignacio, Enrique de la Cruz, Jorge Emmanuel, and Helen Toribio introduce their book on the Philippine-American War, aptly titled *The Forbidden Book*, with the following:

> To the victor goes the privilege of writing history, the glorification of its conquests, and the silencing of the conquered. The history of the Philippine-American War is amassed in volumes of newspaper accounts, military reports, government documents, autobiographies, biographies, and letters by American soldiers. All, however, are part of The Forbidden Book buried in antique collections, libraries, archives, vaults, and private drawers.[45]

Historic places help remind us of the past. However, sometimes they are redeveloped, leaving no trace of what transpired there. Such was the case with Pachappa Camp in Riverside, California. The site of an early Koreatown founded by Ahn Chang Ho in 1904, Pachappa Camp (also known as Dosan's Republic) was home to a Korean immigrant community of families, women, and children. Many of them worked in the local citrus groves and participated in various independence-related activities that took place in Riverside, such as the 1911 Korean National Association of North America convention.

Residents also established a Korean mission and a *hakyo*, or Korean school. While the children also attended American schools, they encountered verbal and physical harassment there as other children sang, "Ching Chong Chinaman, sitting on a wall, along came a white man, and chopped his head off," and then touched their necks to mime chopping their heads off or tackled them.[46] They learned to hide their kimchee and rice lunch boxes from non-Korean classmates to avoid further embarrassment. By contrast, Pachappa Camp's *hakyo* provided a space to learn about their Korean heritage with pride. Ahn Chang Ho often instructed the children: "Be ready, prepare yourself for the coming independence fight for our country!"[47]

The Great Freeze of 1913 devastated Riverside's citrus industry and led to an exodus of many Korean residents to Central and Northern California cities. According to city directories from the mid-1920s, sites formerly occupied by Koreans were now vacant or inhabited by people of Japanese and Mexican descent. By the 1940s, the Korean immigrant pioneers had all but disappeared. Then, in the 1950s, crews bulldozed the area for commercial redevelopment. Oil and gas companies moved in, and their cinderblock buildings and parking lots dotted the landscape. Scholar Edward T. Chang observes:

> Due to development and the physical erasure of Pachappa Camp's built environment, Riverside lost sight of its historic Korean community. For years after the camp's demolition, an insurance map of Riverside, city directories, and a rare newspaper article remained the only written sources about Riverside's Koreatown in the English language, limiting the larger public's knowledge about the significance of the site.[48]

Sometimes historic places remain, but their commemorations are overshadowed by other events. In 2012, the year of the Stockton Gurdwara's centennial, writer Bhira Baukhaus reflected on the significance of the gurdwara's history in relation to devastating hate violence that took place in Wisconsin that same year. A gunman with ties to a white supremacist movement shot and killed six Sikh worshippers in a temple in Oak Creek. What did he see as he stepped through the door and started firing? Baukhaus writes that "presumably he saw the temple as a frightening symbol of otherness."[49] When she first encountered images of the shooting on television, she saw the faces of her own brothers and sisters, her aunties and uncles.

Unlike the Stockton Gurdwara, the construction of the Sikh Temple of Wisconsin was completed more recently, in 2007. However, like the Stockton Gurdwara, the temple serves as a social and cultural hub, housing in its brick building a library, a school for adults and children, and a childcare area. The site also provides Punjabi language instruction, a mentorship program, and accommodations for visiting *ragu jathas* (priests) from around the world. The Sikh Temple also collaborates with the group Rangla Punjab to organize folk dance and popular music events, featuring *gidha*, *bhangra*, and other cultural activities.[50]

Backhaus has a black-and-white photograph of the Stockton Gurdwara that was taken decades after its founding. The photo includes her mother, sister, brothers, cousins, and aunts as well as herself. Her family attended services there for ordinary and major celebrations, like those commemorating births of the gurus who established Sikhism beginning in the fifteenth century. She described the Sikh pioneers who crossed a vast ocean and had the vision to build the gurdwara as "brave."[51] At this concurrence of a centennial celebration of South Asian American resilience and a contemporary act of American racist violence, Baukhaus commented on how far Sikh communities in California had come in terms of younger generations pursuing their American ambitions while preserving their South Asian heritage. Yet, that progress is tempered by the question she herself continues to get from people: Why can't they assimilate more? While Baukhaus does not have a simple answer to that question, she proffers what is at stake when our histories are erased:

> But I do know this: to wipe away what has come before, who we have been over the centuries, also means to forget who our own mothers and fathers were. It means that how they conducted their lives—the families they raised, the homes they built—didn't matter. It denies us that basic human impulse, to remember their stories, the unique timbre of their voices. It would be as if they had never existed at all.[52]

DOCUMENTING, REMEMBERING, ILLUMINATING

Community leaders, researchers, and descendants have used multiple strategies to document, remember, and illuminate these forgotten histories. In 2017, on the fifth-year anniversary of the mass shooting at the Sikh Temple of Wisconsin, Sikh community leader Mandeep Kaur wrote that "for most Americans across our country, this act of terror has been largely forgotten. On the other hand, Sikh Americans will never forget where we were when we learned the news, and will always remember the lives irrevocably altered by this tragedy."[53]

Grief persists, but so too does renewal. Weeks after losing his mother, Harpreet Singh Saini became the first Sikh American to testify in front of the US Senate. His advocacy helped convince the Justice Department to begin tracking hate crimes against Sikhs and other religious minorities who were previously unrepresented in federal hate crime data.

Prabhjot Singh was only twelve years old when he hid in the basement during the shooting and later discovered his slain father. Five years later, he graduated from high school and was about to begin college. Previously, Singh thought that if his father were still alive and had wanted to return to live in India, he would have considered joining him. Encouragement from relatives emboldened Prabhjot to remain in the United States, as did community support. A few days after the shooting, Singh returned with his mother and sisters to the temple and encountered hundreds of people standing vigil with candles. He believed that they were sending his family this message: "We know what happened, and it should not have happened."[54]

Like Prabhjot Singh, Pardeep Kaleka lost his father on August 5, 2012, in the Oak Creek mass shooting, and was moved when so many people of diverse backgrounds came together to speak "this universal language of empathy."[55] The tragic loss gave him a new purpose in life: to keep people together and help them navigate different languages, customs, and cultures. In 2018, Kaleka and former white supremacist Arno Michaelis published their book *The Gift of Our Wounds*, a collaboration that explores the power of forgiveness. In 2019, Kaleka became the first non-white, non-Christian executive director of the Interfaith Conference of Greater Milwaukee. He believes that his Sikh faith illuminates a way forward:

> There is a saying in Sikhism, *Charhdi Kala* which means "we move in relentless optimism." Regardless of hardships in life I'm optimistic about the future. *Charhdi Kala* and compassion go hand in hand. Some people think of compassion as offering forgiveness and all is forgiven, but I think of it as a process, in other words I attach a purpose to what's

happening in life and appreciate the good things when they come. On August 5th, there was a purpose to what happened. Someone came to our temple trying to divide us, saying that we didn't belong and that we weren't wanted in his country. With *Charhdi Kala* the purpose of our response is to reach out, to include the other and say this will not happen again.[56]

In the mid-1990s, Minnesota's Filipino American community began a campaign to correct the historical inaccuracies of the Spanish-American War plaque in the State Capitol. In 2002, the Philippine Study Group together with other Filipino American organizations convinced the Minnesota legislature to install new text acknowledging that the Spanish-American War "was fought to defeat Spain, not to free Filipinos," and that, soon after Spain's surrender to the United States in 1898, Filipinos fought unsuccessfully for their independence against the United States in the Philippine-American War.[57]

The publication of Ignacio, de la Cruz, Emmanuel, and Toribio's *The Forbidden Book* presents another way to resist the cultural amnesia regarding the Philippine-American War and the inaccessibility of related primary source materials: curate and publicize your own collection. *The Forbidden Book* features Ignacio's compilation of over four hundred political cartoons related to the war along with Emmanuel's collection of editorial cartoons. Many of these cartoons are difficult to look at because they portray peoples from the Philippines, Hawai'i, Puerto Rico, Cuba, Samoa, China, Egypt, India, South Africa, and Sudan in buffoonish, savage, and childlike ways. For example, the 1899 political cartoon "The White Man's Burden (Apologies to Kipling)" depicts Uncle Sam and John Bull, the popular national personifications of the United States and England, carrying these peoples up a steep mountain of "barbarism," "ignorance," and "vice" in order to reach "civilization" at the apex.[58] However, confronting the these cartoons reveals an ugly truth: the Philippine-American War is not solely about the conflict between Filipinos and Americans but is also just as much about the dehumanizing impact of imperialist relations throughout the world.

Another 1899 political cartoon illuminates the connection between US continental expansion and Philippine annexation through a message sent by an "American Indian" to a "Filipino": "Be good, or you will be dead!"[59] The coauthors of *The Forbidden Book* note that some of the same US military personnel who subjugated indigenous peoples in the United States—such as Lieutenant Colonel Adna Chaffee, a veteran fighter in the US Indian wars against the Apache, Comanche, and Cheyenne—played leading roles in the Philippine-American War.[60] Furthermore, US conquest of American indigenous peoples through land dispossession and assimilation policies provided ideological justification and legal and institutional models to colonize the Philippines.

The perspectives of Philippine peoples are integral to histories of imperialism. Antonio S. Buangan is a descendant of the Suyoc people from northern Benguet province. In 1904, twenty-five of his Suyoc ancestors lived for several months in the "Igorotte Village" at the St. Louis World's Fair.[61] Buangan writes that, even a century later, "it was a novel idea for many that the Igorot who went to St. Louis even had descendants at all."[62] He decided to conduct his own research on the Suyoc, who had been dehumanized as "objects" of display, with the goal of lifting "those adventurous men, women, and children of my Suyoc great-grandparents' generation out of the anonymity and the obscurity into which they have fallen."[63] Buangan conducted archival research at the Missouri Historical Society (MHS) Museum and Library. Encountering large and detailed photographs of Tugmina (his Aunt Pacita's father's wife) and Oblika (his wife's father's first cousin) was emotionally moving:

> Seeing this large set of my relatives' and ancestors' photographs all spread out in that large room at the MHS was an unforgettable experience. For a moment, spirits of the Suyoc people all seemed to be speaking at once, impatiently scolding and asking me, "Where have you been all this time?" My first wish was to offer them some rice wine, for that was what my parents did at home when they summoned their ancestors or felt their presence. Had I known what I was going to find in St. Louis, I would have brought an appropriate libation.[64]

Buangan shared copies of these photographs with other descendants and, as a result of this communal exchange, learned the names of more Suyoc individuals who had gone to the fair: Buli-e and Bayongasan. Buli-e's daughters and Bayongasan's daughter-in-law were thrilled to see the images, remarking "Y a sanay si ama!" (Oh my, it is father!) The excitement of these findings spurred further research among descendants. Yolanda Lacpap Morita (granddaughter of Buli-e) of Tacoma, Washington, sent Buangan a 1904 newspaper article regarding the arrival of 235 Filipinos aboard the steamship USS *Shawmut* in Tacoma. They were on their way to the fair. Buangan then conducted research at the Tacoma Public Library and found the passenger manifest.

Buangan acknowledges that his research is just beginning, but there is one thing that he knows for sure: the Suyoc people were not a "primitive" group, even though their representation at the fair suggested otherwise. The Suyoc people were skilled in extracting and refining gold and copper. They frequently walked to the coast to trade. In the early 1900s, they met American soldiers who had come to their homeland's mountains to prospect for gold. Some Americans married Suyoc women, who were also known for their skills in mining. These interactions exposed the Suyoc people to the possibility of seeing faraway places, such as St. Louis. In 1904, as they boarded a US steamship on their way to the world's fair, they embarked on the adventure of crossing the expanse of the Pacific Ocean and of visiting lands that they had never traversed before. Among them were Tugmina, Oblika, Buli-e, and Bayongasan. Their individual names are important. "To be 'named' brings ancestors back to their community," explains Buangan.[65]

On March 23, 2017, the city of Riverside held a plaque ceremony to designate the location of Pachappa Camp as a "City Point of Cultural Interest." Scholar Edward T. Chang worked with the city's historic preservation officers, the mayor and city staff, and a coalition of community supporters—including Ahn Chang Ho's youngest son, Ralph Ahn; the Save Our Chinatown Committee; and the Dosan Ahn Chang Ho Memorial Foundation—to obtain the designation, a process that took almost two years. Signage in English and Korean documents that independence activist Ahn Chang Ho founded the Korean American settlement of Pachappa Camp in 1905.[66]

Ralph Ahn sustains the history and memories of this era through editing the newsletters and emceeing the annual gatherings of the Korean American Pioneer Descendants (KAPD) Society. At these gatherings, the descendants and newer generations honor family and community members who participated in the Korean independence struggle. I have had the privilege of attending several of these events because my husband's paternal grandparents, Choi Neung-ik and Kim Chung Shook (also known as Frances Moon Kim), were independence activists and immigrant pioneers. The KAPD newsletter's 2019 issue, commemorating the centennial of Korea's declaration of independence, highlighted Kim's participation in the March First Movement, and her work for the Korean Provisional Government in Shanghai before she immigrated to the United States.[67] During his childhood, my husband, Greg Choy, knew very little about his grandmother, whom he affectionately called Nanny, and her incredible life history as an independence activist. It was not until many years later as Greg earned his doctorate in English, specializing in US multicultural literature and Asian American studies and researching Korean American newspapers with scholar S. E. Solberg, that he started to learn about this history from his father and other relatives.

Some activists were able to return to Korea. Ahn Chang Ho traveled to many parts of the world to organize support for Korean independence and helped establish the Korean Provisional Government in Shanghai until the Japanese arrested him in 1932. After having been imprisoned and tortured, Ahn died in a Korean hospital in 1938. His wife, Helen Ahn, and their children (Philip, Philson, Susan, Soorah, and Ralph) were living in Los Angeles. Their home was a gathering place for the early Korean American community. Today the Ahn House is the site of the University of Southern California's Korean Studies Institute.

Many Korean immigrant pioneers were unable to return to their homeland in their lifetime, and were buried in the United States. However, the Korean government officially recognized some of them as patriots and re-interred their remains in Korean national cemeteries. One of these patriots, Choi Neung-ik, is my husband Greg's grandfather. Choi immigrated to the United States in 1916. He enrolled in the Willows Aviation School, a combat pilot-training unit for the Korean independence movement established in 1920 in Glenn County, California. Choi later served as a representative of the Korean National Revolutionary Corps.[68] He is now buried in Daejeon National Cemetery.

In 2010, thanks to the kindness of Phillip Choi—a former South Korean ambassador and Greg's cousin, once removed—our family was able to visit Choi Neung-ik's gravesite and see Greg's father's name, Howard Choy, which is carved into the gravestone. Howard's name, situated amid a list of key events in Choi's life, is the only part of the gravestone written in English; the rest is engraved in Hangul. As I observed "Uncle" Phillip and Greg reminiscing about Choi Neung-ik's life history while our children Maya and Louis talked with their cousin Jay, I remember feeling awash in gratitude. We were finally able to learn more about our family's history, their hopes and sacrifices that spanned multiple nations, cultures, and generations. We are still learning. The life histories of our ancestors have so much to teach us.

EIGHT

1875: HOMAGE

Xiaojie Tan's daughter Jami described her mom as "petite and fierce!"[1] Daoyou Feng had hoped to return to her hometown in Guangdong and open a business.[2] Delaina Ashley Yaun Gonzalez frequently sang along to gospel music while she worked.[3] Paul Andre Michels was a good-hearted, regular guy.[4] Soon Chung Park's favorite things included towering sunflowers, ceramic owls, and champagne.[5] Hyun Jung Grant was a former elementary school teacher who loved to dance.[6] Suncha Kim was proud to become a US citizen, and her naturalization ceremony was one of the happiest days of her life.[7] Yong Ae Yue denounced racism and called out Asian friends who expressed racism toward Black people.[8]

I write this chapter in their memory. On March 16, 2021, they were killed at three different spas in North Georgia. Six of them were Asian American women.

The board of directors of the Association for Asian American Studies, a professional research and teaching hub founded in 1979, expressed our collective grief and rage: "These murders follow a long history of racist, misogynist violence against Asian women, a history with which we are both professionally and personally familiar."[9]

Their statement resonated with me on a professional and personal level. Professionally, I had done research on the Chicago mass murder of eight female nurses—Gloria Davy, Suzanne Farris, Merlita Gargullo,

Mary Ann Jordan, Patricia Matusek, Valentina Pasion, Nina Schmale, and Pamela Wilkening—by Richard Speck in 1966. Two of his victims—Gargullo and Pasion—were Filipino nurses. The lone survivor, Corazon Amurao, was also a Filipino nurse and the prosecution's star witness. However, most Americans remember the name of the perpetrator, not the women who died nor the brave woman who testified against him.[10]

Personally, while growing up in New York City, I had learned from a young age to hold my keys in my fist during certain situations, such as walking alone or taking the subway at night, in case I needed to use them as a weapon. I cannot recall how I learned to do this, only that it had become second nature, an unspoken rule of our society's normalization of sexual violence.

After the Atlanta murders, Asian American studies scholars, including me, spoke to many journalists. It wasn't an easy thing to do in a time of mourning and anguish. However, having researched and written about sensationalized mass murders, I've learned that featuring the voices and analyses of Asian American women matters, and I hoped it would make a difference.

One of the questions I was asked repeatedly by journalists was what I thought about the perpetrator's claim that race had nothing to do with the mass shooting. The Cherokee County Sheriff's Office spokesman Captain Jay Baker had communicated to the press, "He claims it was not racially motivated. He apparently has an issue, what he considers a sex addiction, and sees these locations as something that allows him to go to these places. And it's a temptation for him that he wanted to eliminate."[11]

When asked this question, I often wondered:

Why should perpetrators of violence dictate the conversation?

Yet, I thought to myself that if his claims were part of the public discourse, then so too should the insights of Asian American women. I responded: "Killing Asian American women to eliminate a man's temptation speaks to the history of the objectification of Asian and Asian American women as variations of the Asian temptress, the dragon ladies and the lotus blossoms, whose value is only in relation to men's fantasies and desires."[12]

REPRESENTATIONS OF US

The history of the objectification of Asian American women is almost 150 years old. One key origin point is an 1875 immigration law known as the Page Act, which prohibited the transport of unfree laborers and women brought for "immoral purposes" to the United States. It created a system of enforcement that conflated Asian women's migration with prostitution. This system obligated the US consul-general or consul residing at ports of embarkation in "China, Japan, or any Oriental country" to "ascertain whether such immigrant has entered into a contract or agreement for a term of service . . . for lewd and immoral purposes."[13] Scholar Kerry Abrams points out that this system treated Asian women differently from European women, as "American consuls in foreign ports had an obligation to screen Chinese and Japanese women before they even left their home countries, and refuse to grant them an immigration certificate if they suspected them of prostitution, a hurdle not imposed on immigrants from other ports, such as those in Europe."[14]

Historian Mae Ngai explains, "The way the law was written, you had to certify that you weren't a prostitute."[15] She asks us to consider:

How do you prove a negative?

Although the Page Act applied to "any Oriental country," it was enforced primarily against Chinese women. As early as the 1850s, the California legislature had attempted to exclude Chinese immigrants by levying heavy fines on steamship companies for transporting unmarried Chinese women, who were assumed to be "lewd and debauched."[16] The enmity directed at Chinese women was heightened by the prevailing nineteenth-century discourses that linked Chinese female bodies with disease. In 1870, Senator Cornelius Cole made clear that continued Chinese female immigration posed a physical as well as moral danger: "When I look upon a certain class of Chinese who come to this land—I mean the females—who are the most undesirable of population, who spread disease and moral death among our white population, I ask myself the question, whether or not there is a limit to this class of immigrants?"[17]

Who represents you?

Before becoming a senator in 1867, Cornelius Cole had served as a representative from California from 1863 to 1865. The author of the Page

Act, Horace F. Page, had also served as a representative from California for five consecutive two-year terms from 1873 to 1883. He dedicated his political career to drafting and advocating for anti-Chinese legislation. Prior to the passage of the Page Act, he had sponsored four anti-Chinese bills and three House resolutions that failed to pass. A key obstacle in his legislative path was the Burlingame-Seward Treaty of 1868 between the United States and China. It promised the Chinese the right to free immigration and travel within the United States.[18] Page's emphasis on excluding immoral women and unfree laborers, supposedly for the purpose of protecting the Western states' moral integrity, enabled him to circumvent the treaty with his eponymous law.[19]

The Page Act had a significant impact in two overlapping ways. First, as the first federal statute restricting immigration, it set a precedent to exclude groups based on their race, national origin, gender, and class. Between 1875 and 1965, the restriction and exclusion of Asian immigrants were prominent features of immigration policy. The 1882 Chinese Exclusion Act barred Chinese laborers from entering the United States for ten years. It was renewed in 1892 for another ten years. In 1902, it was expanded to cover Hawai'i and the Philippines. In 1904, it was extended indefinitely.[20] The 1907 Gentlemen's Agreement between the United States and Japan restricted the immigration of Japanese laborers. The 1917 creation of the Asiatic Barred Zone denied entry from most Asian countries. The passage of the nation's first comprehensive restriction law, the 1924 Johnson-Reed Act, virtually abolished Asian immigration by excluding "aliens" who, because of race or nationality, were ineligible for citizenship. The major exception to the 1924 Immigration Act was Philippine immigration, because Filipinos, as a result of US annexation of the Philippines, had the status of US nationals. However, the passage of the Tydings-McDuffie Act in 1934 changed their status to alien and restricted their immigration to fifty persons per year.[21]

Second, by excluding persons based on filthy and immoral behavior, the Page Act also established a practice of barring persons who did not conform to social norms regarding health, ability, sex, and sexuality. The Immigration Act of 1917 excluded homosexuals as "persons of constitutional psychopathic inferiority," a rationale stemming from pseudoscientific ideas that diagnosed homosexuality as a form of mental illness. During the McCarthy Era, the removal of gays and lesbians from federal employment and the military contributed to the passage of the Immigration and Nationality Act of 1952, which barred homosexuals or immigrants suspected of being homosexuals from entering the United States. In 1965, immigration laws denied entry based on "sexual deviation." It wasn't until the Immigration Act of 1990 that homosexuality was removed as grounds of exclusion from the US. Still, major barriers remain in the twenty-first century.[22]

Despite the significance of Chinese women in US immigration history, they have been overlooked and marginalized as historical subjects. As Abrams observes, "There are many histories of the Chinese in America, but most of them treat male laborers as the standard and women as exceptional."[23] Thus, their objectification in immigration law and its enforcement is not as well known as the 1882 Chinese Exclusion Act. But it should be.

Popular entertainment contributed to the dissemination of these ideas. Throughout the twentieth century and into the twenty-first, Hollywood popularized the objectification of Asian and Asian American women to the masses, depicting them as exotic, sensual, submissive, and mysterious. On-screen, Asian and Asian American women were represented as one-dimensional types, at times scantily dressed, at other times docile and demure, and, more often than not, madly and deeply in love with the film's white male protagonist.[24] Among the most popular types were the dragon lady, the lotus blossom, the geisha girl, and the prostitute, which all became well known in films such as the *Thief of Bagdad* (1924), *Daughter of the Dragon* (1931), *Sayonara* (1957), *South Pacific* (1958), *The World of Suzie Wong* (1960), and *Full Metal Jacket* (1987).

Although these types were relegated to secondary roles or bit parts, they permeated popular culture beyond these specific films as other movies and television shows reproduced the same fantasies about Asian and Asian American women. For example, a segment of the ABC 20/20 special on the Atlanta murders showed how the few spoken lines of a

Vietnamese prostitute in *Full Metal Jacket*—"Me love you long time"—were repeated again in comedic movies like *The 40-Year-Old Virgin* (2005) and the long-running television show *South Park*.[25]

The objectification of Asian American women on-screen, in turn, limited their professional opportunities as actors in Hollywood. Born on January 3, 1905, in Los Angeles, Anna May Wong was the first Chinese American film star in Hollywood. After she was cast as an extra for *The Red Lantern* in 1919, she went on to appear in over sixty movies. Wong auditioned for lead roles, but she was consistently cast as a supporting character. In 1924, she created her own production company, Anna May Wong Productions, but it was short-lived. Anti-miscegenation laws that banned interracial marriages influenced the creation of a 1930 Motion Picture Production Code, which forbade the depiction of miscegenation. As a result, Wong was unable to land leading roles alongside white actors in romantic movies. Wong left Hollywood frustrated by these discriminatory barriers that circumscribed her career. Like other American artists of color in the early twentieth century, she moved to Europe, where she starred in many plays and films including her first talking film in 1930 called *The Flame of Love*. [26]

In a 1933 interview, Wong reflected: "I was so tired of the parts I had to play. Why is it that the screen Chinese is nearly always the villain of the piece, and so cruel a villain—murderous, treacherous, a snake in the grass. We are not like that."[27] She questioned why Chinese people and their culture could not be portrayed with dignity: We have our own virtues. . . . Why do they never show these on the screen?[28]

Although Paramount Studios contacted Wong and promised her leading roles, upon her return, she was still asked to play one-dimensional Asian roles created by white Hollywood directors. At times, Wong refused stereotypical roles and inauthentic direction, such as when one director asked her to use Japanese mannerisms to play a Chinese character. At other times, she agreed to play stereotypical roles in order to work with successful directors of the period, such as Josef von Sternberg. She appeared in the 1932 von Sternberg film *Shanghai Express*, playing a Chinese prostitute alongside her friend Marlene Dietrich.[29]

Who is playing whom?

Compounding this problem of objectification and marginalization on-screen was the centuries-old practice of "yellowface," in which white actors play Asian or Asian American characters. The phenomenon involved white actors taping their eyelids in order to make their eyes appear slanted and wearing buck teeth and heavy makeup. The results were often so exaggerated that their appearances were incredulous and buffoonish. Yet, some of the most prominent American actors performed in yellowface on-screen. These include Katharine Hepburn, who played a Chinese woman, Jade Tan, in the 1944 film *Dragon Seed*; Marlon Brando, portraying Sakini, an Okinawan interpreter, in the 1956 film *Teahouse of the August Moon*; and Mickey Rooney, as Mr. Yunioshi, in *Breakfast at Tiffany's* (1961).

According to scholar Josephine Lee, white actors in theater as well as in film portrayed Asian characters as "villainous despots, exotic curiosities, or comic fools."[30] Yellowface precluded Asian American actors from employment, further hampering the recognition of their talent on stage as well as on-screen. A related practice is "whitewashing," the erasure of Asian or Asian American characters altogether in favor of white casting. In the twenty-first century, examples of yellowface casting and whitewashing include the films *21* (2008), *The Last Airbender* (2010), *Aloha* (2015), *Doctor Strange* (2016), and *Ghost in the Shell* (2017). In other words, for much of the twentieth century and into the twenty-first, Asian Americans couldn't even portray themselves.

How do you make the invisible visible?

One way to make the humanity of Asian American women visible is to foreground their perspectives and experiences. In their 2018 study, scholars Shruti Mukkamala and Karen Suyemoto interviewed Asian American women about their experiences of discrimination through online open-ended surveys as well as in-person group interviews.[31] Out of the 107 participants in the study, only four said they had never experienced discrimination. Mukkamala and Suyemoto identified six types of discrimination that illustrate how race and gender intersect in their lives. These types include being exoticized, objectified, and infantilized, for example, as "geisha girls" with a distinctive sexuality; seen as incapable of being or becoming leaders; perceived to be agreeable and unable to speak up or stand up for themselves; expected to look cute and small; rendered invisible; and assumed to be a service worker, such as a maid or nail salon worker.

The results of Mukkamala and Suyemoto's study complement other research findings that Asian American women face both subtle and blatant discrimination from bosses and coworkers as well as their own partners, family members, and friends. Mukkamala and Suyemoto hope that their research is used to increase public awareness, empower Asian American women, and prevent discrimination against this group. At stake are Asian American women's lives and well-being.

REPRESENTING OURSELVES

We must confront the histories of objectification of Asian American women and the adverse impacts on their lives in order to address these problems. But it is painful to only see yourself through the eyes of others. It might beg the question: Why can't we represent ourselves? However, Asian American women do and have represented themselves, their families, and their communities in a multitude of ways. Given Congressman Horace Page's role in the long history of anti-Asian hostility, and the persistence of the perception that Asian American women are incapable of leadership, the achievements of Asian American female members in Congress warrant a closer look.

Born on the island of Maui, Patsy Takemoto Mink became the first woman of color to serve in Congress when she was elected to the US House of Representatives in 1965. Mink was hailed as a groundbreaking congressmember on the issue of gender equality. Her most well-known legislative work is on the passage of Title IX, which required "all schools that receive federal funding to provide equal opportunities and benefits regardless of gender."[32] Title IX's aims were broad, but its impact on expanding opportunities for women and girls in sports was profound. In 1972, there were just over three hundred thousand women and girls playing college and high school sports in the United States. Forty years after Title IX's passage, the number of girls participating in high school sports nationwide had risen to more than 3 million, and more than 190,000 women were competing in intercollegiate sports—a sixfold increase since 1972.[33]

In 1972, Mink also became the first Asian American to run for US president. A vocal opponent of the Vietnam War, she ran on an antiwar platform. Although her candidacy was unsuccessful, her daughter, Gwendolyn Mink, reflected, "My mother taught me that an election is not an end in itself, but rather an opening to do the hard work of securing justice, peace and the well being of all."[34]

After her long career in Congress, Mink, an environmental advocate, received an appointment from President Jimmy Carter as assistant secretary of state for Oceans and International Environmental and Scientific Affairs in 1972. Mink recognized the connections between nuclear, conventional, and chemical military testing and their adverse ecological impacts across the Pacific in the Aleutian, Marshall, and Hawai'ian archipelagoes. Scholar Judy Tzu-Chun Wu highlights that, during Mink's years as a representative, she repeatedly demanded that the Navy and Department of Defense stop using Kaho'olawe Island as a bombing practice site.[35]

In 1990, Mink was reelected to Congress and served six terms in the House of Representatives. She helped form the Congressional Asian Pacific American Caucus, which was established in 1994. Mink passed away on September 28, 2002, after being hospitalized for pneumonia. Her name was still on the November ballot. She won the election by a landslide and was replaced by Ed Case. The Title IX law was renamed the Patsy Mink Equal Opportunity in Education Act in her honor.[36]

Similarly, current Asian American congresswomen are making history not solely by breaking barriers and becoming "firsts" in various ways, but also by working to address inequities in Asian American and women's histories, among other areas. When Judy Chu was elected to the US House of Representatives in July 2009 to represent the 27th Congressional District of Southern California, she became the first Chinese American woman elected to Congress. One of her proudest accomplishments includes introducing and passing a 2012 congressional resolution of regret for the Chinese Exclusion Act of 1882.[37] In 2013, Senator Mazie

Hirono from Hawai'i became the first Asian American woman in the US Senate, and the first Japanese immigrant member of Congress.[38] A member of the Senate Armed Services and Veterans Affairs Committees, she counts authoring legislation to honor Filipino World War II veterans with the Congressional Gold Medal among her proudest accomplishments.[39]

The daughter of Taiwanese immigrants, Grace Meng became the first Asian American member of Congress from New York, representing its 6th Congressional District, in 2013. One of the pieces of legislation that she has sponsored and passed into law involves striking the use of "Oriental" from federal law. Prior to the passage of the law in 2016, the Department of Energy Act had, for decades, described a "minority" as someone who is "a Negro, Puerto Rican, American Indian, Eskimo, Oriental, or Aleut or is a Spanish speaking individual of Spanish descent." The law changed and finally updated the language to "Asian American, Native Hawai'ian, a Pacific Islander, African American, Hispanic, Puerto Rican, Native American, or an Alaska Native."[40]

In March 2020, Meng also introduced a resolution that denounced the rise in anti-Asian sentiment since the COVID-19 outbreak. The House of Representatives passed the resolution on September 17, 2020. "Since the beginning of the coronavirus pandemic, Asian Americans have been forced to endure demeaning and disgusting acts of bigotry and hate, consisting of everything from verbal assaults to physical attacks," said Meng. "The House needed to take a strong and public stand against this appalling intolerance, discrimination, and violence that has taken place all across the country during this public health crisis, and today it did just that."[41]

After serving as a representative from Illinois, Tammy Duckworth was elected to the Senate in 2016. Senator Duckworth has written about the racism she experienced during political campaigns as well as the challenges she faced as a mixed race child. Growing up in Thailand, she struggled to fit in as the daughter of a white American man. In the United States, she was treated like a perpetual foreigner: "I've had people—Americans—come up to me and ask me where I'm really from, even while I'm wearing a uniform."[42] An Iraq War veteran and Purple Heart recipient who lost her legs in an attack on the helicopter that she was co-piloting, Duckworth was among the first handful of army women to fly combat missions during the war.

In 2018, Duckworth became the first US senator to give birth while serving in office and secured a historic change in Senate rules that allows senators to bring their infant children onto the Senate floor. She expressed her gratitude to her colleagues on both sides of the aisle "for helping bring the Senate into the 21st Century by recognizing that sometimes new parents also have responsibilities at work."[43]

In 2020, Marilyn Strickland became one of the first three Korean American women elected to Congress as well as the first Black representative elected from Washington State. During her swearing-in ceremony in Washington, DC in January 2021, Strickland donned a *hanbok*, a traditional Korean dress, in vibrant colors of red and blue. Strickland was born in South Korea. Her father, Willie Strickland, met her mother, Inmin Kim, while stationed in Korea.

Kim had come of age in Korea under Japanese colonial rule, where she was forced to learn Japanese in grade school. After marrying an African American soldier, she came to "a country where she didn't know anyone, didn't speak the language."[44] Strickland related that her mother endured prejudice, "being 'otherized,' because America has had this habit of treating people of color as the 'other,' especially when your language and your accent doesn't match what they think is the American accent."[45] Strickland observed her mother's ability to focus and to maintain a sense of humor with a growing sense of admiration.

Strickland chose to wear the hanbok during the swearing-in ceremony to honor her mother and her history on the "largest stage" she had ever been on. A hanbok, she explained, "is something that you wear for a very special occasion."[46] On January 3, 2021, Strickland tweeted: "As a woman of both Korean-American and African-American descent, it was deeply personal to wear my #Hanbok, which not only symbolizes my heritage & honors my mother, but also serves as a larger testament to the importance of diversity in our nation, state, and the People's House."[47]

This image resonated with many viewers. Jacob Kim tweeted: "Did I just see Marilyn Strickland @RepStricklandWA, the first Korean-American, Black-American from Washington State elected to the U.S.

House of Representatives wearing hanbok, the traditional Korean dress? I'm ALL for it! Representation MATTERS! Visibility MATTERS!"[48] Mi-ran 미란 Kim responded: "I cannot express to you how much it means to me to see a Hanbok in Congress. Thank you."[49] And Scott Wilson replied: "Blasian representation. On behalf of my kids, I love it."[50] Strickland illustrated one effective way of countering the objectification of Asian American women: having Asian American women create their own images grounded in history, respect, and strength.

"WITH SOFTNESS AND POWER"

"With Softness and Power" is the title of the portrait by artist Amanda Phingbodhipakkiya that graced the cover of *Time* magazine's March 29, 2021, issue. The portrait is of an Asian American woman with a serious, defiant look. Her head is up, her gaze is off to the side but piercing nonetheless. Peonies, chrysanthemums, and hawthorn berries surround her. In the issue's story behind the cover, Phingbodhipakkiya explained that the image "reflects the immeasurable strength of Asian American women who are the connective tissue of our communities, yet too often overlooked, fetishized, dehumanized and underestimated. . . . My hope is to see the beauty of our people reflected in the colors of our communities in a dignified and respectful way."[51]

She further explained that her choice of flowers in the image was purposeful, and that their meanings contest stereotypical notions of Asian American women as docile and submissive lotus blossoms. Rather, the peonies symbolize solidarity and friendship, the chrysanthemums stand for resilience. "It's one of the few flowers that blooms when it's cold— and the hawthorn berries represent longevity and protection."[52]

The news of the Atlanta spa murders hit home for Phingbodhipak-kiya, who was born in Atlanta to Thai and Indonesian immigrants. Currently based in New York City, she studied neuroscience at Columbia and worked at an Alzheimer's research lab before becoming a full-time artist, educator, and STEM advocate. During New York City's COVID-19 lockdown, Phingbodhipakkiya experienced the stigma of anti-Asian racism. After she took a seat in a subway car, the man next to her said, "Ew, gross!" and ran to the other end of the car. She also worried about her parents' safety. Someone had yelled at them to go back to where they came from while they were in a grocery store.

Phingbodhipakkiya has characterized both her artwork and research in neuroscience as the practice of "making the invisible visible—whether it's microscopic worlds or the often unseen struggles of communities of color."[53] Their struggles with being unseen and unsung inspire her to foreground belonging in her work. In November 2020, she created a public art series, "I Still Believe in Our City." Composed of forty-five pieces, it was displayed in the Atlantic Terminal in Brooklyn, a subway hub that serves a diverse group of New Yorkers. The series features vibrant portraits of Black, Asian, and Pacific Islander people alongside messages such as "I did not make you sick," and "I am not your scapegoat."[54]

Phingbodhipakkiya emphasizes that "it's so important to see ourselves." She reminds us that "despite what we have been through as Asian Americans, we're still here. We don't scare easily. We're fighting every day for our shared future."[55]

Xiaojie Tan, Daoyou Feng, Delaina Ashley Yaun Gonzalez, Paul Andre Michels, Soon Chung Park, Hyun Jung Grant, Suncha Kim, and Yong Ae Yue. May we remember your fierceness, good-heartedness, and love for life with softness and power.

1869: THESE WOUNDS

O n January 27, 2021, photographer Corky Lee died due to complications from COVID-19. He was seventy-three years old. The loss was deeply felt by so many in the Asian American community. For the past five decades, Lee had captured key moments of Asian American history, many of which sparked awareness and resistance against violence and injustice.

Among his most well-known photographs is a 1975 photo of Peter Yew with a bloody face as he is dragged away by police. According to writer and scholar Hua Hsu, "They had beaten him after he had tried to stop them from assaulting a teenager who'd been involved in a minor traffic incident."[1] The photo made the cover of the *New York Post* and catalyzed thousands of Chinatown residents to protest police brutality in their community.

A few days after the 9/11 attacks, Lee went to a candlelight vigil in Central Park that raised awareness about the surge in harassment and violence against South Asian Americans, most notably Sikhs, who were being conflated with the terrorists. Lee's photograph of a Sikh man wearing a red turban with a flag draped around his body garnered a New York state journalism award.[2]

Lee's passion for documenting Asian American histories was sparked by an appalling historical omission. In 1869, the completion of the first transcontinental railroad heralded the emergence of the United States as a modern nation. It connected the Atlantic and Pacific Oceans and hastened economic expansion across the continent and beyond. By 1865, Chinese workers made up the vast majority of the Central Pacific Railroad's labor force that built the western portion of the railroad. They placed their lives at risk by working through the blizzards and snowstorms of the 1866–67 winters and tunneling through the Sierra Nevada by blasting rock and carving out tunnels through solid granite. According to the Chinese Railroad Workers in North America Project, the Chinese workers numbered between ten thousand and fifteen thousand, and perhaps as many as twenty thousand between 1865 and 1869. They made up as much as 90 percent of the workforce for much of the construction.[3] Yet, in one of the most egregious examples of the erasure of Asian American history, Chinese railroad workers were excluded from the photograph celebrating the joining of the Central Pacific and Union Pacific railroads in 1869 at Promontory Summit in Utah.

Lee saw this photograph when he was in grade school. He had read that Chinese laborers had worked on that railroad. However, when he examined the photograph, he couldn't find a single Chinese person in it.[4] Not a single Chinese worker.

As I have argued throughout the book, over time, this erasure would form an Asian American historical pattern. It included representing Asian American women as objects of fantasy instead of human beings. It involved the redevelopment of historic places to put up nondescript buildings and parking lots. Historical plaques paid tribute to war veterans under the guise of liberation. Critical photographs were impounded and tucked away in an archive. The passage of dozens of anti-miscegenation laws tried to diminish the presence of interracial families and communities, and the establishment of motion picture codes kept them out of view. News media and social media circulated narratives of Asian and Black enmity when empirical evidence suggested otherwise.

Secret treaties, secret wars, and secret armies contributed to our national amnesia. We have become a nation of not knowing. Not knowing the faces behind the production, preparation, and presentation of our food. Not knowing how the Immigration and Nationality Act of

1965 has changed the face of America. Many Americans cannot name one well-known Asian American. Many don't see Asian American health workers as Americans even though they are literally dying to save us in the age of COVID-19. Many Americans don't see Asian Americans as fellow human beings, but rather as convenient scapegoats in times of crisis. And grave violence, another historical pattern, ensues.

Writing in these years of great hatred, I greeted each chapter of this book with a heavy heart. While I am deeply grateful for the many privileges of my work, confronting histories of violence is emotionally and psychologically difficult. I admit that there were moments when I wished that I could forget the horrors of our past and present. The uncertainty of these pandemic times is so stressful and exhausting. In the most difficult moments, despair creeps in. I worry about what kind of world we are leaving our children and future generations.

And, yet, with the writing of each chapter, I have also encountered something or someone that leaves me in awe. I am especially moved by the creative ways that so many Asian Americans have resisted omission, dismissal, and denigration. They include the organizers who work to stop AAPI hate; the artists who are reminding us that there is more than one way to be Asian American; the students who continue to demand ethnic studies at their schools; the creators of digital platforms that enable immigrants and refugees to share their experiences; the descendants of internees who build memorial gardens where we can remember and reflect; the congressmembers who advocate for our well-being with courage and grace.

They include Corky Lee, who, in 2014 on the 145th anniversary of the transcontinental railroad's completion, gathered a group of Asian Americans, including the descendants of Chinese railroad laborers, at the same spot in Promontory Summit where, in 1869, the celebratory photograph had been taken without the Chinese workers. Herb Tam, curator and director of exhibitions at the Museum of Chinese in America, noted that "the transcontinental-railroad project was him trying to heal a big wound."[5] The group of Asian Americans included young and old, wearing contemporary as well as period clothing. They were smiling big. The joy was palpable. Lee took a photograph. He called these moments "photographic justice."[6]

. . .

The erasure of Asian American histories is painful to confront because they expose wounds, both literal and metaphorical. Yet, for so many Asian Americans over time, knowing what has been omitted has sparked something else. A question can transform into an idea. An idea can inspire the courage to make change. And these actions present multiple ways forward, illuminating a path toward healing.

ACKNOWLEDGMENTS

How do you write a book about Asian American histories during a pandemic and a period of intense anti-Asian sentiment? *First, have an extraordinary editor.* My deep thanks to Gayatri Patnaik, my editor at Beacon Press, for her thoughtful insights on every chapter, steadfast encouragement, and her belief in my writing even when my own confidence waned. I've marveled at how she always knew the right things to say to motivate me to keep writing. Thank you to the Beacon Press team for putting this book out in the world. I'm honored to be part of Beacon Press's ReVisioning History series.

Second, learn from the mentorship of pathbreaking scholars. Thank you, Barbara Posadas, Paul Spickard, Vicki Ruiz, Shelley Fisher Fishkin, Josephine Lee, Elaine Tyler May, Valerie Matsumoto, Michael Salman, Karen Brodkin, George Sanchez, Sidney Lemelle, Antonia Castañeda, Dorinne Kondo, Samuel Yamashita, and Deena González. I have tried and continue to try to emulate your scholarly innovativeness, generosity, and graceful example.

Third, trust the foundation you have gained from having outstanding teachers in your youth. Since an important part of this book is the use of different writing styles, I must acknowledge my teachers at Stuyvesant High School—Barbara Solowey, the late Jacob Irgang, and the late Frank McCourt—for caring about young people's writing and well-being, and nurturing my interest in the craft.

Fourth, listen to and learn from your students. I'm grateful for the engagement of the many undergraduate and doctoral students in my Asian American history classes at UC Berkeley, where I have taught since 2004.

My discussions with the students in my seminar, Asian American History in the Age of COVID-19, during the spring 2021 semester moved me, reminded me of how much Asian American history matters in the present moment, and inspired much of the subject matter of this book. I've had the great fortune of advising many doctoral students—including William Gow, Gladys Nubla, Ethel Regis Lu, Joanne Rondilla, Eric Pido, Jason Oliver Chang, and Ligaya Domingo—with admiration and awe of their achievements in ethnic studies and Asian American history.

Fifth, engage with the media with passion and purpose, because it takes a village to raise public awareness and understanding. In 2020 and early 2021, I communicated with Agnes Constante, Alexander Gonzalez, Anne Brice, Brian Watt, Caitlin Yoshiko Kandil, Cat Sandoval, Catherine E. Shoichet, Charissa Isidro, Charley Lanyon, Christina Thornell, Corryn Wetzel, Currie Engel, David Pierson, Emily Pandise, Ernabel Demillo, Fiona Kelliher, Frank Shyong, Gabrielle Berbey, Ivan Natividad, Jana Katsuyama, Janelle Bitker, Jill Cowen, Jo Ling Kent, Joe Rocha, Josie Huang, Julia Chang Wang, Kimberly Adams, Kimmy Yam, Marc Abizeid, Mina Kim, Mollie Riegger, Nina Martin, Paulina Cachero, Rosem Morton, Saadia Khan, Sarah Titterton, Timothy McLaughlin, Tracie Hunte, Yudi Liu, and more. Thank you for publicizing Asian American history and the insights of Asian American studies scholars.

Sixth, find colleagues and friends who will support you even when things don't go your way, and who will revel in those times when they do. Thank you, Miroslava Chávez-García, Weihong Bao, SanSan Kwan, Laura C. Nelson, Evelyn Nakano Glenn, the late Ronald Takaki, Sau-ling Wong, Michael Omi, Carolyn Chen, Carlos Muñoz Jr., Thomas Biolsi, Shari Huhndorf, Beth Piatote, Raúl Coronado, Juana María Rodríguez, Keith Feldman, Judy Tzu-Chun Wu, Jennifer Ho, Theo Gonzalves, Tammy Ho, David Martinez, Walt Jacobs, Valerie Minor, Barbara Yasue, Leighton Fong, Anna Presler, Max Leung, Jeanette Roan, Jeannie Wang, and Milton Tong, for the great conversations often tinged with laughter. How I miss being in the company of the late Dawn Bohulano Mabalon, Jeffrey Hadler, Yun Won Cho, and Yuji Yasue. UC Berkeley, and its historic Department of Ethnic Studies, has been my professional home for the past seventeen years. I'm grateful to the entire campus community for supporting my research and teaching in Asian American history over many years.

Finally, be grateful for the family—it can be the one you're born into, grow into, and/or the one you create—who loves you. To my mother Patria Ceniza, aunts Lucy Ceniza, Vicky Paragas, Betty Maniego, Onie Ceniza, sister Caroline Ceniza-Levine, and father-in-law Howard Choy, thank you for your support. I write in fond memory of Auntie Mary Hernandez, Lolo Braulio Ceniza, Lola Soledad Ceniza, Uncle Terry Ceniza, my mother-in-law Nellie Choy, Auntie Alice Wong, Auntie Mary Wong, and Uncle Phillip Choi.

I dedicate this book to my husband, Greg Choy, and our children Maya and Louis. Never forget how much I love you. Greg, thank you for being a patient listener and an astute reader, and, perhaps above all, for helping me learn to laugh at myself. Maya and Louis, thank you for simply being who you are—curious and compassionate young people who want to make a difference. You give me hope.

NOTES

PREFACE: WRITING IN THE YEARS OF GREAT HATRED

1. Associated Press, "As Virus-Era Attacks on Asians Rise, Past Victims Look Back," *U.S. News & World Report*, March 2, 2021, www.usnews.com/news/us/articles/2021-03-02/victims-of-anti-asian-attacks-reflect-a-year-into-pandemic.

2. Nicole Hong et al., "Brutal Attack on Filipino Woman Sparks Outrage: 'Everybody Is on Edge,'" *New York Times*, March 30, 2021, https://www.nytimes.com/2021/03/30/nyregion/asian-attack-nyc.html.

3. Kyung Lah and Jason Kravarik, "Family of Thai Immigrant, 84, Says Fatal Attack 'Was Driven by Hate,'" CNN, February 16, 2021, https://www.cnn.com/2021/02/16/us/san-francisco-vicha-ratanapakdee-asian-american-attacks/index.html.

4. T. J. Manotoc, "Elderly Filipino Killed in Arizona in Suspected Hate Crime," ABS-CBN, March 8, 2021, https://news.abs-cbn.com/news/03/08/21/elderly-filipino-killed-in-arizona-feared-to-be-an-asian-hate-crime.

5. According to the Stop AAPI Hate National Report released in March 2021, 68 percent of the approximately 3,800 anti-Asian hate incidents in the United States over the course of the previous year targeted women. Kimmy Yam, "There Were 3,800 Anti-Asian Racist Incidents, Mostly Against Women, in Past Year," NBC News, March 17, 2021, https://www.nbcnews.com/news/asian-america/there-were-3-800-anti-asian-racist-incidents-mostly-against-n1261257.

6. Kimmy Yam, "Racism, Sexism Must Be Considered in Atlanta Case Involving Killing of Six Asian Women, Experts Say," NBC News, March 17, 2021, https://www.nbcnews.com/news/asian-america/racism-sexism-must-be-considered-atlanta-case-involving-killing-six-n1261347.

7. Catherine Ceniza Choy, *Empire of Care: Nursing and Migration in Filipino American History* (Durham, NC: Duke University Press, 2003).

8. Choy, *Empire of Care*, 121–65.

9. Robert K. Wilcox, *The Mysterious Deaths at Ann Arbor* (New York: Popular Library, 1977), 166.

10. James Baldwin, "As Much Truth as One Can Bear," *New York Times Book Review*, January 14, 1962, 148, https://timesmachine.nytimes.com/timesmachine/1962/01/14/118438007.html.

11. Beth Spotswood, "Immigrants' Torment as Angel Island Detainees Re-Created in Dance," *San Francisco Chronicle*, September 14, 2017, https://www.sfchronicle.com/performance/article/Immigrants-torment-as-Angel-Island-detainees-12198419.php.

12. Abby Budiman and Neil G. Ruiz, "Key Facts About Asian Americans, a Diverse and Growing Population," Pew Research Center, April 29, 2021, https://www.pewresearch.org/fact-tank/2021/04/29/key-facts-about-asian-americans.

13. Liz Zhou, "The Inadequacy of the Term 'Asian American,'" *Vox*, May 5, 2021, https://www.vox.com/identities/22380197/asian-american-pacific-islander-aapi-heritage-anti-asian-hate-attacks.

14. Abby Budiman and Neil G. Ruiz, "Asian Americans Are the Fastest-Growing Racial or Ethnic Group in the U.S.," Pew Research Center, April 9, 2021, https://www.pewresearch.org/fact-tank/2021/04/09/asian-americans-are-the-fastest-growing-racial-or-ethnic-group-in-the-u-s.

15. "Profile: Asian Americans," US Department of Health and Human Services, Office of Minority Health, https://minorityhealth.hhs.gov/omh/browse.aspx?lvl=3&lvlid=63, accessed August 15, 2021.

16. Rakesh Kochhar and Anthony Cilluffo, "Income Inequality in the U.S. Is Rising Most Rapidly Among Asians," Pew Research Center, July 12, 2018, https://www.pewresearch.org/social-trends/2018/07/12/income-inequality-in-the-u-s-is-rising-most-rapidly-among-asians.

INTRODUCTION: THE MULTIPLE ORIGINS OF ASIAN AMERICAN HISTORIES

1. "About Stop AAPI Hate," Stop AAPI Hate, https://stopaapihate.org/about.

2. National Nurses United, *Sins of Omission: How Government Failures to Track Covid-19 Data Have Led to More Than 1,700 Health Care Worker Deaths and Jeopardize Public Health*, September 2020, https://www.nationalnursesunited.org/sites/default/files/nnu/graphics/documents/0920_Covid19_SinsOfOmission_Data_Report.pdf.

3. Chen Fu, "'It's Tough to Reconcile Being Both Celebrated and Villainized.' An Asian-American Doctor on the Challenges of the Coronavirus Pandemic," *Time*, April 8, 2020, https://time.com/collection/coronavirus-heroes/5816886/asian-american-doctor-coronavirus.

4. Chia Youyee Vang and Monica Mong Trieu, *Invisible Newcomers: Refugees from Burma/Myanmar and Bhutan in the United States*, Asian & Pacific Islander American Scholarship Fund, 2014, https://apiascholars.org/wp-content/uploads/2019/04/APIASF_Burma_Bhutan_Report.pdf.

5. Anna Purna Kambhampaty, "In 1968, These Activists Coined the Term 'Asian American'—and Helped Shape Decades of Advocacy," *Time*, May 22, 2020, https://time.com/5837805/asian-american-history.

6. Allison O'Connor and Jeanne Batalova, "Korean Immigrants in the United States," *Migration Information Source*, April 10, 2019, https://www.migrationpolicy.org/article/korean-immigrants-united-states-2017.

7. Migration Policy Institute, *The Pakistani Diaspora in the United States*, June 2015, prepared for the Rockefeller Foundation–Aspen Institute Diaspora Program (RAD), https://www.migrationpolicy.org/sites/default/files/publications/RAD-Pakistan.pdf.

8. Abby Budiman and Neil G. Ruiz, "Key Facts About Asian Americans, a Diverse and Growing Population," Pew Research Center, April 29, 2021, https://www.pewresearch.org/fact-tank/2021/04/29/key-facts-about-asian-americans.

CHAPTER ONE: 2020: THE HEALTH OF THE NATION

1. Garrett M. Graff, "An Oral History of the Pandemic Warnings Trump Ignored," *Wired*, April 17, 2020, https://www.wired.com/story/an-oral-history-of-the-pandemic-warnings-trump-ignored.

2. Reis Thebault, Abigail Hauslohner, and Jacqueline Dupree, "U.S. Coronavirus Death Toll Surpasses 100," *Washington Post*, March 17, 2020, https://www.washingtonpost.com/national/us-coronavirus-death-toll-reaches-100/2020/03/17/f8d770c2-67a8-11ea-b313-df458622c2cc_story.html.

3. Katie Mettler and William Booth, "U.S. Deaths from Covid-19 Soar Past 10,000," *Washington Post*, April 6, 2020, https://www.washingtonpost.com/politics/us-deaths-from-covid-19-soar-past-10000/2020/04/06/865feoec-7806-11ea-9bee-c5bf9d2e3288_story.html.

4. "Four Months After First Case, U.S. Death Toll Passes 100,000," *New York Times*, May 27, 2020, https://www.nytimes.com/2020/05/27/us/coronavirus-live-news-updates.html.

5. "1-Month Report," Stop AAPI Hate, April 23, 2020, https://stopaapihate.org/1-month-report.

6. National Nurses United, *Sins of Omission: How Government Failures to Track Covid-19 Data Have Led to More Than 1,700 Health Care Worker Deaths and Jeopardize Public Health*, September 2020, https://www.nationalnursesunited.org/sites/default/files/nnu/graphics/documents/0920_Covid19_SinsOfOmission_Data_Report.pdf.

7. Joan B. Trauner, "Chinese as Medical Scapegoats, 1870–1905," *California History Magazine*, 1978, https://www.foundsf.org/index.php?title=Chinese_as_Medical_Scapegoats,_1870-1905.

8. Nayan Shah, *Contagious Divides: Epidemics and Race in San Francisco's Chinatown* (Berkeley: University of California Press, 2001), 58.

9. Shah, *Contagious Divides*, 51, 53.

10. Shah, *Contagious Divides*, 275n28.

11. Victor G. Heiser, "Unsolved Health Problems Peculiar to the Philippines," *Philippine Journal of Science* 5, no. 2 (July 1910): 177–78, in Record Group 350, box 275, file 2394-25, US National Archives, College Park, Maryland.

12. Natalia Molina, *Fit to Be Citizens? Public Health and Race in Los Angeles, 1879–1939* (Berkeley: University of California Press, 2006), 59.

13. Molina, *Fit to Be Citizens?*, 56.

14. "Hindu Immigration," *Hearings Before the Committee on Immigration, House of Representatives, Sixty-Third Congress, Second Session, Relative to Restriction of Immigration of Hindu Laborers*, part 2, February 19, 1914, p. 71, https://www.lib.washington.edu/specialcollections/collections/exhibits/southasianstudents/docs/hindu-immigration-hearings-before-the-committee-on-immigration.-part-2.

15. Shah, *Contagious Divides*, 58.

16. Shah, *Contagious Divides*, 53.

17. Poem number 48 in *Island: Poetry and History of Chinese Immigrants on Angel Island, 1910–1940*, ed. Him Mark Lai, Genny Lim, and Judy Yung (Seattle: University of Washington Press, 1980), 100.

18. Shah, *Contagious Divides*, 198–99.

19. Kelly Wallace, "Forgotten Los Angeles History: The Chinese Massacre of 1871," *Los Angeles Public Library Blog*, May 19, 2017, https://www.lapl.org /collections-resources/blogs/lapl/chinese-massacre-1871.

20. Tom Rea, "The Rock Springs Massacre," WyoHistory.org, November 8, 2014, https://www.wyohistory.org/encyclopedia/rock-springs-massacre.

21. See Beth Lew-Williams, *The Chinese Must Go: Violence, Exclusion, and the Making of the Alien in America* (Cambridge, MA: Harvard University Press, 2018); Jean Pfaelzer, *Driven Out: The Forgotten War Against Chinese Americans* (Berkeley: University of California Press, 2008).

22. Lew-Williams, *The Chinese Must Go*, 92.

23. Lew-Williams, *The Chinese Must Go*, 98.

24. David Cahn, "The 1907 Bellingham Riots in Historical Context," Seattle Civil Rights & Labor History Project, 2008, https://depts.washington.edu/civilr /bham_history.htm.

25. Richard S. Kim, *The Quest for Statehood: Korean Immigrant Nationalism and U.S. Sovereignty, 1905–1945* (New York: Oxford University Press, 2011), 3–4.

26. Dawn Bohulano Mabalon, *Little Manila Is in the Heart: The Making of the Filipina/o American Community in Stockton, California* (Durham, NC: Duke University Press, 2013), 93.

27. Linda España-Maram, *Creating Masculinity in Los Angeles's Little Manila: Working-Class Filipinos and Popular Culture, 1920s–1950s* (New York: Columbia University Press, 2006), 130.

28. Mary Paik Lee, *Quiet Odyssey* (Seattle: University of Washington Press, 1990), 144–45.

29. Denise Dador, "Coronavirus: Local Boy Bullied, Attacked, Targeted Just Because He's Asian, Officials Say," ABC7, February 14, 2020, https://abc7.com /coronavirus-los-angeles-anti-asian-racism-novel-la-county-public-health/5929456.

30. Kara Takasaki, "Stop AAPI Hate Reporting Center: A Model of Collective Leadership and Community Advocacy," *Journal of Asian American Studies* 23, no. 3 (October 2020): 341–51.

31. Daryl Joji Maeda, "The Asian American Movement," Oxford Research Encyclopedias: American History, published online, June 9, 2016, https://doi.org /10.1093/acrefore/9780199329175.013.21.

32. "About A3PCON," Asian Pacific Policy and Planning Council, http://www .asianpacificpolicyandplanningcouncil.org/about-a3pcon.

33. Takasaki, "Stop AAPI Hate Reporting Center," 343.

34. "Donald Trump's 'Chinese Virus': The Politics of Naming," *The Conversation*, April 21, 2020, https://theconversation.com/donald-trumps-chinese-virus-the -politics-of-naming-136796.

35. Kimmy Yam, "Trump Can't Claim 'Kung Flu' Doesn't Affect Asian Americans in This Climate, Experts Say," NBC News, June 22, 2020, https://www.nbcnews.com /news/asian-america/trump-can-t-claim-kung-flu-doesn-t-affect-asian-n1231812.

36. Yam, "Trump Can't Claim 'Kung Flu' Doesn't Affect Asian Americans in This Climate."

37. World Health Organization, "WHO Issues Best Practices for Naming New Human Infectious Diseases," press release, May 8, 2015, https://www.who.int/news /item/08-05-2015-who-issues-best-practices-for-naming-new-human-infectious-diseases.

38. The Stop AAPI Hate reporting center's various reports, including its state-specific and national reports and those charting the pandemic's first two weeks, first month, and first three months, are available on the Stop AAPI Hate website, at https://stopaapihate.org/reports.

39. According to a 2021 LAAUNCH survey, "Fewer than 1 in 4 Asian Americans feel respected in this country. Meanwhile, close to 1 in 4 white Americans do not believe that anti-Asian American racism is significant enough of a problem that it needs to be addressed." LAAUNCH, "STAATUS Index Report 2021," p. 3, https://uploads-ssl.webflow.com/5f629e7e013d961943d5cec9/6098a7be3d627168e03054da_staatus-index-2021.pdf.

40. Russell Jeung, *Incidents of Coronavirus Discrimination, March 19–25, 2020: A Report for A3PCON and CAA*, March 25, 2020, p. 5, https://stopaapihate.org/wp-content/uploads/2021/04/Stop-AAPI-Hate-Report-Week1-200325.pdf.

41. Russell Jeung, *Incidents of Coronavirus Discrimination, March 26–April 1, 2020: A Report for A3PCON and CAA*, April 3, 2020, p. 3, https://stopaapihate.org/wp-content/uploads/2021/04/Stop-AAPI-Hate-Report-2Weeks-200403.pdf.

42. Stop AAPI Hate, *Stop AAPI Hate National Report: 3.19.20 – 8.5.20*, p. 1, https://stopaapihate.org/wp-content/uploads/2021/04/Stop-AAPI-Hate-Report-National-200805.pdf.

43. "Lost on the Frontline," *The Guardian* and *Kaiser Health News*, 2021, https://www.theguardian.com/us-news/ng-interactive/2020/aug/11/lost-on-the-frontline-covid-19-coronavirus-us-healthcare-workers-deaths-database, accessed January 25, 2021.

44. National Nurses United, *Sins of Omission*.

45. See Jennifer Dixon, "Nurse Who Died from Coronavirus Was a Hero, Risked Her Life for Veterans, Son Says," *Detroit Free Press*, April 3, 2020, https://www.freep.com/story/news/local/2020/04/03/veterans-affair-nurse-coronavirus/2942426001; Alicia Lee, "Beloved Missouri Nurse Died of Coronavirus a Week Before Her 40th Anniversary at Hospital," CNN, April 28, 2020, https://www.cnn.com/2020/04/28/us/missouri-nurse-coronavirus-dies-trnd/index.html; Natacha Larnaud, "Another Nurse on the Front Lines Dies from Coronavirus—This Time, in Miami," CBS News, March 30, 2020, https://www.cbsnews.com/news/coronavirus-nurse-dies-from-covid-19-miami-hospital.

46. Abby Budiman, "Filipinos in the U.S. Fact Sheet," Pew Research Center, April 29, 2021, https://www.pewresearch.org/social-trends/fact-sheet/asian-americans-filipinos-in-the-u-s/#filipino-population-in-the-u-s--2000-2019.

47. Christina Thornell, "Why the US Has So Many Filipino Nurses," Vox, June 30, 2020, https://www.vox.com/2020/6/30/21307199/filipino-nurses-us.

48. Luis Hassan Gallardo and Jeanne Batalova, "Filipino Immigrants in the United States," *Migration Information Source*, July 15, 2020, https://www.migrationpolicy.org/article/filipino-immigrants-united-states-2020.

49. Paul Ong and Tania Azores, "The Migration and Incorporation of Filipino Nurses," in *The New Asian Immigration in Los Angeles and Global Restructuring*, ed. Paul Ong, Edna Bonacich, and Lucie Cheng (Philadelphia: Temple University Press, 1994), 182.

50. Joanne Spetz et al., *2016 Survey of Registered Nurses*, California Board of Registered Nursing, November 1, 2017, https://healthforce.ucsf.edu/sites/healthforce.ucsf.edu/files/publication-pdf/survey2016.pdf.

51. "Filipino Nurses Get a Shout-Out in 70th Emmys Opening Monologue," GMA News Online, September 19, 2018, https://www.gmanetwork.com/news/show biz/showbizabroad/668315/filipino-nurses-get-a-shout-out-in-70th-emmys-opening -monologue/story.

52. Catherine Ceniza Choy, *Empire of Care: Nursing and Migration in Filipino American History* (Durham, NC: Duke University Press, 2003), 41–57.

53. Choy, *Empire of Care*, 61–93.

54. Choy, *Empire of Care*, 62.

55. Choy, *Empire of Care*.

56. Choy, *Empire of Care*, 101.

57. Choy, *Empire of Care*, 67–70.

58. Choy, *Empire of Care*, 84–89.

59. Choy, *Empire of Care*, 114–18.

60. "Meet the Nurse Who Gave World's First COVID-19 Vaccine," *RCN Magazines*, December 24, 2020, https://www.rcn.org.uk/magazines/bulletin/2020/dec/may -parsons-nurse-first-vaccine-covid-19.

61. US Equal Employment Opportunity Commission, "EEOC Announces $2.1 Million Settlement of Wage Discrimination Suit for Class of Filipino Nurses," press release, March 2, 1999, https://www.eeoc.gov/newsroom/eeoc-announces-21-million -settlement-wage-discrimination-suit-class-filipino-nurses.

62. Anh Do, "Filipino Nurses Win Language Discrimination Settlement," *Los Angeles Times*, September 18, 2012, https://www.latimes.com/health/la-xpm-2012 -sep-18-la-me-english-only-20120918-story.html.

63. *The Strength of Many*, dir. Marissa Aroy, 2020, https://vimeo.com/412121963.

64. Jennifer Nazareno et al., "From Imperialism to Inpatient Care: Work Differences of Filipino and White Registered Nurses in the United States and Implications for COVID-19 Through an Intersectional Lens," *Gender, Work & Organization* 28, no. 4 (July 2021): 1426–46, https://doi.org/10.1111/gwao.12657.

65. Sarah Jaffe, "'Horror Story After Horror Story': A Frontline Nurse Discusses the Crisis," *The Nation*, March 26, 2020, https://www.thenation.com/article /society/zenei-cortez-interview.

66. Riza V. Mauricio, "The Power of Touch," in "Frontline Heroes," Philippine Nurses Association of America, 2020, https://mypnaa.wildapricot.org/frontline -heroes.

67. Evangeline Ver Vicente, "COVID-19: Story of an ICU Nurse," *insidePNAA*, May 2020, p. 10, https://mypnaa.wildapricot.org/frontline-heroes.

68. Arlin Fidellaga, "Socially Distant but Spiritually Connected," *insidePNAA*, April 2020, p. 16, https://mypnaa.wildapricot.org/frontline-heroes.

69. Jeanne Batalova, "Immigrant Health-Care Workers in the United States," *Migration Information Source*, May 14, 2020, https://www.migrationpolicy.org /article/immigrant-health-care-workers-united-states-2018.

70. Chen Fu, "'It's Tough to Reconcile Being Both Celebrated and Villainized.' An Asian-American Doctor on the Challenges of the Coronavirus Pandemic," *Time*, April 8, 2020, https://time.com/collection/coronavirus-heroes/5816886/asian -american-doctor-coronavirus.

71. Janelle Bitker, "There's Been a Surge of Attacks Against Asian Americans. Asians in the Bay Area Say the Hostility Isn't New," *San Francisco Chronicle*,

February 25, 2021, https://www.sfchronicle.com/news/article/There-s-been-a-surge
-of-attacks-against-Asian-15969890.php.

72. Ivan Natividad, "Racist Harassment of Asian Health Care Workers Won't
Cure Coronavirus," *Berkeley News*, April 9, 2020, https://news.berkeley.edu/2020
/04/09/racist-harassment-of-asian-health-care-workers-wont-cure-coronavirus.

CHAPTER TWO: 1975: TRAUMA AND TRANSFORMATION

1. Ocean Vuong, *On Earth We're Briefly Gorgeous: A Novel* (New York: Penguin Press, 2019), 35.

2. Vuong, *On Earth We're Briefly Gorgeous*, 35.

3. Martin Wolk, "When Everything Changed: Novelist Ocean Vuong Reflects on a Year of Intense Highs and Lows," *Los Angeles Times*, January 8, 2020, https://www.latimes.com/entertainment-arts/books/story/2020-01-08/ocean-vuong-on-earth-were-briefly-gorgeous.

4. "Do You Remember Glastonbury When . . . ," *Hartford Courant*, March 4, 2016, https://www.courant.com/community/glastonbury/hc-do-you-remember-glastonbury-when-20160304-photogallery.html.

5. Kat Chow, "Going Home with Ocean Vuong," *The Atlantic*, June 4, 2019, https://www.theatlantic.com/entertainment/archive/2019/06/going-home-ocean-vuong-on-earth-were-briefly-gorgeous/590938.

6. "What Is a Refugee?," UNHCR, https://www.unhcr.org/en-us/what-is-a-refugee.html.

7. In their 2014 report on refugees from Burma/Myanmar and Bhutan, scholars Chia Youyee Vang and Monica Mong Trieu explain their use of "Burma/Myanmar": "The usage of the term 'Burma' is consistent with reports released by the U.S. Department of Homeland Security as they track refugees to the United States. We recognize the sensitivity that exists regarding the use of the term. We use Burmese Americans and Burmese refugees to encompass all refugees with origins in Burma/Myanmar with the understanding that there are numerous ethnic groups who prefer to be identified by their respective ethnic identity. We are also sensitive to the use of the country's current official name of the Republic of the Union of Myanmar. Many in the international community use Myanmar because they believe that nations should be referred to by the name that they prefer. We are aware of the recent changes in U.S. relations with the country and that in its May 15, 2013 statement regarding Myanmar President Thein Sein's visit to the United States, the Obama Administration referred to the country as Myanmar, as a courtesy gesture of respect for a government that is pursuing a transformative reform agenda." Chia Youyee Vang and Monica Mong Trieu, *Invisible Newcomers: Refugees from Burma/Myanmar and Bhutan in the United States*, Asian & Pacific Islander American Scholarship Fund, 2014, p. 2, https://apiascholars.org/wp-content/uploads/2019/04/APIASF_Burma_Bhutan_Report.pdf.

8. George Rupp, "The Largest Refugee Resettlement Effort in American History," International Rescue Committee, July 28, 2016, originally published June 27, 2008, https://www.rescue.org/article/largest-refugee-resettlement-effort-american-history.

9. *The Donut King*, dir. Alice Gu (Los Angeles: Logan Industry, 2020).

10. "Transcript of President John F. Kennedy's Inaugural Address (1961)," Our Documents, https://www.ourdocuments.gov/doc.php?flash=false&doc=91&page=transcript.

11. World Peace Foundation, "Cambodia: U.S. Bombing and Civil War," Mass Atrocity Endings, August 7, 2015, https://sites.tufts.edu/atrocityendings/2015/08/07 /cambodia-u-s-bombing-civil-war-khmer-rouge.

12. "Bombing of Cambodia," Ohio History Central, June 13, 2021, https:// ohiohistorycentral.org/w/Bombing_of_Cambodia.

13. "Cambodia," University of Minnesota Center for Holocaust and Genocide Studies, 2021, https://cla.umn.edu/chgs/holocaust-genocide-education/resource -guides/cambodia; Lon Kurashige and Alice Yang Murray, eds., *Major Problems in Asian American History: Documents and Essays* (Boston: Houghton Mifflin, 2003), 388.

14. Louis Elliott, "Monica Sok on Writing the Cambodian Story Beyond Trauma," *Literary Hub*, April 30, 2020, https://lithub.com/monica-sok-on-writing -the-cambodian-story-beyond-trauma.

15. Viet Thanh Nguyen, *Nothing Ever Dies: Vietnam and the Memory of War* (Cambridge, MA: Harvard University Press, 2016), 4.

16. Usha Welaratna, *Beyond the Killing Fields: Voices of Nine Cambodian Survivors in America* (Stanford, CA: Stanford University Press, 1993), 117–35.

17. Welaratna, *Beyond the Killing Fields*, 125.

18. Welaratna, *Beyond the Killing Fields*, 128.

19. Welaratna, *Beyond the Killing Fields*, 127.

20. Robert P. Thayer, *Who Killed Heng Lim? The Southeast Asian Experience of Racial Harassment and Violence in Philadelphia* (Philadelphia: Asian Americans United: Southeast Asian Mutual Assistance Associations Coalition, 1990), 17, https://oac.cdlib.org/view?docId=hb596nb2x7&brand=oac4&doc.view=entire_text.

21. Viet Thanh Nguyen, "The Hidden Scars All Refugees Carry," *New York Times*, September 2, 2016, https://www.nytimes.com/2016/09/03/opinion/the-hidden -scars-all-refugees-carry.html.

22. Abby Budiman and Neil G. Ruiz, "Key Facts About Asian Americans, a Diverse and Growing Population," Pew Research Center, April 29, 2021, https://www .pewresearch.org/fact-tank/2021/04/29/key-facts-about-asian-americans.

23. Abby Budiman, "Cambodians in the U.S. Fact Sheet," Pew Research Center, April 29, 2021, https://www.pewresearch.org/social-trends/fact-sheet/asian-americans -cambodians-in-the-u-s; Abby Budiman, "Hmong in the U.S. Fact Sheet," Pew Research Center, April 29, 2021, https://www.pewresearch.org/social-trends/fact-sheet /asian-americans-hmong-in-the-u-s; Abby Budiman, "Laotians in the U.S. Fact Sheet," Pew Research Center, April 29, 2021, https://www.pewresearch.org/social -trends/fact-sheet/asian-americans-laotians-in-the-u-s.

24. Mike Edgerly, "Minnesota's Global Faces," Minnesota Public Radio, May 16, 2005, http://news.minnesota.publicradio.org/features/2005/05/16_sommerm _globalmap.

25. Kong Pheng Pha, "Two Hate Notes: Deportations, COVID-19, and Xenophobia Against Hmong Americans in the Midwest," *Journal of Asian American Studies* 23, no. 3 (October 2020): 336.

26. Pha, "Two Hate Notes," 337.

27. "Xang Mao Xiong's Life Story as Told to His Daughter, Maijue Xiong," in *Hmong Means Free: Life in Laos and America*, ed. Sucheng Chan (Philadelphia: Temple University Press, 1994), 101.

28. "Xang Mao Xiong's Life Story as Told to His Daughter, Maijue Xiong," 102.

29. "Cover Story," *Laonet Magazine*, April 2006, p. 8, http://www.laonet.com/ISSUE%20102/0102p8-9%20Cover%20Story.pdf.

30. Jerome Kroll et al., "Depression and Posttraumatic Stress Disorder in Southeast Asian Refugees," *American Journal of Psychiatry* 146, no. 12 (December 1989): 1592–97.

31. Centers for Disease Control and Prevention, "Update: Sudden Unexplained Death Syndrome Among Southeast Asian Refugees—United States," *Morbidity and Mortality Weekly Report*, September 23, 1988, https://www.cdc.gov/mmwr/preview/mmwrhtml/00001278.htm.

32. John Burnett, "Decades After Clashing with the Klan, a Thriving Vietnamese Community in Texas," *Weekend Edition Sunday*, NPR, November 25, 2018, https://www.npr.org/2018/11/25/669857481/decades-after-clashing-with-the-klan-a-thriving-vietnamese-community-in-texas.

33. Thayer, *Who Killed Heng Lim?*, 21.

34. Thayer, *Who Killed Heng Lim?*, 25.

35. Thayer, *Who Killed Heng Lim?*, 25–26.

36. Jeff Gammage, "In Philly, Anti-Asian Hate Is Not New," *Philadelphia Inquirer*, May 13, 2021, https://www.inquirer.com/news/a/asian-american-hate-crimes-philadelphia-violence-20210513.html.

37. Frances Kai-Hwa Wang, "Who Is Vincent Chin? The History and Relevance of a 1982 Killing," NBC News, June 15, 2017, https://www.nbcnews.com/news/asian-america/who-vincent-chin-history-relevance-1982-killing-n771291.

38. "M.I.A. = Murdered in America," *CAAAV Voice* 5, no. 1 (Spring 1993): 1, 6, https://caaav.org/wp-content/uploads/2015/01/Voice_Spring_1993.pdf.

39. "New Way Forward Act Would Offer Relief to Many Southeast Asian Refugees Facing a 'Life Sentence' of Deportation," SEARAC (Southeast Asia Resource Action Center), January 27, 2021, https://www.searac.org/immigration/new-way-forward-act-would-offer-relief-to-many-southeast-asian-refugees-facing-a-life-sentence-of-deportation.

40. Jeff Gammage, "Deporting Asian Refugees, Activists Say, Is Anti-Asian Violence—and Removals Are Up," *Philadelphia Inquirer*, March 27, 2021, https://www.inquirer.com/news/immigration-immigrant-southeast-asia-asian-violence-cambodia-vietnam-laos-deportation-detention-20210327.html.

41. Sanjoy Mazumdar et al., "Creating a Sense of Place: The Vietnamese-Americans and Little Saigon," *Journal of Environmental Psychology* 20, no. 4 (2000): 319–33.

42. Beth Nguyen, "Preserving Vietnamese Tradition in Silicon Valley," MOFAD (Museum of Food and Drink) and *Eater*, 2016, https://www.eater.com/a/mofad-city-guides/san-jose-vietnamese-history.

43. "Our History," Lee's Sandwiches, 2021, https://leesandwiches.com/about-us.

44. "Our History," Phở Hòa, https://phohoa.com, accessed June 13, 2021.

45. Karen J. Leong et al., "Resilient History and the Rebuilding of a Community: The Vietnamese American Community in New Orleans East," *Journal of American History* 94, no. 3 (December 2007): 770–79.

46. *The Donut King*.

47. Nikki Tundel, "Preserving a Tradition That Prepares Hmong Souls for Eternity," MPR News, May 6, 2013, https://www.mprnews.org/story/2013/05/06/preserving-a-tradition-that-prepares-hmong-souls-for-eternity.

48. Cynthia Schuster, "Wisconsin Hmong-Americans Look to Preserve Cultural Heritage in New Generations," Wisconsin Public Radio, June 26, 2014, https://www.wpr.org/wisconsin-hmong-americans-look-preserve-cultural-heritage-new-generations.

49. "Education," Angkor Dance Troupe, 2021, https://www.angkordance.org.

50. Instagram post, Lao Student Association, Fresno State University, May 15, 2021, https://www.instagram.com/p/CO6n8jfA9Ve.

51. "Herstory," HAWA (Hmong American Women's Association), 2021, https://www.hawamke.org/herstory.

52. "The State of Laotian Americans," LANA (Laotian American National Alliance), 2021, https://lanausa.org/about-laotian-americans.

53. "Outreach," Laotian American Society, https://www.lasga.org/outreach.

54. Rady Mom as told to Ted Siefer, "Cambodian-American Rady Mom's House Win Makes History," *Boston Globe*, November 13, 2014, https://www.bostonglobe.com/magazine/2014/11/05/cambodian-american-rady-mom-house-win-makes-history/5eGOk46Dno9HtlV410Vg8K/story.html.

55. "Overview," Legacies of War, 2021, http://legaciesofwar.org/about/overview.

56. Tina Maharath, "Tina Maharath for Ohio State Senate 2018," *Lao American Magazine*, September 1, 2017, http://www.laoamericanmagazine.com/2017/09/tina-maharath-for-ohio-state-senate-2018.

57. Felicia R. Lee, "A New Literature with Asian Roots," *New York Times*, February 22, 2003, https://www.nytimes.com/2003/02/22/books/a-new-literature-with-asian-roots.html.

58. "About Us," *Little Laos on the Prairie*, 2021, https://littlelaosontheprairie.org/the-bloggers.

59. "About Us," *Little Laos on the Prairie*.

60. Monica Sok, "The Cambodian American Writers Who Are Reimagining Cambodian Literature: 5 Writers Discuss Subverting Conventions and Writing Against the Trauma Narrative," *Electric Lit*, June 11, 2019, https://electricliterature.com/there-is-more-than-one-way-to-be-cambodian.

61. Andru Defeye, "Poetry Is Changing the World. And Two Sacramento Youth Poets Are Leading the Renaissance," *Sacramento Bee*, March 2, 2021, https://www.sacbee.com/news/local/sacramento-tipping-point/community-voices/article249513370.html.

62. "Refugee Act of 1980," National Archives Foundation, 2021, https://www.archivesfoundation.org/documents/refugee-act-1980.

63. David A. Martin, "The Refugee Act of 1980: A Forlorn Anniversary," *Lawfare*, March 19, 2020, https://www.lawfareblog.com/refugee-act-1980-forlorn-anniversary.

64. "Statement by President Joe Biden on Refugee Admissions," White House, May 3, 2021, https://www.whitehouse.gov/briefing-room/statements-releases/2021/05/03/statement-by-president-joe-biden-on-refugee-admissions.

65. Vang and Trieu, *Invisible Newcomers*, 7.

66. Taylor Tedford, Kimberly Kindy, and Jacob Bogage, "Trump Orders Meat Plants to Stay Open in Pandemic," *Washington Post*, April 29, 2020, https://www .washingtonpost.com/business/2020/04/28/trump-meat-plants-dpa.

67. Kate Payne, "Iowa's Burmese Community Devastated by COVID-19," *Weekend Edition Sunday*, NPR, June 21, 2020, https://www.npr.org/2020/06/21 /881173373/iowas-burmese-community-devastated-by-covid-19.

CHAPTER THREE: 1968: WHAT'S IN THE NAME "ASIAN AMERICAN"?

1. Anna Purna Kambhampaty, "In 1968, These Activists Coined the Term 'Asian American'—and Helped Shape Decades of Advocacy," *Time*, May 22, 2020, https://time.com/5837805/asian-american-history.

2. "The Third World Liberation Front and the History of Ethnic Studies and African American Studies," University of California, Berkeley Library, August 4, 2021, https://guides.lib.berkeley.edu/twlf/oralhistories.

3. Edward W. Said, *Orientalism* (New York: Pantheon, 1978).

4. See Eiichiro Azuma, *Between Two Empires: Race, History, and Transnationalism in Japanese America* (New York: Oxford University Press, 2005); and Yen Le Espiritu, *Asian American Panethnicity: Bridging Institutions and Identities* (Philadelphia: Temple University Press, 1992).

5. Yuji Ichioka, *The Issei: The World of the First Generation Japanese Immigrants, 1885–1924* (New York: Free Press, 1988), 219.

6. Espiritu, *Asian American Panethnicity*, 26.

7. Ryan Masaaki Yokota, "Interview with Pat Sumi," in *Asian Americans: The Movement and the Moment*, ed. Steve Louie and Glenn K. Omatsu (Los Angeles: UCLA Asian American Studies Center Press, 2001), 17–31. See also Judy Tzu-Chun Wu, *Radicals on the Road: Internationalism, Orientalism, and Feminism During the Vietnam Era* (Ithaca, NY: Cornell University Press, 2013).

8. "Activist Amy Uyematsu Proclaims the Emergence of 'Yellow Power,' 1969," in *Major Problems in Asian American History: Documents and Essays*, ed. Lon Kurashige and Alice Yang Murray (Boston: Houghton Mifflin, 2003), 421, used with permission from Amy Uyematsu, "The Emergence of Yellow Power in America," *Gidra*, October 1969, from *Roots: An Asian American Reader*.

9. Esther Wang, "The Counterculturalists: Alex Hing," *The Margins*, October 9, 2014, https://aaww.org/counterculturalist-alex-hing.

10. Philippine-American Collegiate Endeavor (PACE), "Statement of the Philippine-American Collegiate Endeavor (PACE) Philosophy and Goals," Asian American Movement 1968, January 16, 2008, http://aam1968.blogspot.com/2008 /01/philippine-american-collegiate-endeavor.html.

11. Daryl J. Maeda, *Chains of Babylon: The Rise of Asian America* (Minneapolis: University of Minnesota Press, 2009), 104.

12. Catherine Ceniza Choy, "Towards Trans-Pacific Social Justice: Women and Protest in Filipino American History," *Journal of Asian American Studies* 8, no. 3 (Fall 2005): 293–307.

13. Augusto Espiritu, foreword to *A Time to Rise: Collective Memoirs of the Union of Democratic Filipinos (KDP)*, ed. Rene Ciria Cruz, Cindy Domingo, and Bruce Occena (Seattle: University of Washington Press, 2017), xiv.

14. See Maeda, *Chains of Babylon*; *Who Killed Vincent Chin?*, dir. Christine Choy and Renee Tajima-Peña (New York: Filmakers Library, 1990); Yasuko I. Takezawa, *Breaking the Silence: Redress and Japanese American Ethnicity* (Ithaca, NY: Cornell University Press, 1995); and Estella Habal, *San Francisco's International Hotel: Mobilizing the Filipino American Community in the Anti-Eviction Movement* (Philadelphia: Temple University Press, 2007).

15. Kevin L. Nadal, "The Brown Asian American Movement: Advocating for South Asian, Southeast Asian, and Filipino American Communities," *Asian American Policy Review* 29 (Spring 2019): 2–11.

16. "A Skit on Sexism Within the Asian American Movement, 1971," in *Major Problems in Asian American History*, ed. Lon Kurashige and Alice Yang Murray, p. 425, from Miya Iwataki, "The Asian Women's Movement—A Retrospective," *East Wind* 2, no. 1 (Spring/Summer 1983): 37.

17. Daniel C. Tsang, "Slicing Silence: Asian Progressives Come Out," in Louie and Omatsu, *Asian Americans*, 220–39.

18. "Interview with Jeff Leong, 2018," Asian American Political Alliance Oral History Project, 2018, p. 6, UC Berkeley, Ethnic Studies Library, https://calisphere.org/item/2c92e2bf-0034-41a6-ab53-69a961ad4c95.

19. "Interview with Steve Wong, 2018," Asian American Political Alliance Oral History Project, 2018, p. 1, UC Berkeley, Ethnic Studies Library, https://calisphere.org/item/290ff150-769c-49a1-a911-70d5ddfc09fa.

20. Abe Ignacio, Enrique de la Cruz, Jorge Emmanuel, and Helen Toribio, *The Forbidden Book: The Philippine-American War in Political Cartoons* (San Francisco: T'boli Publishing, 2004), 3.

21. Paolo Chua, "The 15 Best Jose Rizal Quotes," *Esquire Philippines*, December 27, 2019, https://www.esquiremag.ph/culture/lifestyle/best-jose-rizal-quotes-a00297-20191227-lfrm2.

22. Meredith Eliassen, "On Display: The 1968 San Francisco State Student Strike," *Process: A Blog for American History*, December 18, 2018, http://www.processhistory.org/eliassen-1968.

23. Maeda, *Chains of Babylon*, 50.

24. "Success Story of One Minority Group in U.S.," *U.S. News and World Report*, December 26, 1966.

25. "People v. Hall (1854)," Immigration History, online resource, Immigration and Ethnic History Society, https://immigrationhistory.org/item/people-v-hall.

26. Frederick Douglass, "Our Composite Nationality," December 7, 1869, Teaching American History, https://teachingamericanhistory.org/library/document/our-composite-nationality.

27. Michael Morey, "The 19th-Century African American Soldier Who Fought for Filipino Liberation," Zócalo Public Square, April 16, 2019, https://www.zocalopublicsquare.org/2019/04/16/19th-century-african-american-solider-fought-filipino-liberation/ideas/essay.

28. Igancio et al., *The Forbidden Book*, 82.

29. Barbara M. Posadas, "The Hierarchy of Color and Psychological Adjustment in an Industrial Environment: Filipinos, the Pullman Company, and the Brotherhood of Sleeping Car Porters," *Labor History* 22, no. 3 (Summer 1982): 349–73.

30. Posadas, "The Hierarchy of Color and Psychological Adjustment in an Industrial Environment," 363.

31. Don Villar, "Remembering Chicago Asian American Activist Cipriano Samonte," Chicago Federation of Labor, https://chicagolabor.org/cfl/chicago-asian -american-activist-cipriano-samonte.

32. "Visitors in the Pomona Assembly Center—Takashi Hoshizaki," YouTube video, posted by Densho, February 9, 2016, https://www.youtube.com/watch?v =aMvhKDb3g7Y.

33. "Life of Kiyoshi Kuromiya: From Selma Marcher to AIDS Activist," NBC News, March 7, 2015, https://www.nbcnews.com/storyline/selma-50th-anniversary /selma-marcher-aids-activist-life-steven-kuromiya-n318876.

34. Tsang, "Slicing Silence," 222.

35. DeNeen L. Brown, "Thurgood Marshall's Interracial Love: 'I Don't Care What People Think. I'm Marrying You,'" *Washington Post*, August 18, 2016, https://www.washingtonpost.com/local/thurgood-marshalls-interracial-love-i-dont -care-what-people-think-im-marrying-you/2016/08/18/84f636be-54d5-11e6-bbf5 -957ad17b4385_story.html.

36. "Interviewee: Cecilia Suyat Marshall," June 29, 2013, Falls Church, Virginia, Interviewer: Emilye Crosby, Videographer: John Bishop, Civil Rights History Project Interview completed by the Southern Oral History Program under contract to the Smithsonian Institution's National Museum of African American History and Culture and the Library of Congress, 2013, p. 13, https://tile.loc.gov/storage-services /service/afc/afc2010039/afc2010039_crhp0097_Marshall_transcript/afc2010039 _crhp0097_Marshall_transcript.pdf.

37. "Interviewee: Cecilia Suyat Marshall," 5.

38. Robert D. McFadden, "Grace Lee Boggs, Human Rights Advocate for 7 Decades, Dies at 100," *New York Times*, October 5, 2015, https://www.nytimes .com/2015/10/06/us/grace-lee-boggs-detroit-activist-dies-at-100.html.

39. Michelle Chen, "Grace Lee Boggs: Small Rebellions," *Guernica*, July 15, 2014, https://www.guernicamag.com/small-rebellions.

40. "Yuri Kochiyama," *Densho Encyclopedia*, June 3, 2014, https://encyclopedia .densho.org/Yuri_Kochiyama.

41. William Yardley, "Yuri Kochiyama, Rights Activist Who Befriended Malcolm X, Dies at 93," *New York Times*, June 4, 2014, https://www.nytimes.com/2014 /06/05/us/yuri-kochiyama-civil-rights-activist-dies-at-93.html.

42. "Yuri Kochiyama"; Y. Vue, "The Unerasing of Asian American Civil Rights History," *Medium*, August 30, 2020, https://yiavue.medium.com/the-unerasing-of -asian-american-civil-rights-history-3c13d4a33848.

43. "STAATUS Index Report 2021," LAAUNCH, pp. 30–31, https://uploads-ssl .webflow.com/5f629e7e013d961943d5cec9/6098a7be3d627168e03054da_staatus -index-2021.pdf.

44. Melissa Borja and Jacob Gibson, "Anti-Asian Racism in 2020," Virulent Hate Reports, 14–16, https://virulenthate.org/wp-content/uploads/2021/05/Virulent -Hate-Anti-Asian-Racism-In-2020-5.17.21.pdf.

45. Kimmy Yam, "Viral Images Show People of Color as Anti-Asian Perpetrators. That Misses the Big Picture," NBC News, June 15, 2021, https://www.nbcnews

.com/news/asian-america/viral-images-show-people-color-anti-asian-perpetrators-misses-big-n1270821.

46. Edward Taehan Chang, "Confronting *Sa-i-gu*: Twenty Years After the Los Angeles Riots," *American Studies* 35, no. 2 (2012): 1, http://dx.doi.org/10.18078/amstin.2012.35.2.001, retrieved from https://escholarship.org/uc/item/17h713dj.

47. Rev. Samuel Rodriguez, Rev. Mark Whitlock, and Rev. Hyepin Im, "Editorial: Faith Leaders Reflections on Race, 25 Years after the LA Riots," NBC News, April 19, 2017, https://www.nbcnews.com/news/nbcblk/editorial-faith-leaders-reflections-race-25-years-after-la-riots-n752636.

48. "About," Letters for Black Lives, *Medium*, July 11, 2016, https://lettersforblacklives.com/about-the-letter-ed27ea67eb2e.

49. Sathvik Nair, "Letters for Black Lives: South Asian American Version," Letters for Black Lives, Medium, August 2, 2016, https://lettersforblacklives.com/letters-for-black-lives-south-asian-american-version-f5d8ec9a46ac.

50. KPIX CBS Bay Area, "Bay Area Rappers Unite to Condemn Rise in Attacks Against Asian-American Seniors," February 10, 2021, https://www.youtube.com/watch?v=DqvUZr4htyo.

51. KPIX CBS Bay Area, "Bay Area Rappers Unite to Condemn Rise in Attacks Against Asian-American Seniors."

52. Agnes Constante, "After 50 Years, Asian American Studies Programs Can Still Be Hard to Find," NBC News, June 27, 2019, https://www.nbcnews.com/news/asian-america/after-50-years-asian-american-studies-programs-can-still-be-n1022331.

53. Madeline Holcombe, "Most US Schools Teach Little to Nothing About Asian American History and It Hurts Everyone, Experts Say," CNN, May 31, 2021, https://www.cnn.com/2021/05/31/us/asian-american-pacific-islander-history-schools/index.html.

54. "Full Text of HB0376," Illinois General Assembly, https://www.ilga.gov/legislation/fulltext.asp?DocName=&SessionId=110&GA=102&DocTypeId=HB&DocNum=0376&GAID=16&LegID=128327&SpecSess=&Session=.

55. Kate Taylor and Amelia Nierenberg, "The Fight to Teach Asian American History," *New York Times*, June 2, 2021, https://www.nytimes.com/2021/06/02/us/asian-american-history.html; and Susan Dunne, "Senators Push to Mandate Asian American Studies in Connecticut Public Schools amid Surge of Racist Attacks," *Hartford Courant*, February 26, 2021, https://www.courant.com/coronavirus/hc-news-coronavirus-connecticut-anti-asian-racism-20210225-7skl3dxpvna4phd3jebtcyb53e-story.html.

CHAPTER FOUR: 1965: THE MANY FACES OF POST-1965 ASIAN AMERICA

1. "My Name Is Krishna Chandrasekhar," interviewed by Kamala Gururaja, First Days Project, SAADA (South Asian American Digital Archive), https://firstdays.saada.org/story/krishna-chandrasekhar.

2. "My Name Is Lakshmi Kalapatapu," interviewed by Jaisal Kalapatapu, First Days Project, SAADA (South Asian American Digital Archive), https://firstdays.saada.org/story/lakshmi-kalapatapu.

3. "My Name Is Lakshmi Kalapatapu."

4. "My Name Is Lakshmi Kalapatapu."

5. Bill Ong Hing, *Making and Remaking Asian America Through Immigration Policy, 1850–1990* (Stanford, CA: Stanford University Press, 1993), 38–41, 198–200.

6. Rebekah Barber, "How the Civil Rights Movement Opened the Door to Immigrants of Color," *Facing South*, February 3, 2017, https://www.facingsouth.org /2017/02/how-civil-rights-movement-opened-door-immigrants-color.

7. Rose Cuison Villazor, "The Immigration Act of 1965 and the Creation of a Modern, Diverse America," *HuffPost*, October 28, 2015, https://www.huffpost .com/entry/the-immigration-act-of-19_b_8394570; and Tom Gjelten, "In 1965, A Conservative Tried to Keep America White. His Plan Backfired," *Weekend Edition Saturday*, NPR, October 3, 2015, https://www.npr.org/2015/10/03/445339838/the -unintended-consequences-of-the-1965-immigration-act.

8. Muzaffar Chishti, Faye Hipsman, and Isabel Ball, "Fifty Years On, the 1965 Immigration and Nationality Act Continues to Reshape the United States," *Migration Information Source*, October 15, 2015, https://www.migrationpolicy.org/article /fifty-years-1965-immigration-and-nationality-act-continues-reshape-united-states.

9. Abby Budiman and Neil G. Ruiz, "Key Facts About Asian Origin Groups in the U.S.," Pew Research Center, April 29, 2021, https://www.pewresearch.org/fact -tank/2021/04/29/key-facts-about-asian-origin-groups-in-the-u-s.

10. Budiman and Ruiz, "Key Facts About Asian Origin Groups in the U.S."

11. Karthick Ramakrishnan, "How 1965 Changed Asian America, in 2 Graphs," *Data Bits*, AAPI Data, September 28, 2015, http://aapidata.com/blog/1965 -two-graphs.

12. Budiman and Ruiz, "Key Facts about Asian Origin Groups in the U.S."

13. Abby Budiman, "Nepalese in the U.S. Fact Sheet," Pew Research Center, April 29, 2021, https://www.pewresearch.org/social-trends/fact-sheet/asian-americans -nepalese-in-the-u-s.

14. "My Name Is Tariq Akmal," interviewed by Sindya N. Bhanoo, First Days Project, SAADA (South Asian American Digital Archive), https://firstdays.saada.org /story/tariq-akmal.

15. "My Name Is Tariq Akmal."

16. "My Name Is Tariq Akmal."

17. "This Is the Story of My First Day," interviewed by Anjli Shah, First Days Project, SAADA (South Asian American Digital Archive), https://firstdays.saada.org /story/980. The story's contributor asked that their name be withheld.

18. "My Name Is Viji Raman," interview by Eshaan Mani, First Days Project, SAADA (South Asian American Digital Archive), https://firstdays.saada.org/story /viji-raman.

19. "Women We Admire: Viji Raman," Daya, March 8, 2021, https://www.daya houston.org/post/women-we-admire-viji-raman.

20. Catherine Ceniza Choy, *Empire of Care: Nursing and Migration in Filipino American History* (Durham, NC: Duke University Press, 2003).

21. Jennifer Nazareno, "Welfare State Replacements: Deinstitutionalization, Privatization and the Outsourcing to Immigrant Women Enterprise," *International Journal of Health Services* 48, no. 2 (April 2018): 260.

22. Rakesh Kochhar and Anthony Cilluffo, "Income Inequality in the U.S. Is Rising Most Rapidly Among Asians," Pew Research Center, July 12, 2018, https://

www.pewresearch.org/social-trends/2018/07/12/income-inequality-in-the-u-s-is
-rising-most-rapidly-among-asians.

23. Karthick Ramakrishnan and Sono Shah, "One Out of Every 7 Asian Immigrants Is Undocumented," *Data Bits*, AAPI Data, September 8, 2017, http://aapidata.com/blog/asian-undoc-1in7.

24. Vanessa Williams, "'You Feel Invisible': How America's Fastest-Growing Immigrant Group Is Being Left Out of the DACA conversation," *Washington Post*, September 8, 2017, https://www.washingtonpost.com/news/post-nation/wp/2017/09/08/an-asian-daca-recipient-reminds-us-that-not-all-immigrant-families-are-from-south-of-the-u-s-border.

25. Preeti Sharma, Saba Waheed, Vina Nguyen, Lina Stepick, Reyna Orellana, Liana Katz, Sabrina Kim, and Katrina Lapira, *Nail File: A Study of Nail Salon Workers and Industry in the United States*, UCLA Labor Center and California Healthy Nail Salon Collaborative, 2018, p. 4.

26. Sharma et al., *Nail File*, 14.

27. Sharma et al., *Nail File*, 15.

28. Sharma et al., *Nail File*, 40.

29. Andy Kiersz, "Asian Americans Still Aren't Reaching the C-Suite—and It All Comes Down to Promotions. These 4 Charts Put the Problem in Perspective," *Insider*, May 26, 2021, https://www.businessinsider.com/asian-american-ceos-rare-lack-of-promotions-2021-5. See also Buck Gee and Denise Peck, "The Illusion of Asian Success: Scant Progress for Minorities in Cracking the Glass Ceiling from 2007–2015," Ascend: Pan Asian Leaders, November 2018, https://www.ascendleadershipfoundation.org/research/the-illusion-of-asian-success. Gee and Peck created the Executive Parity Index (EPI), defined as a ratio of the percentage representation of a company's executive workforce relative to that company's percentage representation of its entry-level professional workforce, as a key analytical tool. They also introduced a Management Parity Index (MPI), a tool similar to the EPI, to compare the mid-level management representation against the professional representation for an assessment of the lower-level management pipeline flows.

30. Jennifer Liu, "How the Model Minority Myth Holds Asian Americans Back at Work—and What Companies Should Do," CNBC, May 3, 2021, https://www.cnbc.com/2021/05/03/how-the-model-minority-myth-holds-asian-americans-back-at-work.html.

31. Michel Marriott, "In Jersey City, Indians Protest Violence," *New York Times*, October 12, 1987, https://www.nytimes.com/1987/10/12/nyregion/in-jersey-city-indians-protest-violence.html.

32. Janice Lobo Sapigao, *microchips for millions* (San Francisco: Philippine American Writers and Artists, 2016).

33. Sapigao, *microchips for millions*, 17.

34. Sapigao, *microchips for millions*, 43.

35. Budiman and Ruiz, "Key Facts About Asian Origin Groups in the U.S."

36. Nancy Wang Yuen, Dr. Stacy L. Smith, Dr. Katherine Pieper, Marc Choueiti, Kevin Yao, and Dana Dinh, *The Prevalence and Portrayal of Asian and Pacific Islanders across 1,300 Popular Films*, USC Annenberg Inclusion Initiative, May 2021, p. 10, https://assets.uscannenberg.org/docs/aii_aapi-representation-across-films-2021-05-18.pdf.

37. Jayanth Kumar, "Did You Know California Has a Dental Czar?," Zócalo Public Square, September 30, 2019, https://www.zocalopublicsquare.org/2019/09/30/did-you-know-california-has-a-dental-czar/ideas/essay/.

38. Ka-Kit Hui, "Defining Health as a 'State of Complete Physical, Mental, and Social Well-Being,'" Zócalo Public Square, September 30, 2019, https://www.zocalopublicsquare.org/2019/09/30/defining-health-as-a-state-of-complete-physical-mental-and-social-well-being/ideas/essay.

39. Hui, "Defining Health."

40. Erika Lee, *America for Americans: A History of Xenophobia in the United States* (New York: Basic Books, 2019).

41. Catherine Ceniza Choy, "When the Reporter Asks You Why There Are So Many Filipino Nurses in the U.S.," *The Margins*, May 17, 2021, https://aaww.org/when-the-reporter-asks-catherine-ceniza-choy.

42. Richard Gonzales, "America No Longer a 'Nation of Immigrants,' USCIS Says," *The Two-Way*, NPR, February 22, 2018, https://www.npr.org/sections/thetwo-way/2018/02/22/588097749/america-no-longer-a-nation-of-immigrants-uscis-says.

INTERLUDE: 1965 REPRISE: THE FACES BEHIND THE FOOD

1. *The Delano Manongs: Forgotten Heroes of the United Farm Workers*, dir. Marissa Aroy (New York: Media Factory, 2014).

2. Sasha Khokha, "Leaving a Legacy: Dawn Bohulano Mabalon, Filipino-American Champion and Historian," *The California Report*, KQED, August 17, 2018, https://www.kqed.org/news/11687433/leaving-a-legacy-dawn-bohulano-mabalon-filipino-american-champion-and-historian.

3. Ronald Takaki, *Strangers from a Different Shore: A History of Asian Americans*, updated and rev. ed. (New York: Little, Brown, 1998), 132–35.

4. Milton Murayama, *All I Asking for Is My Body* (San Francisco: Supa Press, 1975).

5. George Chu, "Chinatowns in the Delta: The Chinese in the Sacramento-San Joaquin Delta, 1870–1960," *California Historical Society Quarterly* 49, no. 1 (March 1970): 24.

6. "Ah Bing," Museum of Chinese in America (MOCA), 2021, https://www.mocanyc.org/collections/stories/ah-bing.

7. David R. Shipman, "The Citrus Wizard of Florida," US Department of Agriculture, February 21, 2017, https://www.usda.gov/media/blog/2012/05/16/citrus-wizard-florida.

8. Chris Friday, *Organizing Asian American Labor: The Pacific Coast Canned-Salmon Industry, 1870–1942* (Philadelphia: Temple University Press, 1994), 2.

9. Valerie J. Matsumoto, *Farming the Home Place: A Japanese American Community in California, 1919–1982* (Ithaca, NY: Cornell University Press, 1993), 22.

10. Takaki, *Strangers from a Different Shore*, 189.

11. Chrissy Lee Yau, "'Ashamed of Certain Japanese': The Politics of Affect in Japanese Women's Immigration Exclusion, 1919–1924," in *Gendering the Trans-Pacific World*, ed. Catherine Ceniza Choy and Judy Tzu-Chun Wu (Leiden, Netherlands: Brill, 2017), 213.

12. Matsumoto, *Farming the Home Place*, 17.

13. Suzanne McMahon, curator, "Chapter 3: From Laborers to Landowners," in "Echoes of Freedom: South Asian Pioneers in California, 1899–1965," University of California, Berkeley Library, July 6, 2020, https://guides.lib.berkeley.edu/echoes -of-freedom/laborers-to-landowners.

14. Heather R. Lee, "A Life Cooking for Others: The Work and Migration Experiences of a Chinese Restaurant Worker in New York City, 1920–1946," in *Eating Asian America: A Food Studies Reader*, ed. Robert Ji-Song Ku, Martin F. Manalansan IV, and Anita Mannur (New York: New York University Press, 2013), 53–77.

15. Christine R. Yano (with Wanda Adams), "Tasting America: The Politics and Pleasures of School Lunch in Hawai'i," in *Eating Asian America*, 41.

16. Carlos Bulosan, *America Is in the Heart* (Seattle: University of Washington Press, 1946), 136.

17. "SAUND, Dalip Singh (Judge)," U.S. House of Representatives, History, Art & Archives, https://history.house.gov/People/Detail/21228.

18. Mark Padoongpatt, *Flavors of Empire: Food and the Making of Thai America* (Oakland: University of California Press, 2017).

19. Dawn Bohulano Mabalon, *Little Manila Is in the Heart: The Making of the Filipina/o American Community in Stockton, California* (Durham, NC: Duke University Press, 2013), 88, 98–99, 254–58.

20. Arleen de Vera, "Without Parallel: The Local 7 Deportation Cases, 1949–1955," *Amerasia Journal* 20, no. 2 (1994): 1–25.

21. Carly Stern, "The 'DoorDash' for Leftover Food Takes Flight amid New York Lockdown," *OZY*, April 7, 2020, https://www.ozy.com/the-new-and-the-next /the-doordash-for-leftover-food-takes-flight-amid-new-york-lockdown/288490.

22. "Our Story," Heart of Dinner, https://www.heartofdinner.org/our-story.

23. Jaweed Kaleem, "Where Are Asian American Communities Growing the Fastest? Not California," *Los Angeles Times*, April 29, 2021, https://www.latimes .com/world-nation/story/2021-04-29/asian-americans-north-dakota.

CHAPTER FIVE: 1953: MIXED RACE LIVES

1. Catherine Ceniza Choy, *Global Families: A History of Asian International Adoption in America* (New York: New York University Press, 2013), 15–45.

2. Maggie Jones, "Why a Generation of Adoptees Is Returning to South Korea," *New York Times Magazine*, January 14, 2015, https://www.nytimes.com/2015/01/18 /magazine/why-a-generation-of-adoptees-is-returning-to-south-korea.html.

3. Bettijane Levine, "For Orphans of the Forgotten War, the Past Is Shrouded with Questions," *Los Angeles Times*, June 21, 2000.

4. "A White American Woman Compares Marriage to Chinese and Japanese Husbands, circa 1924," in *Major Problems in Asian American History: Documents and Essays*, ed. Lon Kurashige and Alice Yang Murray (Boston: Houghton Mifflin, 2003), 219. The document is from Fisk University, Social Science Institute, *Orientals and Their Cultural Adjustment: Interviews, Life Histories and Social Adjustment Experiences of Chinese and Japanese of Varying Backgrounds and Length of Residence in the United States* (Nashville: Social Science Institute, Fisk University, 1946), 42–50, 72–73.

5. "A White American Woman Compares Marriage."

6. "A White American Woman Compares Marriage," 220.

7. Velina Hasu Houston, "Rising Sun, Rising Soul: On Mixed Race Asian Identity That Includes Blackness," in *Red and Yellow, Black and Brown: Decentering Whiteness in Mixed Race Studies*, ed. Joanne L. Rondilla, Rudy P. Guevarra, and Paul Spickard (New Brunswick, NJ: Rutgers University Press, 2017), 21.

8. Choy, *Global Families*, 18–19.

9. Choy, *Global Families*, 18–19. See also Catherine Ceniza Choy, "Race at the Center: The History of American Cold War Asian Adoption," *Journal of American-East Asian Relations* 16, no. 3 (2009): 1–20; and Susie Woo, *Framed by War: Korean Children and Women at the Crossroads of Empire* (New York: New York University Press, 2019).

10. Richard H. Weil, "International Adoptions: The Quiet Migration," *International Migration Review* 18, no. 2 (Summer 1984): 276–93; and Kirsten Lovelock, "Intercountry Adoption as a Migratory Practice: A Comparative Analysis of Intercountry Adoption and Immigration Policy and Practice in the United States, Canada, and New Zealand in the Post WWII Period," *International Migration Review* 34, no. 3 (Fall 2000): 907–49.

11. Yukiko Koshiro, *Trans-Pacific Racisms and the U.S. Occupation of Japan* (New York: Columbia University Press, 1999), 183–84.

12. Gladys Nubla, "The Sexualized Child and Mestizaje: Colonial Tropes of the Filipina/o," in *Gendering the Trans-Pacific World*, ed. Catherine Ceniza Choy and Judy Tzu-Chun Wu (Leiden, Netherlands: Brill, 2017), 165–95.

13. Evangeline Canonizado Buell, *Twenty-Five Chickens and a Pig for a Bride: Growing Up in a Filipino Immigrant Family* (San Francisco: T'Boli, 2006), 18.

14. Choy, *Global Families*, 27.

15. Choy, *Global Families*, 27–28.

16. Choy, *Global Families*, 30–35.

17. Choy, *Global Families*, 22.

18. Choy, *Global Families*, 39.

19. Allison Varzally, *Children of Reunion: Vietnamese Adoptions and the Politics of Family Migrations* (Chapel Hill: University of North Carolina Press, 2017).

20. John Kuo Wei Tchen, *New York Before Chinatown: Orientalism and the Shaping of American Culture, 1776–1882* (Baltimore: Johns Hopkins University Press, 1999).

21. Tchen, *New York Before Chinatown*, 76.

22. Tchen, *New York Before Chinatown*, 77.

23. Tchen, *New York Before Chinatown*, 85.

24. Tchen, *New York Before Chinatown*, 86.

25. Vivek Bald, *Bengali Harlem and the Lost Histories of South Asian America* (Cambridge, MA: Harvard University Press, 2015).

26. Bald, *Bengali Harlem and the Lost Histories of South Asian America*, 203–4.

27. Bald, *Bengali Harlem and the Lost Histories of South Asian America*, 7.

28. "Researcher Traces Early Nineteenth-Century Origins of Filipino American Family, 1988," in *Major Problems in Asian American History*, ed. Lon Kurashige and Alice Yang Murray, 46–47. The document is from Marina E. Espina, *Filipinos in Louisiana* (New Orleans: A. F. Laborde, 1988), 58–59, 61, 63, 65.

29. "Researcher Traces Early Nineteenth-Century Origins," 47.

30. Rachel Moran, *Interracial Intimacy: The Regulation of Race and Romance* (Chicago: University of Chicago Press, 2001), 17.

31. See Peggy Pascoe, *What Comes Naturally: Miscegenation Law and the Making of Race in America* (New York: Oxford University Press, 2009).

32. "A White American Woman Compares Marriage," 222.

33. "A White American Woman Compares Marriage," 222.

34. Barbara M. Posadas, "Hmm, You Don't Look Polish!," *Polish American Studies* 74, no. 2 (Autumn 2017): 38.

35. Posadas, "Hmm, You Don't Look Polish!," 40.

36. Posadas, "Hmm, You Don't Look Polish!"

37. Allison Varzally, "Romantic Crossings: Making Love, Family, and Non-Whiteness in California, 1925–1950," *Journal of American Ethnic History* 23, no. 1 (Fall 2003): 4.

38. Karen Isaksen Leonard, *Making Ethnic Choices: California's Punjabi Mexican American Community* (Philadelphia: Temple University Press, 1992), 62.

39. Leonard, *Making Ethnic Choices*, 68.

40. Leonard, *Making Ethnic Choices*, 123.

41. Leonard, *Making Ethnic Choices*.

42. Leonard, *Making Ethnic Choices*, 66.

43. Leonard, *Making Ethnic Choices*, 126.

44. Leonard, *Making Ethnic Choices*, 123.

45. Rudy P. Guevarra Jr., *Becoming Mexipino: Multiethnic Identities and Communities in San Diego* (New Brunswick, NJ: Rutgers University Press, 2012).

46. Guevarra, *Becoming Mexipino*, 27.

47. Guevarra, *Becoming Mexipino*, 151.

48. Guevarra, *Becoming Mexipino*, 154.

49. Guevarra, *Becoming Mexipino*, 156.

50. Guevarra, *Becoming Mexipino*, 161.

51. Sabrina Tavernise, Tariro Mzezewa, and Giulia Heyward, "Behind the Surprising Jump in Multiracial Americans, Several Theories," *New York Times*, August 13, 2021, https://www.nytimes.com/2021/08/12/us/us-census-population-growth-diversity.html.

52. Kimmy Yam and Dartunorro Clark, "Black, Asian, American: Kamala Harris' Identity, How It Shaped Her and What It Means for Voters," NBC News, August 13, 2020, https://www.nbcnews.com/news/nbcblk/black-asian-american-kamala-harris-identity-how-it-shaped-her-n1236563.

53. Gretchen Livingston, "The Rise of Multiracial and Multiethnic Babies in the U.S.," Pew Research Center, June 6, 2017, https://www.pewresearch.org/fact-tank/2017/06/06/the-rise-of-multiracial-and-multiethnic-babies-in-the-u-s.

54. See Paul R. Spickard, *Mixed Blood: Intermarriage and Ethnic Identity in Twentieth-Century America* (Madison: University of Wisconsin Press, 1989); and Maria P. P. Root, ed., *Racially Mixed People in America* (Newbury Park, CA: Sage Publications, 1992).

55. "Maria P. P. Root, PhD: Clinical Psychologist and Independent Scholar," *American Psychological Association* 37, no. 2 (February 2006), https://www.apa.org/monitor/feb06/root.

56. Maria P. P. Root, "Bill of Rights for People of Mixed Heritage," 1993, https://www.apa.org/pubs/videos/4310742-rights.pdf.

57. See Celeste Katz Marston, "'What Are You?' How Multiracial Americans Respond and How It's Changing," NBC News, February 28, 2021, https://www.nbcnews.com/news/asian-america/what-are-you-how-multiracial-americans-respond-how-it-s-n1255166; and Akemi Johnson, "Who Gets To Be 'Hapa'?," *Code Switch*, NPR, August 8, 2016, https://www.npr.org/sections/codeswitch/2016/08/08/487821049/who-gets-to-be-hapa.

58. *Part Asian, 100% Hapa*, portraits by Kip Fulbeck with foreword by Sean Lennon and afterword by Paul Spickard (San Francisco: Chronicle Books, 2006), 248.

59. *Part Asian, 100% Hapa*, 200.

60. "About This Exhibition: 'Hapa.me: 15 Years of the Hapa Project,'" Japanese American National Museum, April 7–October 28, 2018, https://www.janm.org/exhibits/hapa-me.

61. *Hapa.me: 15 Years of the Hapa Project*, portraits by Kip Fulbeck with essays by Velina Hasu Houston, Cindy Nakashima, Keao Nesmith, and Paul Spickard (Los Angeles: Japanese American National Museum, 2018), 166–67, 96–97.

62. Kip Fulbeck, introduction to *Part Asian, 100% Hapa*, 16.

63. Michelle Ye Hee Lee, "Atlanta Shooting Victim's Biracial Sons Seek to Unite Black, Asian Communities in Shared Fight Against Hate," *Washington Post*, August 8, 2021, https://www.washingtonpost.com/national/atlanta-spa-shootings-yong-ae-yue/2021/08/08/9b8460b0-d1fb-11eb-9f29-e9e6c9e843c6_story.html.

CHAPTER SIX: 1941 AND 1942: THE DAYS THAT YOU REMEMBER

1. Brian Niiya, "Asian Americans and World War II," in *Finding a Path Forward: Asian American Pacific Islander National Historic Landmarks Theme Study*, ed. Franklin Odo (Washington, DC: National Historic Landmarks Program, National Park Service, US Department of the Interior, 2017), 207.

2. I am indebted to Gary Y. Okihiro for this account and several others cited in this chapter from his remarkable essay "An American Story," in *Impounded: Dorothea Lange and the Censored Images of Japanese American Internment*, ed. Linda Gordon and Gary Y. Okihiro (New York: W. W. Norton, 2006), 47–84. The story of Yoshiaki Fukuda appears on pages 54–55.

3. "Following evacuation orders, this store, at 13th and Franklin Streets, was closed. The owner, a University of California graduate of Japanese descent, placed the I AM AN AMERICAN sign on the store front on December 8, the day after Pearl Harbor. Evacuees of Japanese ancestry will be housed in War Relocation Authority centers for the duration. Photographer: Lange, Dorothea. Oakland, California. Date: 1942-03-13," University of California, Berkeley, Bancroft Library, https://oac.cdlib.org/ark:/13030/ft367nb1xv/?brand=oac4.

4. Okihiro, "An American Story," 54.

5. Niiya, "Asian Americans and World War II," 207.

6. Alice Yang Murray, "The Internment of Japanese Americans," in *Major Problems in Asian American History: Documents and Essays*, ed. Lon Kurashige and Alice Yang Murray (Boston: Houghton Mifflin, 2003), 312.

7. "Exclusion Order posted at First and Front Streets directing removal of persons of Japanese ancestry from the first San Francisco section to be affected

by evacuation. Evacuees will be housed in War Relocation Authority centers for the duration. Photographer: Lange, Dorothea. San Francisco, California. Date: 1942-04-11," University of California, Berkeley, Bancroft Library, https://oac.cdlib .org/ark:/13030/ft796nb45t/?brand=oac4.

8. Jeanne Wakatsuki Houston and James D. Houston, *Farewell to Manzanar: A True Story of Japanese American Experience During and After the World War II Internment* (Boston: Houghton Mifflin, 1973), 13.

9. Yoshiko Uchida, *Desert Exile: The Uprooting of a Japanese American Family*, with a new introduction by Traise Yamamoto (Seattle: University of Washington Press, 1982), 61.

10. Uchida, *Desert Exile*, 90.

11. Kelly A. Spring, "Miné Okubo," National Women's History Museum, https://www.womenshistory.org/education-resources/biographies/mine-okubo.

12. Okihiro, "An American Story," 69.

13. Okihiro, "An American Story."

14. Christopher Capozzola, *Bound by War: How the United States and the Philippines Built America's First Pacific Century* (New York: Basic Books, 2020), 168.

15. Mary Paik Lee, *Quiet Odyssey: A Pioneer Korean Woman in America* (Seattle: University of Washington Press, 1990), 94–95.

16. Niiya, "Asian Americans and World War II," 208.

17. Capozzola, *Bound by War*, 166–67.

18. Catherine Clifford, "What 83-Year-Old George Takei Learned About Resilience from His Dad Making Art in Japanese Internment Camp," CNBC, October 16, 2020, https://www.cnbc.com/2020/10/16/what-george-takei-learned-about-resilience -in-japanese-internment-camp.html.

19. "Japanese-American Internment During World War II," National Archives, Educator Resources, July 8, 2021, https://www.archives.gov/education/lessons /japanese-relocation#background.

20. Franklin Odo, "442nd Regimental Combat Team," *Densho Encyclopedia*, October 16, 2020, https://encyclopedia.densho.org/442nd_Regimental_Combat_Team.

21. John Okada, *No-No Boy: A Novel* (Rutland, VT: C. E. Tuttle, 1957). See also John Okada, *No-No Boy* with a new foreword by Ruth Ozeki, introduction by Lawson Fusao Inada, and afterword by Frank Chin (Seattle: University of Washington Press, 2014); and Frank Abe, Greg Robinson, and Floyd Cheung, eds., *John Okada: The Life and Rediscovered Work of the Author of* No-No Boy (Seattle: University of Washington Press, 2018).

22. Stephanie Buck, "Overlooked No More: Mitsuye Endo, a Name Linked to Justice for Japanese-Americans," *New York Times*, October 9, 2019, https://www .nytimes.com/2019/10/09/obituaries/mitsuye-endo-overlooked.html.

23. Mae M. Ngai, *Impossible Subjects: Illegal Aliens and the Making of Modern America* (Princeton, NJ: Princeton University Press, 2004), 175–201.

24. I am indebted to Brian Niiya for this haunting image and the historical information I have included in this paragraph from his astute essay "Asian Americans and World War II," 212.

25. John H. Fong, "Rosie the Riveter, World War II Home Front Oral History Project," conducted by Robin Li in 2011, Regional Oral History Office, Bancroft Library, University of California, Berkeley, 2012, p. 11.

26. Fong, "Rosie the Riveter," 4.

27. "Chinese Americans Picket Scrap Metal to Japan," Oregon History Project, March 17, 2018, https://www.oregonhistoryproject.org/articles/historical-records /chinese-americans-picket-scrap-metal-to-japan/#.YRP-_dNKj-Y.

28. Dorothy Cordova, "Rosie the Riveter WWII American Home Front Oral History Project," conducted by Robin Li in 2012, Regional Oral History Office, Bancroft Library, University of California, Berkeley, 2013, p. 15.

29. Cordova, "Rosie the Riveter," p. 17.

30. Niiya, "Asian Americans and World War II," 212.

31. K. Scott Wong, Americans First: Chinese Americans and the Second World War (Cambridge, MA: Harvard University Press, 2005), 60.

32. Wong, Americans First, 61.

33. Wong, Americans First, 171.

34. Wong, Americans First, 2.

35. Wong, Americans First, 167.

36. Maggie Gee, "Rosie the Riveter World War II American Homefront Oral History Project," conducted by Leah McGarrigle, Robin Li, and Kathryn Stine, 2003, Regional Oral History Office, Bancroft Library, University of California, Berkeley, 2007, p. 84.

37. An Untold Triumph: The Story of the 1st and 2nd Filipino Infantry Regiments, U.S. Army, dir. Noel Izon (San Francisco: Center for Asian American Media, 2005), https://video.alexanderstreet.com/watch/an-untold-triumph.

38. See Capozzola, Bound by War, 165–66; Dawn Bohulano Mabalon, Little Manila Is in the Heart: The Making of the Filipina/o American Community in Stockton, California (Durham, NC: Duke University Press, 2013), 233; and Theo Gonzalves, "'We Hold a Neatly Folded Hope': Filipino American Veterans of World War II on Citizenship and Political Obligation," Amerasia Journal 21, no. 3 (Fall 1995): 155–74.

39. An Untold Triumph.

40. An Untold Triumph.

41. Capozzola, Bound by War, 147.

42. Catherine Ceniza Choy, "Remembering the Filipino Veterans of World War II," Berkeley Blog, November 9, 2017, https://blogs.berkeley.edu/2017/11/09 /remembering-the-filipino-veterans-of-world-war-ii.

43. Bong-Youn Choy, Koreans in America (Chicago: Nelson Hall, 1979), 172.

44. Choy, Koreans in America, 174.

45. "Young Oak Kim: Hero and Humanitarian," A Story Map, http://bit.ly /NvAMYc.

46. "For Susan Ahn, WWII Was a Fight for America and Korea," Asian Americans, video clip, aired April 21, 2020, on PBS, https://www.pbs.org/video/susan-ahn -cudd-korean-american-pioneer-and-woman-warrior-akb.

47. Wong, Americans First, 49.

48. Wong, Americans First, 51.

49. Wong, Americans First, 54.

50. Wong, Americans First, 50–51.

51. Evangeline Canonizado Buell, Twenty-Five Chickens and a Pig for a Bride (San Francisco: T'Boli Publishing, 2006), 58.

52. Buell, *Twenty-Five Chickens*, 59.

53. Mabalon, *Little Manila Is in the Heart*, 243.

54. Wong, *Americans First*, 164–65.

55. Capozzola, *Bound by War*, 152.

56. Mabalon, *Little Manila Is in the Heart*, 246.

57. Okihiro, "An American Story," 80.

58. Linda Gordon, "Dorothea Lange Photographs the Japanese American Internment," in *Impounded: Dorothea Lange and the Censored Images of Japanese American Internment*, ed. Linda Gordon and Gary Y. Okihiro (New York: W. W. Norton, 2006), 6.

59. Miné Okubo, *Citizen 13660* (New York: Columbia University Press, 1946); see also Miné Okubo, *Citizen 13660*, 2nd ed., with a new introduction by Christine Hong (Seattle: University of Washington Press, 2014); Houston and Houston, *Farewell to Manzanar*; Yoshiko Uchida, *Desert Exile: The Uprooting of a Japanese-Amerian Family* (Seattle: University of Washington Press, 1982); Yoshiko Uchida, *Desert Exile: The Uprooting of a Japanese American Family*, 2nd ed. (Seattle: University of Washington Press, 2015); George Takei, Justin Eisinger, Steven Scott, and Harmony Becker, *They Called Us Enemy* (Marietta, GA: Top Shelf Productions, 2019).

60. Traise Yamamoto, "Introduction: An Uncommon Spirit," in Uchida, *Desert Exile*, 2nd ed., xx.

61. Ralph Frammolino, "Ferguson's View on Japanese-American Internment Blasted," *Los Angeles Times*, August 29, 1990, https://www.latimes.com/archives/la-xpm-1990-08-29-mn-309-story.html.

62. Lauren Batten, "From Japanese Incarceration to COVID: The Fight for Justice," *Pacific Council Magazine*, May 11, 2020, https://www.pacificcouncil.org/newsroom/japanese-incarceration-covid-fight-justice.

63. Choy, "Remembering the Filipino Veterans of World War II."

64. Antonio Raimundo, "The Filipino Veterans Equity Movement: A Case Study in Reparations Theory," *California Law Review* 98, no. 2 (2010): 575–623.

CHAPTER SEVEN: 1919: DECLARATION OF INDEPENDENCE

1. "Korean Congress Declares Independence from Japanese Rule, 1919," in *Major Problems in Asian American History*, ed. Lon Kurashige and Alice Yang Murray (Boston: Houghton Mifflin, 2003), 155–56. This document is from "First Korean Congress: Held in the Little Theatre, 17th and Delancey Streets (Philadelphia), 1919" (Sŏul Tŭkpyŏlsi: Pŏmhan Sŏjŭk Chusik Hosea, 1986).

2. "Manuel Quezon Calls for Filipino Independence (1919)," *The American Yawp Reader*, https://www.americanyawp.com/reader/21-world-war-i/manuel-quezon-calls-for-filipino-independence-1919.

3. Gyan Prakash, "The Massacre That Led to the End of the British Empire," *New York Times*, April 13, 2019, https://www.nytimes.com/2019/04/13/opinion/1919-amrtisar-british-empire-india.html.

4. "Indian Immigrant Mohan Singh Recounts His Education in the United States, circa 1924," from Miss Secord, "The Life History of Mohan," in *Major Problems in Asian American History*, 153. This document is from the papers of William C. Smith (A-237, A-102, 84-A), Special Collections and University Archives, University of Oregon.

5. Lili Kim, "Korean Independence Movement in Hawai'i and the Continental United States," 2001, in *Major Problems in Asian American History*, 172–73.

6. Kim, "Korean Independence Movement in Hawai'i," 173.

7. Kim, "Korean Independence Movement in Hawai'i," 174–75; and Edward T. Chang, *Pachappa Camp: The First Koreatown in the United States* (Lanham, MD: Lexington Books, 2021), 35–36.

8. Richard Kim, *The Quest for Statehood: Korean Immigrant Nationalism and U.S. Sovereignty, 1905–1945* (New York: Oxford University Press, 2011), 15.

9. Kim, *The Quest for Statehood*.

10. Kim, *The Quest for Statehood*, 3–4.

11. Kim, *The Quest for Statehood*, 26.

12. Kim, "Korean Independence Movement in Hawai'i and the Continental United States," 177.

13. Kim, "Korean Independence Movement in Hawai'i and the Continental United States."

14. Margaret K. Pai, *The Dreams of Two Yi-min* (Honolulu: University of Hawai'i Press, 1989), 20–21.

15. Edward T. Chang and Woo Sung Han, *Korean American Pioneer Aviators: The Willow Airmen* (Lanham, MD: Lexington Books, 2015), xiv.

16. Chang and Han, *Korean American Pioneer Aviators*, xvi. See also David K. Yoo, *Contentious Spirits: Religion in Korean American History, 1903–1945* (Stanford, CA: Stanford University Press, 2010).

17. "Korean Congress Declares Independence from Japanese Rule, 1919," 155.

18. "Korean Congress Declares Independence from Japanese Rule, 1919," 156.

19. Kim, *The Quest for Statehood*, 64.

20. Kim, *The Quest for Statehood*, 18; Kim, "Korean Independence Movement in Hawai'i and the Continental United States," 174.

21. Dawn Bohulano Mabalon, *Little Manila Is in the Heart: The Making of the Filipina/o American Community in Stockton, California* (Durham, NC: Duke University Press, 2013), 30.

22. "Modern History Sourcebook: Rudyard Kipling, The White Man's Burden, 1899," Internet History Sourcebooks Project, Fordham University, January 26, 1996, https://sourcebooks.fordham.edu/mod/kipling.asp.

23. Christopher Capozzola, *Bound by War: How the United States and the Philippines Built America's First Pacific Century* (New York: Basic Books, 2020), 56–57.

24. Mabalon, *Little Manila Is in the Heart*, 30–31.

25. Abe Ignacio, Enrique de la Cruz, Jorge Emmanuel, and Helen Toribio, *The Forbidden Book: The Philippine-American War in Political Cartoons* (San Francisco: T'boli Publishing, 2004), 1–2.

26. Mark Twain, "The War Prayer," https://www.people.vcu.edu/~toggel/prayer.pdf.

27. See Catherine Ceniza Choy, "A Filipino Woman in America: The Life and Work of Encarnacion Alzona," *Genre: Forms of Discourse and Culture* 3 (Fall 2006): 127–40.

28. See Robert Rydell, *All the World's a Fair: Visions of Empire at American International Expositions, 1876–1916* (Chicago: University of Chicago Press, 1985).

29. Benito M. Vergara Jr., *Displaying Filipinos: Photography and Colonialism in Early 20th Century Philippines* (Quezon City: University of the Philippines Press, 1995), 112.

30. Greg Allen, "'Living Exhibits' at 1904 World's Fair Revisited," *Morning Edition*, NPR, May 31, 2004, https://www.npr.org/templates/story/story.php?story Id=1909651.

31. Allen, "'Living Exhibits' at 1904 World's Fair Revisited."

32. Suzanne McMahon, curator, "Chapter 6: At the University," in "Echoes of Freedom: South Asian Pioneers in California, 1899–1965," UC Berkeley Library, last updated July 6, 2020, https://guides.lib.berkeley.edu/echoes-of-freedom/university.

33. McMahon, "Chapter 6: At the University."

34. "Taraknath Das," in "New, Thinking, Agile, and Patriotic: 'Hindu' Students at the University of Washington, 1908–1915," University of Washington Libraries, Special Collections, 2006, https://www.lib.washington.edu/specialcollections/collections/exhibits/southasianstudents/das.

35. Joan M. Jensen, "Exporting Independence to Colonial India," in *Major Problems in Asian American History*, 170. This essay is from Joan M. Jensen, *Passage from India: Asian Indian Immigrants in North America* (New Haven, CT: Yale University Press, 1988).

36. Seema Sohi, "The Ghadar Party," SAADA: South Asian American Digital Archive, May 8, 2018, https://www.saada.org/tides/article/the-ghadar-party. See also Seema Sohi, "Repressing the 'Hindu Menace': Race, Anarchy, and Indian Anticolonialism," in *The Sun Never Sets: South Asian Migrants in an Age of U.S. Power*, ed. Vivek Bald et al. (New York: New York University Press, 2013), 50–74.

37. Sohi, "The Ghadar Party."

38. Suzanne McMahon, curator, "Chapter 7: Ghadar," in "Echoes of Freedom," in "Echoes of Freedom: South Asian Pioneers in California, 1899–1965," UC Berkeley Library, last updated July 6, 2020, https://guides.lib.berkeley.edu/echoes-of-freedom/university.

39. Judy Yung, "Student and Revolutionist," Angel Island Immigration Station Foundation, 2021, https://www.immigrant-voices.aiisf.org/stories-by-author/875-student-and-revolutionist.

40. Sohi, "The Ghadar Party."

41. Kartar Singh Sarabha, "On the Way to the Gallows," in Yung, "Student and Revolutionist."

42. Karen Leonard, *Making Ethnic Choices: California's Punjabi Mexican Americans* (Philadelphia: Temple University Press, 1992), 131.

43. Leonard, *Making Ethnic Choices*.

44. "New Plaque at State Capitol Gives New Perspective to War in Philippines," *Brainerd Dispatch*, February 6, 2002, https://www.brainerddispatch.com/news/3420410-new-plaque-state-capitol-gives-new-perspective-war-philippines.

45. Ignacio et al., *The Forbidden Book*, 1.

46. Chang, *Pachappa Camp*, 63–64.

47. Chang, *Pachappa Camp*, 64.

48. Chang, *Pachappa Camp*, 114.

49. Bhira Baukhaus, "A Sikh Temple's Century," *New York Times*, August 7, 2012, https://www.nytimes.com/2012/08/08/opinion/a-sikh-temples-proud-history.html?_r=1.

50. "About Sikh Temple of Wisconsin," Sikh Temple of Wisconsin, 2021, http://sikhtempleofwisconsin.com/about-us.

51. Baukhaus, "A Sikh Temple's Century."

52. Baukhaus, "A Sikh Temple's Century."

53. Mandeep Kaur, "Sikhs Remain Resilient After Five Years of Living with Tragedy," *Milwaukee Independent*, August 8, 2017, https://www.milwaukee independent.com/articles/sikhs-remain-resilient-five-years-living-tragedy.

54. Julie Zauzmer Weil, "He Was 12. He Had Just Moved to America. Then His Sikh Father Was Murdered," *Washington Post*, August 4, 2017, https://www .washingtonpost.com/news/acts-of-faith/wp/2017/08/04/his-father-was-murdered -hes-still-grappling-with-what-it-means-to-be-sikh-in-america.

55. Elly Fishman, "2021 Unity Awards Honoree: Pardeep Singh Kaleka," *Milwaukee*, February 8, 2021, https://www.milwaukeemag.com/2021-unity-awards -honoree-pardeep-singh-kaleka.

56. Pardeep Kaleka, "Stories: Pardeep Kaleka," The Forgiveness Project, February 16, 2016, https://www.theforgivenessproject.com/stories/pardeep-kaleka.

57. Philippine Study Group of Minnesota, Capitol Area Architectural and Planning Board, Minnesota Historical Society, and Minnesota Department of Administration, "Text for the Corrective Spanish-American War Plaque," 2001, http://www .crcworks.org/newtext.pdf.

58. "The White Man's Burden (Apologies to Kipling)," *Judge* (New York: Judge Publishing Company, 1899), artist: Victor Gillam, in Ignacio et al., *The Forbidden Book*, 25.

59. "Speaking from Experience (Through Professor Marconi's Wireless Telegraphy): American Indian (to Filipino)—'Be Good, or You Will Be Dead!'" *Judge* (New York: Arkell Publishing Company, c. 1899), artist: Victor Gillam, in Ignacio et al., *The Forbidden Book*, 96.

60. Ignacio et al., *The Forbidden Book*, 10.

61. Antonio S. Buangan, "The Suyoc People Who Went to St. Louis 100 Years Ago: The Search for My Ancestors," *Philippine Studies* 52, no. 4 (2004): 474–98.

62. Buangan, "The Suyoc People Who Went to St. Louis," 480.

63. Buangan, "The Suyoc People Who Went to St. Louis."

64. Buangan, "The Suyoc People Who Went to St. Louis," 481.

65. Buangan, "The Suyoc People Who Went to St. Louis," 479.

66. Chang, *Pachappa Camp*, 111–14.

67. "Centennial: Korea's Declaration of Independence March 1, 1919–March 1, 2019," *Korean American Pioneers Descendants Newsletter*, February 2019, p. 2.

68. "Choi, Neung-ik: He Was in Charge of Diplomatic Business as a Representative of Korean National Revolutionary Corps," KNA Memorial Foundation, January 25, 2019, https://knamf.org/choi-neung-ik. For the history of the Willows Aviation School, see Chang and Han, *Korean American Pioneer Aviators*.

CHAPTER EIGHT: 1875: HOMAGE

1. Lauren Mellone, "ATL Spa Shooting Family Survivor Fund: Jami Webb," GoFundMe, https://www.gofundme.com/f/atl-spa-shooting-family-survivor-fund -jami-webb.

2. Joshua Sharpe, "With No Family in U.S., Local Asian Americans Hold Service for Spa Shooting Victim," *Atlanta Journal-Constitution*, April 4, 2021, https:// www.ajc.com/news/crime/with-no-family-in-us-local-asian-americans-hold-service -for-spa-shooting-victim/XKXBRJDDXRD4JOLSHI4QG4EDWU.

3. "Delaina Ashley Yaun Gonzalez," in "Victims Lost to Recent Anti-AAPI Hate Crimes," Stanford Libraries, https://exhibits.stanford.edu/riseup/feature/delaina-ashley-yaun-gonzalez.

4. Jewel Wicker and Victoria Bekiempis, "Paul Andre Michels: 'Very Good-Hearted' Handyman Killed in Atlanta Shootings," *Guardian*, March 18, 2021, https://www.theguardian.com/us-news/2021/mar/18/paul-andre-michels-atlanta-spa-shootings.

5. Hanna Park, "Soon Chung Park Worked Long Days as Single Mom to Bring 5 Kids from Korea to U.S.," NBC News, March 25, 2021, https://www.nbcnews.com/news/asian-america/soon-chung-park-worked-long-days-single-mom-bring-5-kids-korea-us-rcna514.

6. Victoria Bekiempis, "Hyun Jung Grant: Ex-Teacher Who Loved to Dance Killed in Atlanta Spa Shootings," *Guardian*, March 19, 2021, https://www.theguardian.com/us-news/2021/mar/19/hyun-jung-grant-atlanta-spa-shootings.

7. Michelle Ye Hee Lee, "America Was Always Where She Felt She Belonged," *Washington Post*, April 20, 2021, https://www.washingtonpost.com/nation/2021/04/20/suncha-kim-atlanta-spa-shooting.

8. Michelle Ye Hee Lee, "Atlanta Shooting Victim's Biracial Sons Seek to Unite Black, Asian Communities in Shared Fight Against Hate," *Washington Post*, August 8, 2021, https://www.washingtonpost.com/national/atlanta-spa-shootings-yong-ae-yue/2021/08/08/9b8460b0-d1fb-11eb-9f29-e9e6c9e843c6_story.html.

9. Board of the Association for Asian American Studies, "Response to the Atlanta Murders," Association for Asian American Studies, March 2021, https://aaastudies.org/response-to-the-atlanta-murders.

10. Catherine Ceniza Choy, *Empire of Care: Nursing and Migration in Filipino American History* (Durham, NC: Duke University Press, 2003), 121–39.

11. Lisa Hagen, "'Sex Addiction' Cited as Spurring Spa Shooting, but Most Killed Were of Asian Descent," NPR, March 17, 2021, https://www.npr.org/2021/03/17/978288270/shooter-claimed-sex-addiction-as-his-reason-but-most-victims-were-of-asian-desce.

12. Kimmy Yam, "Racism, Sexism Must Be Considered in Atlanta Case Involving Killing of Six Asian Women, Experts Say," NBC News, March 17, 2021, https://www.nbcnews.com/news/asian-america/racism-sexism-must-be-considered-atlanta-case-involving-killing-six-n1261347.

13. "Page Law (1875)," Immigration History, 2019, https://immigrationhistory.org/item/page-act.

14. Kerry Abrams, "Polygamy, Prostitution, and the Federalization of Immigration Law," *Columbia Law Review* 105, no. 3 (April 2005): 695–96.

15. Mari Uyehara, "The Roots of the Atlanta Shooting Go Back to the First Law Restricting Immigration," *The Nation*, March 22, 2021, https://www.thenation.com/article/society/atlanta-shooting-history.

16. Uyehara, "The Roots of the Atlanta Shooting."

17. Abrams, "Polygamy, Prostitution, and the Federalization of Immigration Law," 663.

18. US Department of State, Office of the Historian, Foreign Service Institute, "The Burlingame-Seward Treaty, 1868," https://history.state.gov/milestones/1866-1898/burlingame-seward-treaty.

19. Abrams, "Polygamy, Prostitution, and the Federalization of Immigration Law," 690–91.

20. K. Scott Wong, *Americans First: Chinese Americans and the Second World War* (Cambridge, MA: Harvard University Press, 2005), 128–29.

21. Bill Ong Hing, *Making and Remaking Asian America Through Immigration Policy, 1850–1990* (Stanford, CA: Stanford University Press, 1993).

22. According to University of California, Berkeley Library's "We're Here, We're Queer, and We're in the Public Record! The LGBTQ Movement and Life as Seen Through Government Information": "It was still legal to ban people living with HIV from immigrating; this ban was not overturned until January 2010. In 1994, 'homosexuals' were added as a social group that could qualify for asylum, but LGBTQ+ people still face significant barriers to receiving refuge. Though federal recognition of same-sex marriage in 2015 extended the protections of immigration laws for lawfully married people to LGBTQ+ couples, groups that don't fit heteronormative models, such as trans* immigrants, face disproportionate discrimination." See "Immigration," in "We're Here, We're Queer, and We're in the Public Record! The LGBTQ Movement and Life as Seen Through Government Information," University of California, Berkeley Library, 2018, https://exhibits.lib.berkeley.edu/spotlight /queer/feature/immigration.

23. Abrams, "Polygamy, Prostitution, and the Federalization of Immigration Law," 648.

24. Herb Wong, Deborah Gee, and Pamela Porter, *Slaying the Dragon*, video (San Francisco: CrossCurrent Media, NAATA, 2007). Originally broadcast by KQED, San Francisco, in 1987.

25. *A Special Edition of 20/20*, season 43, episode 18, "Murder in Atlanta," ABC News, aired March 19, 2021.

26. Kerri Lee Alexander, "Anna May Wong," National Women's History Museum, 2019, https://www.womenshistory.org/education-resources/biographies /anna-may-wong. See also Karen Leong, *The China Mystique: Pearl S. Buck, Anna May Wong, Mayling Soong, and the Transformation of American Orientalism* (Berkeley: University of California Press, 2005); and Shirley Jennifer Lim, *Anna May Wong: Performing the Modern* (Philadelphia: Temple University Press, 2019).

27. Edward Sakamoto, "Anna May Wong and the Dragon-Lady Syndrome," *Los Angeles Times*, July 12, 1987, https://www.latimes.com/archives/la-xpm-1987 -07-12-ca-3279-story.html.

28. Sakamoto, "Anna May Wong and the Dragon-Lady Syndrome."

29. Alexander, "Anna May Wong."

30. Josephine Lee, "Yellowface Performance: Historical and Contemporary Contexts," *Oxford Research Encyclopedia of Literature*, February 25, 2019, https:// doi.org/10.1093/acrefore/9780190201098.013.834.

31. Shruti Mukkamala and Karen Suyemoto, "Racialized Sexism/Sexualized Racism: A Multimethod Study of Intersectional Experiences of Discrimination for Asian American Women," *Asian American Journal of Psychology* 9, no. 1 (2018): 32–46, http://dx.doi.org/10.1037/aap0000104.

32. Kerri Lee Alexander, "Patsy Mink," National Women's History Museum, 2019, https://www.womenshistory.org/education-resources/biographies/patsy-mink.

33. Sarah Pruitt, "How Title IX Transformed Women's Sports," *History*, June 11, 2021, https://www.history.com/news/title-nine-womens-sports.

34. Gwendolyn Mink, "My Mother Was One of the First Women to Run for President," *Time*, June 9, 2016, https://time.com/4362066/hillary-clinton-democratic-nominee-patsy-mink.

35. Judy Tzu-Chun Wu, "The Dead, the Living, and the Sacred: Patsy Mink, Antimilitarism, and Reimagining the Pacific World," *Meridians* 18, no. 2 (2019): 310.

36. Alexander, "Patsy Mink."

37. "H.Res. 683 (112th): Expressing the Regret of the House of Representatives for the Passage of Laws That Adversely Affected the Chinese in the United States, Including the Chinese Exclusion Act," GovTrack, June 18, 2012, https://www.govtrack.us/congress/bills/112/hres683/text.

38. Brian Niiya, "Mazie Hirono," *Densho Encyclopedia*, https://encyclopedia.densho.org/Mazie%20Hirono.

39. "About Mazie," Mazie K. Hirono, https://www.hirono.senate.gov/about.

40. Kamala Kelkar, "Obama Signs Bill Eliminating 'Negro,' 'Oriental' from Federal Laws," PBS, May 22, 2016, https://www.pbs.org/newshour/nation/obama-signs-bill-eliminating-negro-spanish-speaking-oriental-from-federal-laws.

41. "House Passes Meng Resolution to Denounce Anti-Asian Sentiment Related to the Coronavirus," Rep. Grace Meng, September 17, 2020, https://meng.house.gov/media-center/press-releases/house-passes-meng-resolution-to-denounce-anti-asian-sentiment-related-to.

42. Jessica Smith, "Sen. Duckworth: Anti-Asian Hate Crimes 'Notoriously Underreported,'" *Yahoo! Finance*, April 9, 2021, https://news.yahoo.com/sen-duckworth-anti-asian-hate-crimes-notoriously-underreported-152929640.html.

43. "Historic Senate Rules Change Allows New Parents to Bring Their Children onto Senate Floor for First Time," Tammy Duckworth, April 18, 2018, https://www.duckworth.senate.gov/news/press-releases/historic-senate-rules-change-allows-new-parents-to-bring-their-children-onto-senate-floor-for-first-time.

44. Kimmy Yam, "Congresswoman Wears Hanbok at Swearing-In Ceremony, Honors Korean Immigrant Mom," NBC News, January 4, 2021, https://www.nbcnews.com/news/asian-america/congresswoman-wears-hanbok-swearing-ceremony-honors-korean-immigrant-mom-n1252786.

45. Yam, "Congresswoman Wears Hanbok at Swearing-In Ceremony."

46. Yam, "Congresswoman Wears Hanbok at Swearing-In Ceremony."

47. Marilyn Strickland (@RepStricklandWA), Twitter, January 3, 2021, https://twitter.com/repstricklandwa/status/1345913491186716672?lang=en.

48. Jacob Kim (@fullofhype), Twitter, January 3, 2021, https://mobile.twitter.com/fullofhype/status/1345872010694565892, quoted in Yam, "Congresswoman Wears Hanbok at Swearing-In Ceremony."

49. Miran 미란 Kim (@mirankinsays), Twitter, January 4, 2021, https://twitter.com/mirankimsays/status/1345997140410167297?s=20, quoted in Yam, "Congresswoman Wears Hanbok at Swearing-In Ceremony."

50. Scott Wilson (@RScottWilson), Twitter, January 3, 2021, https://twitter.com/RScottWilson/status/1345933064950505583300.

51. Olivia B. Waxman, "The Story Behind Time's Cover on Anti-Asian Violence and Hate Crimes," *Time*, March 18, 2021, https://time.com/5947622/time-cover-anti-asian-american-violence-atlanta-shooting.

52. Waxman, "The Story Behind Time's Cover on Anti-Asian Violence."

53. Waxman, "The Story Behind Time's Cover on Anti-Asian Violence."

54. Lauren Messman, "'I Still Believe in Our City': A Public Art Series Takes On Racism," *New York Times*, November 2, 2020, https://www.nytimes.com/2020/11 /02/arts/design/public-art-covid-race-subway.html.

55. Waxman, "The Story Behind Time's Cover on Anti-Asian Violence."

CONCLUSION: 1869: THESE WOUNDS

1. Hua Hsu, "Corky Lee's Photographs Helped Generations of Asian-Americans See Themselves," *New Yorker*, January 30, 2021, https://www.newyorker.com /culture/postscript/corky-lees-photographs-helped-generations-of-asian-americans -see-themselves.

2. Emil Guillermo, "Chinese American History Professors Gave Photographer Corky Lee His Calling," *Diverse Issues in Higher Education*, February 2, 2021, https://www.diverseeducation.com/demographics/asian-american-pacific-islander /article/15108588/chinese-american-history-professors-gave-photographer-corky -lee-his-calling.

3. "Introduction," Chinese Railroad Workers in North America Project, Stanford University, 2018, https://web.stanford.edu/group/chineserailroad/cgi-bin/website /virtual. See also Gordon H. Chang and Shelley Fisher Fishkin, eds., *The Chinese and the Iron Road: Building the Transcontinental Railroad* (Stanford, CA: Stanford University Press, 2019).

4. Junru Huang, "Not on the Menu: Corky Lee's Life and Work," video, https:// vimeo.com/65482946.

5. Ming Lin and Alexandra Tatarsky, "Corky Lee 'Was Chinatown to Me,'" *Vulture*, February 3, 2021, https://www.vulture.com/article/corky-lee-photographer -obituary.html.

6. "Photographic Justice: Rest in Power Corky Lee," Center for Asian American Media, February 24, 2021, https://caamedia.org/blog/2021/02/24/photographic -justice-rest-in-power-corky-lee.

INDEX

ABOUT THE AUTHOR

C atherine Ceniza Choy has studied and taught Asian American history for more than twenty years. She is the author of the book *Empire of Care: Nursing and Migration in Filipino American History* (2003), which explores how and why the Philippines became the leading exporter of professional nurses to the United States. *Empire of Care* received the 2003 American Journal of Nursing History and Public Policy Book Award and the 2005 Association for Asian American Studies History Book Award. Her second book, *Global Families: A History of Asian International Adoption in America* (2013), unearthed the little-known historical origins of Asian international adoption in the United States beginning with the post–World War II presence of the US military in Asia. Choy also co-edited the anthology *Gendering the Trans-Pacific World* (2017), with Judy Tzu-Chun Wu. An engaged public scholar, Choy has been interviewed in many media outlets, including ABC's *20/20*, *The Atlantic*, CNN, the *Los Angeles Times*, NBC News, the *New York Times*, ProPublica, the *San Francisco Chronicle*, *Time*, and *Vox*, about the history of anti-Asian hate and violence, the disproportionate toll of COVID-19 on Filipino nurses in the United States, and racism and misogyny in the March 16, 2021, Atlanta murders.

Choy is professor of ethnic studies at the University of California, Berkeley, and associate dean of Diversity, Equity, Inclusion, Belonging, and Justice in the Division of Computing, Data Science, and Society. She is a former chair of the Department of Ethnic Studies and associate dean of the Undergraduate Studies Division. The daughter of Filipino immigrants, Choy was born and raised in New York City. She received her PhD in history from the University of California, Los Angeles, and her BA in history from Pomona College. She lives in Berkeley with her husband and their two children.